MISSION ACCOMPLISHED: STOP THE CLOCK

SECOND EDITION

*To Mel, my life partner and mentor,
with love and gratitude for your
unending patience, interest and support.
If not for your hundreds of hours spent dealing with
the mechanical aspects of getting this manuscript
to the publisher, my life story would remain untold.*

ACCLAIM FOR *Mission Accomplished: Stop the Clock*

*A wry, erudite octogenarian's memoir tells of surviving a
Great Depression childhood, serving as a U.S. Army nurse during
World War II in Europe and celebrating her decades-long,
post-war career as a loving wife, mother and grandmother.*

First-time author Engelman is a gifted natural storyteller—the kind
of charismatic lady who effortlessly holds sway over a card table or kaffee-
klatsch with her fascinating tales of life's triumphs and tragedies, personal
and universal. Alone, the breadth of her experiences as a healthcare professional both in the United States and abroad would make her book at least
interesting to someone studying midcentury social history, but it offers
much more. Instead of the glib, self-aggrandizing yarns and social propa-
gandizing that plague most memoirs, the author focuses her sharp mind
and pen on chatty, candid impressions of life in a variety of extraordinary
situations: as a student nurse, dealing with the maddening, petty bureaucra-
cy of academia and cranky patients; as a young Jew, encountering insidious
racism in society and the workplace; as an Army nurse, facing the profound
absurdities and horrors of life on a battlefield far from home; and always as
a compassionate, quick-witted observer. Though the stories of her stint in
France after D-Day and later in Belgium make great reading—especially
a selection of the letters she sent home to loved ones—Engelman's remi-
niscences of civilian life are just as fascinating, if less dramatic. Here the
book takes on a more relaxed tone, as if the anecdotes have been perfected by endless telling and polishing. Though less self-consciously exquisite
as work by writers like M.F.K. Fisher, these well-told tales bring to mind
Fisher's belief in the art of storytelling as a major element in the art of life.

A must-read for WWII history buffs and lovers of homespun
storytelling.

— **Kirkus Discoveries**

For more information please visit:

www.murielengelman.com

CONTENTS

ILLUSTRATIONS

PREFACE

The original purpose of this book was to relate some of my unusual and stranger-than-fiction experiences during World War II, an era that impacted the rest of my life. My very supportive spouse, Mel, a war and history buff, encouraged me to keep writing, if only for my children and grandsons, so that they could learn the facts of my life as a U.S. Army nurse.

When I finally arrived home after being discharged, I needed time to unwind and to learn to become a civilian again. I was far from the young girl who had left home for nursing school, and my maturation had been molded by forces more powerful than those faced by the usual high school graduate going off to college.

Despite living with buzz bombs, strafing, and the threat of capture, lighter moments in off-duty time balanced out wartime horrors. Then, life was enjoyable—when we were able to laugh, dance, and sing, and enjoy the companionship of other female and male officers, all with the same goal: doing what we came for—and surviving.

Once that page had been turned and military life was suddenly reduced to memories, I knew that I needed to record those memories, along with the faces, so that I would have them forever. I set out to create a photo album with detailed captions of much that I had experienced as an army nurse; that album became the nucleus of *Mission Accomplished: Stop the Clock*.

To hone my skills, I enrolled in writing classes. One in particular, which I took for several years at the University of South Florida, was "Personal Narrative," led by Evelyn Lerman. Through this class I broadened my subject material to encompass other well-remembered funny or sad episodes over the years. Often, for a class assignment, Evelyn dictated a three- or four-word subject that we had to fit into a story, fact or fiction.

All of my stories found here are about actual situations that occurred in different phases of my life; the cast of characters are friends, patients, family, or acquaintances. Many of these people are still alive, so to ensure anonymity, names, locale, and minor facts pertaining to their identification have been changed. Because the stories were written over a period of years, there is some repetition of certain events which may not be in chronological order. This is especially obvious when discussing dates, as in birthdays or years of marriage.

In the chapter titled "Letters Home," which are excerpts from my letters to family members, the text is reproduced here exactly as written at the time, including grammatical and punctuation errors. When writing by the dim light of a kerosene lantern or flashlight, which occurred frequently, punctuation and grammatical perfection was the last thing on my mind.

ACKNOWLEDGMENTS

I couldn't have reached this point without the continual encouragement from Mel, who corrected my grammatical errors (e.g., when to use whom instead of who). He worked out my never-ending computer problems with the patience of ten saints and spent hours scanning old photographs for use.

Another mentor to whom I am deeply indebted is Lane Gutstein, a personal friend and dedicated English teacher, who was responsible for teaching me about such unknown or forgotten items as split infinitives and gerunds, as well as punctuation. (Split infinitives had a familiar ring to them, but gerunds …? I'm sure they hadn't been invented some seventy or more years ago.)

Lane's husband, Dr. Walter Gutstein, was also an enthusiastic supporter, quick to acknowledge his enjoyment, and how could you not love a guy who quoted from *my* stories months and years after reading them?

Others who must be thanked are my California friends, MariJan Vested and Margaret Lemmon, who served as sounding boards and offered helpful suggestions. Also Joe Florsheimer, Sarasota, Florida, for his gracious assistance in resolving computer questions beyond Mel's skills.

My fourteen year old grandson Aaron, who effortlessly, closed the generation gap, by obtaining a domain name and creating a website for this book.

The surprised and happy response to my life stories from my children, Suzy and Curtis (a.k.a. Corky), and their spouses, Dennis O'Reilly and Anita, as well as our many friends who actually asked to read them, encouraged me to "go for publication."

SECOND EDITION ACKNOWLEDGMENTS

Over the years since the first publication of *Mission Accomplished: Stop the Clock*, I realized, especially after addressing various groups of people, students, veterans, church and social organizations, etc., that I failed to include many memories and facts about the Battle of the Bulge and the history leading up to it. So by publishing this second edition I hope to satisfy my readers with more details about the most important battle of World War II.

For this second edition I want to acknowledge with gratitude the help of my friend Robin Meader, Ph.D., and my loving daughter, Suzy Engelman, Ph.D., both of whom provided the answers to my constant computer problems, and my one-in-a-million son-in-law, Dennis O'Reilly, J.D., who spent hours correcting, formatting, and proofing. In my next life, I will return completely computer literate.

PART ONE

PRE-WAR

CHAPTER ONE

MEMORY BANK RETRIEVED

MY BRAIN is shortchanging me. Familiar words desert me in the middle of a sentence, and I can't remember where I put something five minutes earlier, yet my memory functions well enough that I can remember incidents and family living patterns that occurred when I was four years old, a long eighty years ago. Attempts to penetrate earlier layers of my life prove futile, with no memories to recall; age four, however, brings such a flood of experiences that I have to slow them down in order to assimilate them.

I have a visual picture of our home—which was on the second floor of my grandparents' home—with its large front porches and a scattering of rocking chairs. There was a large hemp hammock swinging gently in the side yard, and the backyard was shaded by three fruit trees, lush with cherries, peaches, and apples in season. At the far end of the yard was a grape arbor, laden with purple Concord grapes in late August and September, and I can still see the dark stains on my fingers after I gorged myself on them.

My grandmother had a big black stove in her kitchen, with round, flat discs on top that were removed by a pronged metal holder when she needed to throw coal into the stove. A black coal hod sat on the floor next to the stove. Upstairs, we had a gas stove and an icebox, which had one compartment just for the big slab of ice that the iceman delivered each week; my mother would put the "ice" sign in our front window to let him know when we needed a delivery. He used tongs to carry the hunk of ice upstairs, slinging it over his rubber-covered shoulder and depositing it in the ice box. When my father came home, he would remove the water-filled pan that was under the icebox. Even though we had a gas stove, our house was heated by coal, and every few weeks in the winter, the coal truck would stop in front of the house. The delivery man had a heavy canvas sack filled with coal that he hooked over his shoulders. He would pause at the cellar window that overlooked the coal bin and empty his sack of coal down the chute into the bin.

The memories of my fifth year are overshadowed by one big event: my operation. My parents drove me in our green four-door Essex to Hartford Hospital, eighteen miles away, where my tonsils and adenoids were to be removed—and it was scary. The hospital was so big and endless-looking, and the admitting nurse didn't seem to like kids. She was as stiff and cold as her heavily starched white uniform. She asked, "Did you have a bath before you came?"

"Yes," I replied, "my mother gave me a bath this morning."

"Well, she didn't do a very good job cleaning your belly button," charged my captor, who was, by then, digging out my belly button—and even at age five, I realized that was nowhere near my tonsils.

Maybe they are going to take out my tonsils and adenoids through my belly button instead of my mouth, I thought.

Once installed in bed, wearing a hospital gown that tied in back and didn't cover my behind, the nurse barked, "Do you know how to count?"

"Sure, I know how to count" was my quick reply. "I'm five years old." "Start counting, then, and we'll see how smart you are," she ordered.

I hadn't gotten past six before she clamped a mask over my nose that had a sweetish-foul smell. I screamed for her to remove it—and then woke up some time later, still screaming. My throat was so sore that I knew—without having to feel my belly button—that my tonsils had come out through my mouth. My neck was draped with an ice bag, and when I stopped throwing up from the ether, the nurses fed me chips of ice. After the ice melted on my tongue, it was still very painful to swallow. The one bright spot about this operation was … *ice cream*! Every night until my throat was better, my father would come home with a box of ice cream, and I was a little sorry when it didn't hurt any more. Ice cream was such a treat; we usually had it only in the summertime. Sometimes we drove to the ice cream parlor for an ice cream cone, and sometimes, when my parents returned from a drive, they would wake up my sister and me for a dish of ice cream.

The next few years were eventful, for my grandparents bought a duplex up-and-down house on Bradley Boulevard, a WASP enclave. We were the first Jewish family to venture into this prestigious area. My grandparents lived on one side of the house, and our family lived on the other. We shared a joint front door and hallway. The cooking smells emanating from the grandparents' side of the house were so much more enticing than my mother's cooking smells. That was because my grandmother cooked with chicken fat, the way they did in the Old Country. My mother believed in healthy, non-fattening recipes, which were not as tasty as my grand-mother's—the precursors to cholesterol issues.

My grandparents were very religious, and on Saturdays, the Sabbath, I had to light the gas stove for my grandmother so she could heat their precooked dinners. When the paper boy came on Saturday mornings, I gave him the coins she had previously wrapped up in a scrap of newspaper. Lighting the stove and handling money wasn't permissible on the Sabbath, because that came under the heading of "work." My grandmother could speak English and had successfully operated her own dry goods store for years, but she couldn't read or write English. When I came home from school, we sat at the kitchen table, and she laboriously copied the Palmer lessons in writing and words from my spelling book. I felt very important.

There were several boys and girls in the neighborhood for playmates, and we roller skated and rode our bikes together. Only the girls were inter-ested in playing hopscotch and jump rope on the sidewalk in front of our house. I didn't realize it at the time, as I wasn't aware of anti-Semitism, but Nancy, whose father was a lawyer, remarked many times, "Even though my father has a Jewish nose, we are Protestants, not Jews." I didn't know what made a nose "Jewish" because my father's nose was smaller than her father's, and my father really was Jewish. When Nancy was in a good mood, she would invite me to her church on Saturday afternoons for a cowboy movie, but when she was mad at me for some reason, she stuck out her tongue at me and called me "Jew Beggel." Then she would run home as I called after her, "Nancy Pancy!" It took me twenty years to figure out that she was equating Jews with bagels.

I loved going to my friend Mary's house, where every room held pastel-painted statues of the Virgin Mary, and the walls were hung with

CHAPTER TWO

CLASS BEAUTY

"BETTY," I panted in exasperation, "let's slow down; you're killing me."

"No!" Betty replied breathlessly. "We have to keep running, or we'll never lose weight."

I couldn't possibly run and answer her at the same time, but I thought as I trotted along beside her that Betty, my best friend, was overdoing this weight business. I'd told her fifty times a day that she wasn't fat, that I would give my eye teeth to be as "fat" as she was, but she'd only respond with, "The mirror doesn't lie."

This illusion, that she was fat, had possessed her completely since starting our junior year in high school, and nothing could change her opinion about herself. We were both 5 feet 5½ inches tall, but I weighed 148 pounds, as compared to Betty's weight of 118 pounds. I wore a size 16 dress, and she wore a size 10. Betty's hip bones were visible in tight skirts, but if I had hip bones, I could not find them under my layers of adipose tissue. And yet, Betty honestly believed she was fat!

Aware that I needed the exercise more than she, I acceded to her commands each day as we made our way up the hills to our high school: "*Run; don't walk.* Hop up and down the curbs. Don't take the elevators in the building; use the stairs! And don't just walk up the stairs, run up."

The fact that she was drop-dead gorgeous didn't affect her erroneous opinion of her body, and when I tried to point out that people (especially males) stared appreciatively at her ethereal beauty, she insisted they stared because she was fat. Every student in the junior class, with the exception of Betty, knew without any doubt that she would be the winning candidate for the Class Beauty category in our class elections. She was blessed with an abundance of shoulder-length, shiny, almost black, natural wavy hair that

The next few years were eventful, for my grandparents bought a duplex up-and-down house on Bradley Boulevard, a WASP enclave. We were the first Jewish family to venture into this prestigious area. My grandparents lived on one side of the house, and our family lived on the other. We shared a joint front door and hallway. The cooking smells emanating from the grandparents' side of the house were so much more enticing than my mother's cooking smells. That was because my grandmother cooked with chicken fat, the way they did in the Old Country. My mother believed in healthy, non-fattening recipes, which were not as tasty as my grand-mother's—the precursors to cholesterol issues.

My grandparents were very religious, and on Saturdays, the Sabbath, I had to light the gas stove for my grandmother so she could heat their precooked dinners. When the paper boy came on Saturday mornings, I gave him the coins she had previously wrapped up in a scrap of newspaper. Lighting the stove and handling money wasn't permissible on the Sabbath, because that came under the heading of "work." My grandmother could speak English and had successfully operated her own dry goods store for years, but she couldn't read or write English. When I came home from school, we sat at the kitchen table, and she laboriously copied the Palmer lessons in writing and words from my spelling book. I felt very important.

There were several boys and girls in the neighborhood for playmates, and we roller skated and rode our bikes together. Only the girls were inter-ested in playing hopscotch and jump rope on the sidewalk in front of our house. I didn't realize it at the time, as I wasn't aware of anti-Semitism, but Nancy, whose father was a lawyer, remarked many times, "Even though my father has a Jewish nose, we are Protestants, not Jews." I didn't know what made a nose "Jewish" because my father's nose was smaller than her father's, and my father really was Jewish. When Nancy was in a good mood, she would invite me to her church on Saturday afternoons for a cowboy movie, but when she was mad at me for some reason, she stuck out her tongue at me and called me "Jew Beggel." Then she would run home as I called after her, "Nancy Pancy!" It took me twenty years to figure out that she was equating Jews with bagels.

I loved going to my friend Mary's house, where every room held pastel-painted statues of the Virgin Mary, and the walls were hung with wooden crucifixes and framed pictures of Christ with the crown of thorns upon His head, with drops of blood dripping ominously down the canvas. I stood transfixed before these pictures, visualizing the terrible pain He must have suffered, with the nails going through His hands and feet and the thorns penetrating His scalp. Mary's father owned the Yellow Cab Company at the railroad station, and on rainy days he would send a cab to school to pick her up. If she saw me walking home in the rain, she would have the cab stop for me.

My friend Malcolm, whose mother was the only woman I knew who drove a car, also picked up Malcolm at school on rainy days, and if I was lucky, I was invited to ride home in their big Packard touring car with isinglass windows. On Malcolm's ninth birthday, his parents' gift to him was a ride in an airplane. They piled a bunch of us kids in the car and drove us to the airport to share in the thrill of watching Malcolm board the plane for his fifteen-minute plane ride, which cost five dollars. Malcolm had loaded the pockets of his leather pilot's jacket with scraps of paper that he'd planned to throw out the window of the plane from aloft, but in his excitement, he forgot and still had the loaded pockets when the plane landed.

I remember my ninth year as the year that my mother bought a girdle for me to wear—not like her long, whale-boned corset with steel hooks but an elasticized panty with a strip of cloth between the legs that tried to work its way up to where my tonsils had been. I didn't like it, but my mother said I was getting too fat and had to stop sneaking food. I did love to eat and always wanted seconds at mealtime, which my mother refused me, so I'd sneak it out of the refrigerator when she wasn't in the kitchen. My sister, Ruth, was skinny and didn't like to eat most foods, which should have pleased my mother, but I can still see her chasing Ruth around the dining room table with a wooden spoon, trying to force her to eat. It was about this time that I remember my parents talking in low tones about something called "Depression," and they didn't seem very happy about it.

My tenth birthday was coming up, the only birthday when we kids were allowed to have a real party with kids invited, for parties were too expensive. That year, my birthday fell on a Saturday, which was piano-lesson day. I set off for the two-mile walk downtown to my piano teacher, happily anticipating the afternoon party. At the conclusion of the lesson, I dug in my pocket for the little red-felt purse that held three one-dollar bills to pay for one month of lessons, but it wasn't there. I frantically checked all my pockets with no sign of it, while the teacher tried to appease me by saying that I must have left it at home. I retraced my footsteps home, eyes to the ground, checking the gutters as well as the sidewalks, crying and praying as I walked, but there was no sign of the purse. It wasn't at home either, yet—surprisingly—my mother didn't even scold me. That afternoon I played Pin the Tail on the Donkey and Musical Chairs with the kids with false gaiety. I opened my gifts and ate the ice cream and cake, but the loss of that three dollars weighed heavily on my heart. I had looked forward to this milestone birthday for so long, and now it was ruined. ❧

CHAPTER TWO

CLASS BEAUTY

"BETTY," I panted in exasperation, "let's slow down; you're killing me."

"No!" Betty replied breathlessly. "We have to keep running, or we'll never lose weight."

I couldn't possibly run and answer her at the same time, but I thought as I trotted along beside her that Betty, my best friend, was overdoing this weight business. I'd told her fifty times a day that she wasn't fat, that I would give my eye teeth to be as "fat" as she was, but she'd only respond with, "The mirror doesn't lie."

This illusion, that she was fat, had possessed her completely since starting our junior year in high school, and nothing could change her opinion about herself. We were both 5 feet 5½ inches tall, but I weighed 148 pounds, as compared to Betty's weight of 118 pounds. I wore a size 16 dress, and she wore a size 10. Betty's hip bones were visible in tight skirts, but if I had hip bones, I could not find them under my layers of adipose tissue. And yet, Betty honestly believed she was fat!

Aware that I needed the exercise more than she, I acceded to her commands each day as we made our way up the hills to our high school: "*Run; don't walk. Hop up and down the curbs. Don't take the elevators in the building; use the stairs! And don't just walk up the stairs, run up.*"

The fact that she was drop-dead gorgeous didn't affect her erroneous opinion of her body, and when I tried to point out that people (especially males) stared appreciatively at her ethereal beauty, she insisted they stared because she was fat. Every student in the junior class, with the exception of Betty, knew without any doubt that she would be the winning candidate for the Class Beauty category in our class elections. She was blessed with an abundance of shoulder-length, shiny, almost black, natural wavy hair that framed a sun-tanned, high-cheek-boned face. Her deep-set, dreamy-looking dark brown eyes were fringed with long, curly lashes that imparted an air of childlike innocence, setting off to good advantage Betty's sculpted patrician nose. A generous mouth, which smiled languidly and frequently, displayed perfect white teeth, completing the picture of a beautiful girl on the cusp of womanhood. And yet she couldn't see herself as others saw her.

Physical beauty wasn't Betty's only attribute; she had a happy, easygoing disposition and was never one to criticize others—she only found fault with her own body. It was amazing that her disposition remained as sweet as it was, for her family background left more to be desired. Betty never knew Her father, as her parents were divorced when she was a baby, and she and her mother, Edna, lived in her widowed grandmother's home.

Edna was employed as a secretary in one of the silver factory offices in town. Not only was she one of the few women of that time to drive a car, but she also played golf. This was pretty much unheard of in those days, especially because she was the only woman golfer among the men from her office. Edna's social life was paramount, so she wasn't around too much for any mothering that Betty might need; that task fell to Edna's mother, Hattie, who was out of touch with the times and tried to inflict her outmoded method of child-rearing on Betty, along with her constant criticism.

On our walks to school (or I should say our *runs* to school), Betty often unburdened herself to me and was frequently in tears, because nothing she did pleased her mother or her grandmother. Though she was an excellent student, they would tell her that she should have gotten an A+, rather than A; that her hair looked like a rat's nest; or that her choice in clothes was disgraceful, "like that of a streetwalker." The only thing Betty did right—at least in Edna's and Hattie's eyes—was to be beautiful. "She had better not mess up her chances to be the Class Beauty with all her crazy dieting," they'd say. Betty and I both knew they loved her, but their choice of words was often hurtful.

It wasn't surprising at all that the shoe-in for The Most Handsome category was a certain Matthew Peck, who became Betty's constant partner at school dances. He joined our talks in the hallway between classes; he kept her on the phone for hours at night, much to her grandmother's disgust; and he often joined us on our walk home from school—Matthew's joining us meant that it was a more sedate walk, with no running or hopping up and down curbs. Sometimes the sidewalk narrowed so only two could walk abreast, and I would then pull behind them. But Betty, loyal as ever, would motion for Matt to fall behind and for me to take my place beside her.

The running-and-hopping bit was only a small part of the picture. Food—or lack of it—was high on Betty's list of priorities, and at home, the hue and cry of her mother (when she was home) and grandmother was, "Betty, why are you starving yourself?" Or, "Betty, you're just skin and bones; you look terrible." Betty ate next to nothing, despite their entreaties and threats. I can still see her, sitting at her dining room table, a huge plate of mashed potatoes in front of her, with the tears running down her face.

"Listen, young lady," Betty's grandmother proclaimed, jabbing a pointed finger at her, "you eat all those potatoes, or you're not going to that football game today."

As her grandmother stalked into the kitchen, I whispered to Betty, "Eat them already, or we're going to miss the game."

A paper bag magically appeared from beneath the tablecloth, into which Betty pushed the contents of her plate. Then the bag disappeared back under the tablecloth. As Grandmother emerged from the kitchen, Betty winked at me as she displayed her empty plate.

"Hmm," her grandmother puffed out, "it's just too bad you have to aggravate me to death by not eating, when you know all along you're going to finish it if you want to get out of this house." With that, she flounced out of the dining room.

Betty sashayed into the bedroom that she shared with her mother, hiding the bag in the folds of her skirt. She held it there until she could dump it into a trash container as we made our way down the street.

There was one place where Betty ate—in fact, she gorged herself, as did I—and that was at the monthly club meeting at school, where sinful, fattening goodies were served in abundance—potato chips, chocolate-covered ice cream bars, Hostess cupcakes with frosting, Milky Way bars, Old Nick candy bars, sodas—and we had three and four helpings of each. These were all forbidden foods in my home for the following reasons: they were fattening, they were fattening, and they were an unnecessary expenditure in the always-tight food budget. My mother's idea of a wild dessert was a spice cake without any frosting. Is it any wonder that I was all too happy to be Betty's food-bingeing partner? And I needed all that food a lot less than she did.

The first time I was privy to Betty's stuffing herself on all those forbidden foods, I couldn't quite reconcile it to the fact that she literally ate no food at home except black coffee. "Betty," I inquired, "why are we eating all this fattening food? We'll never lose the weight this food is going to pile on us."

"You'll see," she promised, "after school, when we go to your house."

My mother worked, so our house was always empty when I arrived home from school. After club meetings, it became routine for Betty to accompany me home. Then, she'd unload her school briefcase with the likes of Milk of Magnesia, senna leaf tea, Ex-Lax, mineral oil, and cascara tablets.

"First off, we'll get rid of the top layer," she instructed. With that, she walked into the downstairs bathroom, where she proceeded to put her finger down her throat, which initiated the gagging reflex. In no time, the "top layer" was disgorged. I was an apt pupil and worked the upstairs bathroom while she did the downstairs one. Once that procedure was finished, she introduced me to the murderously horrible taste of senna leaf tea, which was almost bad enough in itself to activate the gagging reflex. Following the tea, we each swallowed two Ex-Lax squares, and then Betty gave me a cascara tablet to take at bedtime, just in case nothing else worked.

I enjoyed my food too much to give up eating the way she did, and though I tried following her cathartic regime for a few weeks, I ended up gaining four pounds. I was now up to 152, but by the end of our school year, Betty was down to 100 pounds.

When we started our senior year in September, our classmates were appalled with Betty's appearance, and some made cautious remarks to the effect that she should stop dieting because it was showing in her face. Indeed, her face was gaunt, with those dark eyes sunk deep into the sockets. She truly resembled a walking skeleton. As the year progressed, her weight dropped to 92 pounds, her menstrual periods ceased, and her family physician threw up his hands in despair each time she declared she was too fat. In those days, no one ever heard of anorexia or bulimia, although now it seems clear that one or both of those could have been her diagnosis.

At some point along the way, the Most Handsome candidate, Matthew Peck, gradually ceased his attentions at the school dances. The nightly phone calls were no more (to the relief of Betty's grandmother), and so it was just the two of us again, walking home from school. Matt took the winner of the Class Beauty contest to the senior prom, but it wasn't my dear friend Betty. Betty seemed unruffled by the fact that she hadn't won the title of Class Beauty, though her mother and grandmother were certainly annoyed. She wasn't upset, either, by Matt's lack of attention. In fact, she was relieved—by springtime she had met Jim, who lived in a neighboring town, and the chemistry between the two was instantaneous. Jim saw her innate beauty under the bony exterior and was smitten by her warm, loving, and outgoing personality. In a matter of weeks, they were going steady, and in his eyes, she was truly the Class Beauty. Where others noted her broomstick-like arms and jutting shoulder blades, Jim was oblivious. At the senior prom, Jim gazed deeply into Betty's eyes as they danced to the romantic hit songs of our day.

As her confidante, I knew that Betty was in love, and I was happy that she had found someone who still appreciated her and returned her love, in spite of her wraithlike appearance. His entrance in her life ended Betty's ambition to become a nurse. Although she entered nursing school the September following graduation, she left at the end of her first year to marry Jim, who was about to be inducted into the Army. Apparently, Jim's entry into her life ended the eating problems too, for one of the photographs she sent me while I was in nurses training in Cambridge showed that Betty was, once again, drop-dead gorgeous. She became pregnant in the third month of marriage, which may have contributed to the ethereal glow that emanated from her face. Of course, her mother and grandmother were furious that she had become pregnant so soon. "People will talk and count the months," they said.

I wish I could say that Betty and Jim lived happily ever after, but that wasn't meant to be. Evidently, marriage vows didn't mean too much to Jim. On his return from the service, after an absence of two years overseas and at a time when their marriage should have been comparatively carefree, trouble was brewing in their household. Jim had not suffered from lack of female companionship during his stint in Europe, and he still desired variety once he returned home. At one point, a confused and unhappy Betty came to spend a few days with Mel and me to try to sort out her feelings and future direction. But all it took was one phone call from Jim to send her flying back to him and their two children. Jim didn't change over the next few years, and eventually, Betty decided she'd had her fill of his philandering, which, most regrettably, she demonstrated to him by committing suicide. ❧

CHAPTER THREE

MISSING: ONE CHAPTER

IF THE STORY OF MY LIFE is ever written, it is imperative that one certain chapter be deleted. To this day, over sixty-three years later, I cringe with mortification at the mere thought of that painful episode.

It started off innocently enough, right after high school graduation, when we were still flushed with self-importance and the excitement of reaching this milestone. Several classmates and I, in the throes of separation pangs, banded together to produce a musical variety show, with talent garnered from former performers in school musicals.

For those functions I was always relegated to the first-soprano side of the chorus and never given a starring role. Granted, I had done my share of singing as class comedienne with a male counterpart—the more off-key we sang, the funnier the act. But I did yearn to be a singer of more import, and now was my chance. I was one of the directors of this variety show, and I was determined to sing, no matter what! I still can't believe my chutzpah.

Because I was a director, I waived my turn at rehearsing on stage with the other performers. After all, I reasoned to myself, I practiced at home—when I had the house to myself—and my voice sounded pretty good to me. I thought that I sang my chosen romantic number, "I'm Getting Sentimental Over You," with pathos.

Came the big night, and every one of the five hundred seats in the City Hall auditorium was filled. Our singers, dancers, and musicians, who had been honing their skills for years in school productions, drew thunderous applause from the appreciative audience; they were good! I was backstage, reveling in the enthusiastic reception they were getting, when someone poked my arm and whispered, "You're next."

Cold reality set in as I made my way to center stage and the spotlight focused on me. As the orchestra began the introduction to my song, I looked out over that sea of faces and was instantly paralyzed with stage fright. I opened my mouth to sing, but no sound issued forth. Something was wrong: the sounds that had come out so readily and sweetly at home were now mute. The orchestra played a few opening bars again, and I could feel a sympathetic audience mentally urging my vocal cords into action. Again, the orchestra played some opening bars, and I finally managed to warble some thin sounds to the musical accompaniment. Where was that confident voice that, prior to this night, had sounded so pretty in my ears? I managed to finish my number, barely able to squeak out the lyrics, but I was overcome with humiliation at my own stupidity for not rehearsing on stage with the others.

I ran offstage to a smattering of polite applause and cowered backstage until the end of the show, neither hearing nor seeing the rest of the performance. It was difficult participating in the after-show party, realizing that I, one of the directors, was the only dud of the evening. I learned the hard way that wanting to sing does not a singer make.

I was dining recently with old friends from my hometown who winter in Florida. While reminiscing about mutual friends, my ugly past caught up with me. The host ruined my dinner by suddenly asking, "Hey, whatever happened to you at that variety show?"

I reiterate: that chapter of my life must be deleted. 🙒

CHAPTER FOUR

BANDAGE POWER

IT SEEMS RIDICULOUS that something as innocuous as rolls of cotton bandage could define a good portion of my life, but that's what happened, according to my mother (and if my mother said it, then it was the gospel truth). I don't have any recollection (although I was reminded dozens of times over the next half century) of my early years, when I brought home injured dogs, cats, and playmates for bandaging. This probably was inspired by my visit to a doctor's office.

Early photos of me usually showed a bandage on one of my extremities, so I was apparently impressed enough by the sympathy and attention garnered by this bandage to pass on the good deed to animals and friends in need of a fix. We didn't have money to waste on "bandages for the whole world," according to my mother, so when our household supply ran out, I'd go to her rag bag and tear up strips of clean white rags, which served the purpose, though they lacked the éclat and professionalism of a Curity bandage. A generous swab of mercurochrome preceded my applying the bandage, and then the patient was as good as new.

As a result of my preoccupation, it was ordained that I would become a nurse. My paternal grandmother in Russia was a midwife with her own clinic, so the medical bent was definitely in my blood. I had no intention of spending eight to ten years of my young life in the rigorous medical school and internship regime, but the idea of a three-year nursing course, bandaging those in need, suited me just fine. This, then, was my goal throughout my public school years—that is, until my senior year in high school, when I took to heart the horror stories of former upperclassmen with regard to the ogre who taught chemistry and the difficulties of passing that course. No way was I going to take the course only to flunk it.

So I took typing instead, declaring that I would be a secretary, much to the disappointment of my mother, who kept insisting I was born to be a nurse.

Surprisingly, I liked typing and was good at it, but upon graduation, I learned that one year of high school typing didn't qualify me to be a secretary. I enrolled in a local business college to ratchet up my typing speed and learn the Gregg method of shorthand. All those little squiggles that looked like hieroglyphics had meaning, and I was fascinated by them. My speed and proficiency increased rapidly, and I was able to transcribe to the typewriter the long business letters I'd taken in shorthand at maximum speed—without error. It was always a source of amazement to me that I could do this, because I could never paint or draw and always said my hands were like feet.

I sailed through the first half of the next semester, which was too easy. There were no challenges for me to overcome. Then, strange sensations of ennui began to emerge, and at this point, the nursing profession started enticing me again. I castigated myself repeatedly for not having taken chemistry, but what could I do about it?

A family friend, who had been a nurse in the Boston area, encouraged me to apply to a nursing school for the fall semester and to take a summer course in chemistry to acquire the necessary credits. Because I wanted so badly to attend nursing school, I finally was able to conquer my fear that I would flunk chemistry.

In short order, I was accepted at Northeastern University in Boston for chemistry classes three nights a week; this gave me the option of finding a day-time job. I also was accepted into the fall nursing class at Cambridge Hospital (contingent upon my attaining the necessary credits in chemistry). Cambridge Hospital was a private hospital, beautifully located on the banks of the Charles River, with huge expanses of lawn between the buildings. I had chosen to apply to this hospital, based on the supposition that it would allow me to see more of my then boyfriend, Ted, who was a sophomore at Harvard. The location of the nursing school, just a few blocks from Harvard Square and the Harvard dormitories, would be advantageous to furthering our budding romance, a romance that'd had difficulty attaining full bloom because we saw each other only during his few school vacations. Ironically, once he was available to me on a steady basis, the anticipation and thrill of the chase was gone, and we remained just good friends.

Now that my future was decided, the next step was to find inexpensive, safe housing for a nineteen-year-old female who was living away from home in a strange city. This turned out to be the YWCA on Berkley Street, an old but imposing brick building that was a couple of miles from my classes at Northeastern University—easy walking distance for me. The fee for renting a small six-by-eight bedroom was minimal, about three dollars per week. In addition to my other expenses for food and transportation for job hunting, the three dollars was about all my mother could afford at the time.

My room was on the second floor; it contained a small but comfortable cot-sized bed, a chair, a small chest of drawers, and an armoire, sufficient for holding my three-month supply of clothing. My one window overlooked Berkley Street, and immediately across the street was an enormous stone edifice that seemed to swallow up half of the block. Glaring at me each time my gaze wandered out the window was a startling sign, three feet high, in black gothic letters on a white background: *Jesus is coming. Are you ready?* Each morning as I raised my head from my pillow, the message on that sign was enough to keep me from falling back to sleep.

While living at the YWCA, my diet consisted of peanut butter sandwiches, as I could easily keep a jar of peanut butter and loaf of bread in my room. Another treat I allowed myself was sandwich spread, ground pickles, and mayonnaise on white bread—even without the benefit of refrigeration, I suffered no ill effects. A few times a week, I splurged on a hot meal—usually Chinese food—for twenty-five cents (or even thirty-five cents) at a food counter or inexpensive restaurant. I had to ration myself, because I could have eaten Chinese food three times a day. I did not lose weight that summer.

Once food and shelter were accounted for, the next step was to find a job where I could use my typing and shorthand skills and which was within a decent commuting distance. When I found an ad in the *Boston Globe*, seeking a secretary for the Cambridge Roofing Company, I knew this was my chance. Armed with my references from business college, I set out for the interview and found my way to the Cambridge Roofing Company, via subway and bus. On arrival, I was greeted by the office manager, Sarah, a warm, bespectacled, buxom redhead, who was about thirty years old. She was the only female on the premises—the place was populated with male truck drivers and engineers and the owner, Mr. Feldman, who had a marked speech impediment.

After dictating a letter to me, which I immediately transcribed and typed up without problem, Sarah, who was overwhelmed with work, hired me on the spot. As she later confided to me, she was delighted to have another female to converse with, especially a Jewish one. It was common to inquire about one's religious affiliation on job applications in those days and on my job application, I had listed Protestant as my religious denomination because Jews weren't readily hired. After I had proven my secretarial skills, I divulged the truth to Sarah, who chuckled and said she had a feeling all along that I was a "member of the tribe."

Work at Cambridge Roofing was enjoyable, and my only secretarial goof occurred when I took dictation one day from Mr. Feldman. "Merrill," he began (although my name is Muriel), "please take a letter." I transcribed his message as I heard it, which was "Please sip us a barrel of pits." When I gave it to him to sign, he exploded, "Good grasis, Merrill! I said 'Sip us a barrel of pits'!"

Suddenly, it dawns on me: Not only could he not pronounce my name, but he also couldn't pronounce the *sh* sound! And I didn't know enough about roofing materials at that point to realize he'd meant "Ship us a barrel of pitch." I learned quickly after that episode.

Chemistry classes were not as difficult as I had feared. In fact, I hated to admit it—especially after my year of procrastination—but the subject really was interesting (even though my total enthusiasm for chemistry would never be earth-shattering).

I received an A on my final exams, along with a congratulatory letter from my professor, to whom I'd expressed my deep-seated fear of flunking.

My superintendent of nurses was extremely pleased with the results of my summer course, and the last stumbling block was removed from my much-detoured road to nursing school. It had been a long journey from my neighborhood bandaging days, but I had arrived. And my mother had been right—I was born to be a nurse. 🙾

CHAPTER FIVE

BITS AND PIECES

"THIS MEANS I'LL HAVE TO COOK, and clean out the guest room closet and drawers," I complained to Mel, "but I'm really thrilled that they are coming." My nursing school classmate, dating back sixty-six years, had just e-mailed the unexpected but good news that she and her husband were coming for a weekend visit in March. This simple announcement from Doris set the wheels of my brain in motion, recalling bits and pieces of my life as a student nurse for three years, another lifetime ago, and little tableaux of certain incidents kept popping up on my memory screen.

How clearly I see myself during those first several weeks, when I and my fellow "probationers" learned the ins and outs of bed-making, bathing patients, and taking blood pressure, temperature, pulse, and respiration. Then the day came when we were finally allowed on the wards to deal with real patients (instead of Mary Lou, the dummy), and we were all in a state of nervous anticipation. After I'd bathed my three assigned patients and changed the linens on their beds, I was given an additional duty of cleaning the thermometer tray, an easy enough chore—or so I thought, as I carried the chrome rack that held thirty thermometers into the utility room.

Each thermometer was held in a test tube filled with blue disinfecting solution, with a cotton wad at the bottom to cushion the sensitive mercury-containing tip of the thermometer. I removed each thermometer gently and placed it in a shallow tray; then I thoroughly cleansed the tubes and refilled them with clean cotton and solution. I filled the tray of thermometers with steaming hot, soapy water, cleaning each one thoroughly, and then rinsed them under hot running water before inserting them into the sparkling clean test tubes.

At that point, the head nurse entered the utility room, and I proudly pointed to the gleaming thermometer rack. She picked one out of its test-tube holder, looked closely at it, and then replaced it in its holder. She repeated this operation with three or four more thermometers before announcing severely, "Miss Phillips, you have just ruined thirty thermometers, which will be charged to your breakage fee. Didn't you realize the thermometer is only graded to 106 degrees, and the hot water you cleaned them in was close to boiling—212 degrees?"

No, I hadn't; no one ever told me.

I also remember Miss Conroy, the youngest and most animated among the rest of the moth-eaten-looking nursing instructors. She looked perky and cute in her starched white uniform, with her cap pinned to her curly reddish-gold hair. She taught anatomy and physiology, and because we loved her, we always looked forward to this class.

One day, she asked an unusual question: "Does anyone here know the meaning of the word *masturbate?*" Furtive glances passed between some nurses, while others stared blankly at the teacher. Then, one arm shot up in response to the question. "Yes, Miss McDermott?" said Miss Conroy. "You know the meaning of the word?"

Triumphant in her knowledge, Miss McDermott, known to us as Mac, stated, "It means to chew rapidly."

Miss Conroy's only reply was "I believe you are thinking of the word *masticate.*" The subject was not pursued.

And then there was my six weeks spent in the diet kitchen, learning to prepare both special and house diets. One day, I had a sudden inspiration as I whipped the tubs of bland-looking mashed potatoes that would be served throughout the hospital. Certainly, some drops of red vegetable dye in the potatoes would make them more colorful and appealing to the eye and appetite. My esthetic senses were satisfied by the mounds of fluffy clouds of pink mashed potatoes that emerged. I anticipated accolades for my ingenuity from the diet-kitchen director. Instead, when all the trays were returned to the diet kitchen with the potatoes largely uneaten, I received her scathing reprimand: "Miss Phillips, in the future you will direct your artistic bent in other directions than the diet kitchen."

Some bits and pieces of nurses training memories always bring a smile to my face. One such memory is of the time I fixed up my classmate Stephanie with the roommate of my date, a Harvard sophomore. Stephanie was to meet the three of us in the Nurses Lounge at 7 p.m. When she hadn't appeared by 7:20, I went to her room to hurry her up. The door to her room was partially open, so I walked in. She stood in front of the mirror in her bra and panties. Her head was down, and she seemed intent on pinning something to her panties. Then I saw that there was a line of big hospital-size safety pins all around her waist.

"What in the world are you doing?" I asked testily. "You're twenty minutes late and holding us up."

"Well, I've heard these Harvard guys are all wolves" she replied defensively. "I'm pinning my pants to my bra, so I won't be taking any chances."

In our second year, we had Miss Conroy again for ob-gyn classes, which coincided with our working on the maternity floor. I was confounded by a question posed to me by my patient, Mrs. Burns. I promised to relay her question to my nursing instructor, which I did in class the next day. "Miss Conroy, my patient, Mrs. Burns, has been on the maternity floor six times in eight years, and she is exhausted and depressed from so many pregnancies. She has asked me how she can stop them." Mrs. Burns surely picked a fine one to ask for advice—I was naïve about certain facts of life; until I became a student nurse I'd thought pregnancy could be "caught" from toilet seats.

Miss Conroy was visibly agitated. "Miss Phillips, in this state of Massachusetts, there are such things known as "blue laws," which prohibit us from dispensing any advice about birth control. Tell her to discuss it with her physician."

I felt rebuked, but I also was sad for poor Mrs. Burns, whose physician couldn't or wouldn't ease her dilemma. I often wondered how many kids she unwillingly produced over the years.

In those days, the physician ruled supreme in the hospital. We treated them as gods, and they really thought they were. We nurses had to stand to relinquish our seat whenever one of the gods approached the nurses' desk, and when we saw them coming down the hall, even if they were several yards away, it was standard protocol to stop what we were doing to hold the door open for them. Most were pleasant to work with, but there was an occasional rotten apple in the barrel. One particular obstetrician was known for his volatile temper and penchant for throwing instruments on the floor of the delivery room. He was quickly identified via the hospital grapevine on the day he threw a weighted speculum through the delivery room window, shattering the glass and lining the floor with thousands of shards.

In this same time period, we saw maternity patients hospitalized for two weeks after their deliveries; and cataract surgery patients who had to remain at flat bed rest for ten days, with sand bags around their heads to minimize all head movement. Cancer patients were a rarity at that time, and when one was admitted to the hospital, the word traveled quickly around the hospital. "Did you hear that there is a CA patient on Ward A?"

Doris, my friend who was coming to visit, was the one true intellectual in our class of thirty nurses. She read every single page of the daily *Boston Globe* newspaper in the Nurses Lounge. The rest of us only read the funnies or the entertainment page. Doris was the only one able to discourse on happenings in the world outside of the hospital, but that held no interest for the other nurses. Coming from a family of extreme poverty, she was concerned with the starving poor of the world, as well as the underdogs and the plight of the blacks (known then as "colored people").

She once invited me to accompany her to a free lecture in Boston, the topic of which was way above my head. The fiery speakers kept repeating the same words: entitlement, the masses, equality, capitalism, socialism. It was very boring for me and a waste of an afternoon. I didn't know then that Doris was a card-carrying Communist. At our senior-class dance, she was severely reprimanded for dancing with a "colored" member of the band, a friend of hers from the Communist Party. When she married a well-to-do businessman, she dropped her Communist Party membership, although for years she was head of the NAACP in her state. This was Doris, true to her ideals.

Oh, I couldn't wait for her to arrive so we could rehash all these bits and pieces—and more—all over again. ❧

Muriel as a student nurse.

CHAPTER SIX

CELIA AND THE MADHOUSE

"THEY'LL WORK YOU TO DEATH, and Celia is the worst!"

"Good luck, and try not to get Celia!"

"That place is a real madhouse!"

"Stay away from Celia; she's a bitch on wheels!"

Senior-class nursing students, just returned from their three-month affiliation in communicable diseases at Boston City Hospital, were regaling us with wild tales of their experiences there. I was about to leave for the same affiliation with five other class members, and we listened in horrified fascination to the stories about the worst head nurse, the floors with the worst facilities, and who were the worst patients—and Celia, it was unanimously determined, was the worst of the worst patients! The twelve weeks looming before us felt like a lifetime sentence, when we would leave the familiar environs of our own hospital in Cambridge for the unknown, just a few miles away; it might as well have been Siberia.

The Communicable Disease section of City really did seem like a madhouse, because the beds never cooled off. The very early 1940s had not yet seen vaccines for the prevention of measles, whooping cough, scarlet fever, or polio, and these diseases were rampant. We couldn't disinfect the beds and remake them fast enough before there'd be more incoming patients.

One student nurse was faced with orders to disinfect a bed for an extremely ill patient who'd been newly admitted to the floor. The morgue attendants, however, hadn't yet come to claim the body of the patient who had expired in that bed some time before. What to do? The need for the bed was paramount, so the dead patient was placed in an arm chair adjacent to the bed, which could now be made up for the incoming patient. By the time the morgue attendants arrived, rigor mortis had set in, and it was most strange to see them wheel off a draped sitting figure.

I had been at City for three weeks without a sign of Celia—so far, so good. And then my worst fears were realized when I was assigned to the polio wing. I got Celia—the "bitch on wheels"—and I found out that she actually was on wheels, for Celia was a twenty-six-year-old polio victim, encased in a full-body respirator on wheels. She was to be my morning-care patient for the next several weeks.

Being on the polio ward for six years gave Celia seniority over the other patients, and she barked her orders to this quaking student nurse: "Where have you been?" "I'm hungry; feed me now!" "Scratch my nose!" "Move my little finger on my left hand—no, not *that* finger, stupid. The little finger!"

Celia was completely paralyzed from the neck down, and the only muscles she had control of were her muscles for chewing and swallowing, blinking, and talking. And talk she did!

Great, I'm defeated before I start, I thought. *But I might as well give it a try.* "Celia, I am Miss Phillips," I began, "and I will be your nurse for morning care for the next three or four weeks. You are my first polio patient, and I'll do my best to keep you satisfied." *That should soften her,* I thought. I was pleased with my attempt at diplomacy—until she quickly deflated me with her comeback:.

"You won't satisfy me while you're letting the coffee dribble down my neck into my ear," she shot back.

I had a lot to learn about the care of a polio patient, but between Celia's continual carping about her daily care and my true desire to make her as comfortable as possible, Celia and I became friends. My empathy for Celia knew no bounds, particularly when I learned that she had been engaged to marry a young law student at the time she was stricken with this dread disease. She'd been just nineteen but was destined to spend the rest of her life entombed in a mechanical breathing machine. To my way of thinking, death would have been preferable to this kind of existence, but she had no choice.

As the days passed, I became more proficient in my nursing care, and I looked forward to my time with her. We discussed past experiences, our families, the latest news items, and hospital personalities. Celia had a keen mind and was still interested in the happenings of the outside world. A reading apparatus had been placed at the top of the respirator, and she could turn the pages of a book by a thread held between her teeth. A bedside radio kept her informed about the world she had left almost seven years ago.

Even after I was transferred to another wing of the hospital, I would go back to visit Celia when not on duty. One day, I arrived at her room and was horrified to find her respirator empty. Then I was told that Celia was sitting out on the porch with a new portable chest respirator. Rushing out to the porch, I found Celia proudly ensconced in a wheelchair, enjoying the sun with other wheelchair patients. After the six years spent on her back with only a dirt-gray hospital ceiling for her view, this was a radical change in Celia's life.

There may have been later improvements, and my mind is hazy as to the mechanics of the respirator, but at that time, sixty years ago, Celia could use this portable chest respirator only for half-hour periods, as inspirations had to be consciously taken at regular intervals; otherwise, she could lapse into unconsciousness and death. If Celia had been so inclined, her release from the iron-lung prison could have been at hand; she could have just "forgotten" to breathe during one of her half-hour daily sessions.

In my position as a nurse, it was part of our creed to inspire and give hope to sick patients and to encourage them to get better, to live. *But is Celia's existence in that iron machine really living?* I pondered. *What can she look forward to?* I compared the bedside photograph of a vibrant, brown-eyed, lovely woman with shoulder-length dark wavy hair to this sunken-cheeked, sunken-eyed patient with the hospital pallor face, and hospital-shorn hairdo, peeking out from the collar of the respirator. Five years, ten years, twenty years?

I finally broached the subject that had been on my mind for days. "Celia, I really admire your guts and tenacity in making the best of your situation," I told her, "particularly when it is within your power to be free."

Celia's reply reverberates in my ears to this day. "Muriel, don't think I haven't been aware of my opportunity to escape this life ever since I have been able to use the chest respirator. I keep thinking that my deliverance is at hand, and each day I promise myself, 'Today is the day', and yet, in the final analysis, I really want to be around. I know my case is hopeless and yet, I have hope. Maybe something will be invented tomorrow or next week. Maybe I'll wake up some day, and I'll be cured, miraculously. It's not guts that I have; it's hope."

Some fifteen or twenty years later, I read Celia's obituary in the *New York Times*. She was credited as being one of the iron lung patients to have survived the longest. ❧

CHAPTER SEVEN

DELUSIONS

IN 1941 THE UNITED STATES was still in the throes of the Depression, and our superintendent of nurses was in the throes of delusions of martyrdom. If she harbored those same ideas today, she'd be out of a job—or, more likely, in a mental institution.

At a time in history when the nursing profession was at the tail end of the salary scale of all the professions, and nurses worked the craziest hours and did the dirtiest of work, it was considered unethical to unionize nurses. The biggest proponent of this notion was our Miss Lawson, whose responsibility was to teach the senior nursing class the subject of nursing ethics one day a week. After all the exciting, thrilling, and undreamed of facets of nursing we had learned over the past two and a half years, her class was *boring*!

She would stand ramrod straight in front of the class. Her heavily starched white uniform was buttoned tightly to her neck and had wide accordion pleats that flared over her ample bosom. Perched on her severely combed-back gray hair, which was gathered in a tight bun, was the Massachusetts General Hospital pleated, inverted-cup-like cap. This cap was a symbol of superiority then (and now), as Mass General Hospital was one of the oldest and most renowned of hospitals, and any nurse of distinction at that time was, of course, a Mass General graduate.

Miss Lawson's oval-shaped face was heavily wrinkled, and her pointed chin and her two protruding upper front teeth gave her a beaver-like appearance. She would drone on and on during each class period, enumerating what a good nurse should do or should not do. When she got to the Should Not Do's, she would toss her head back, bare her teeth in a semi-grin that was more of a grimace, and murmur through those beaver teeth,

"We don't do that, do we, girls?"

Money was Miss Lawson's nemesis. She preached endlessly about the evils of money. "Money is truly the root of all evils." or "Money is dirty, filthy lucre!"

Time and again, she instilled in us the idea that any jobs we should take upon graduation should be for humanitarian reasons only. "Don't ever let me hear that any of my nurses would accept a job based upon the salary she would receive," she warned us. "Your job is to alleviate pain and suffering, not to consider financial gain."

Did this woman suffer from delusions, or could she have been so altruistic that she really believed in what she preached? I'll never know. ❧

PART TWO

THE-WAR

CHAPTER EIGHT

MESSAGE TO HARRY

WORLD WAR II was in full swing in 1943, when our U.S. Army general hospital was scheduled for overseas duty. A full complement of equipment, clothing, and emergency food rations (K-rations) had been issued to us, but our most important item of equipment was the steel helmet and liner. We nurses complained bitterly about the weight of that helmet on our heads, but we soon learned that this helmet would be our best friend. In time, it would serve as our wash basin, bathtub, and portable toilet, as well as our only body protection during bombings (at which time we would worm as much of ourselves as possible into those helmets) and wish they were bigger.

For six months, our hospital unit trained intensively at Fort Devens, Massachusetts, for this overseas mission. Finally, we were ready to go. The nurses had drilled for hours daily. ("Hut, two, three, four; to the rear, march!") We straggled through fifteen-mile hikes, learned compass reading, and studied diseases, from Yaws to Tsutsugamushi fever. We went through gas-mask drill, learned to pitch tents, practiced ascending and descending a rope ladder, and went through the infiltration course. The infiltration course included crawling on our bellies under live ammunition, and I can still hear the drill sergeant bellowing, "Get your butts down, or you'll get 'em creased." We got our butts down.

Preparatory to boarding the ship, our hospital personnel (one hundred nurses, fifty medical, dental, and medical administrative officers; and five hundred enlisted men) spent three days in quarantine at a staging area near Boston. Troop movements required the utmost secrecy, and we were forbidden to make phone calls, write letters, or divulge any information about imminent departure. "Loose lips sink ships" had been pounded into us.

On our last night in the staging area, while doing a final luggage check, a voice called out from the barracks doorway, "Phone call for Lieutenant Phillips." I was catapulted into a state of panic. Who knew I was here? And how did that person get my phone number? I raced to the wall phone and became weak with relief when I heard the voice of my newest romantic interest, a handsome dentist named Harry, who was serving on a naval troop transport. We had only seen each other twice since we first met aboard a troop train, but we kept the military post office busy with our voluminous correspondence. Harry's ship, the USS *Dorothea Dix*, had been involved in military landings in North Africa and Europe and was apparently just returning from a naval operation.

A dozen questions ran through my head, but I was quickly silenced. "Don't ask questions because I cannot answer you," Harry said. "I just want you to know that I know where you are going, and you will be sailing in my convoy."

Whoopee! My trepidations over leaving the United States the next day vanished in the euphoria of hearing Harry's voice and the miraculous news that I would be traveling in his ship's convoy.

It was a cold, bleak late-December day when we boarded our ship, the USS *E.B. Alexander*, in Boston Harbor. We learned the name of our ship only after we boarded it, as names of all ships during the war were obliterated from their bows for security reasons; the ships were identified only by numbers. Our destination was unknown to us, though weeks earlier we had been issued clothing for tropical climes. We assumed that this meant we were headed for the Pacific Theater of Operations. Wrong! After five days at sea, the tropical clothing was replaced with cold-weather clothing for the Atlantic Theater of Operations—this was to confuse the enemy.

The convoy of ships was enormous, with sixty to seventy ships strung out to the horizon, each carrying thousands of troops and supplies. Our flanks were guarded by destroyers. Harry was somewhere in this vast armada, but where?

I was assigned to an eight-by-ten-foot stateroom. It had one porthole, which quickly became almost covered by the mounds of equipment from the seven other nurses who shared this tiny space with me. We slept in two and three tiers of cots, and with all our hand luggage stacked on the floor, there was room for only one person at a time to be moving about in the stateroom. Complaining about our space shortage was not the order of the day, as we felt strong sympathy for the enlisted men, who were jammed by the thousands into the hold of the ship, where seasickness was rampant, and the stench of vomitus emanating from the hold was overpowering.

Days one and two at sea passed quickly enough, as we got indoctrinated into the physical layout of this huge, floating navy installation. Meal assignments were given in what must have been a luxuriously appointed dining room during peace time. Now, however, it was outfitted with long wooden tables, which were edged with molding to keep dishes from sliding off in stormy weather.

Huge galvanized garbage cans were strategically placed in the room, as well as throughout the ship, and put to good use when the going got rough.

First on the ship's agenda was lifeboat drill, which was a serious exercise and held daily. Then I was ready for my own agenda, trying to locate Harry's ship in the convoy. I wandered about the ship, questioning every naval officer I encountered, and eventually found myself in the communications office. When I explained my mission to the communications officers and asked about the USS *Dorothea Dix*, both officers chuckled and pointed to the ship directly in front of us. "There's your ship," one said. "The lead ship of this convoy. And the admiral of the fleet is on that ship."

It was too good to be true! Of all the sixty to seventy ships in this convoy, Harry's ship was the one before my very eyes. I spent the rest of the voyage at the railing, peering through binoculars, hoping to get a glimpse of Harry among the thousands of troops aboard his ship. I never realized that while I was at leisure on my ship, he was on duty in the dispensary of his ship. Still, I thought it was so thrilling and romantic for the two of us to be in the mid-Atlantic at the same time, so near and yet so far apart. In my frequent letters to family, written on deck and to be mailed when we landed, I attempted to tell the story of Harry being on the ship in front of us. For security reasons, there could be no mention in our mail of other ships, so my family was completely mystified when they received one of my letters, which stated "I spend my days looking at Harry's behind."

By day five, there still was no sign of Harry at the railing of his ship, so I took my one bottle of Canadian Club to the communications deck, and with a lot of persuasion on my part (plus the bottle), the naval officers agreed to flash a message to Harry aboard the *Dorothea Dix*.

The word of Harry's proximity had traveled quickly throughout our hospital unit, and a large group of our staff gathered on deck to watch my message being flashed to the ship preceding us. The blinking signal lights from that ship acknowledged receipt of my message which read:

"Please inform Lieut. (jg) Harry G. that Lieut. Phillips is aboard the *E.B. Alexander.*"

Two days later, a response was handed to me in the form of a yellow cablegram: "Please deliver following message to Lieut. Muriel Phillips. Will try to contact you ashore. Lieut. (jg) Harry G."

To this day, this cablegram is treasured among my wartime souvenirs and photos.

What was there to do now but wait out the rest of the voyage until our ship landed? I hoped that Harry, at that point, would rush up the gangplank of our ship for a highly anticipated reunion. This Atlantic crossing took twelve days to complete, rather than the usual five days, because the convoy had to zigzag to avoid German submarines, and we also encountered fierce winter storms, with waves washing wildly over the decks. Everyone aboard ship was seasick for days on end, and those galvanized garbage cans that were stationed so conveniently on every deck drew a lot of customers.

On day twelve, the *Dorothea Dix* and our ship pulled into the Mersey Docks in Liverpool, England, after parting with the rest of our convoy en route to Glasgow, Scotland. The Associated Press newsreel photographers were on hand to photograph our nurses disembarking from the ship, and the newsreel photos were soon shown in movie theaters all over the United States. I didn't appear in any of them, though, because I was still hanging over the ship's rail, looking for Harry, who never showed up.

The nurses were trucked to a railroad siding, where we had our first taste of European trains—compartment cars, with six nurses to a compartment. After we were stowed inside, each compartment door was locked, and then we waited and we waited. Eventually, the train started up and went ahead two miles ... but backed up three. At this point in time, we realized the value of our steel helmets as portable toilets.

After endless hours of the train, advancing and retreating, we traveled the necessary mileage and were deposited at Oulton Park, a staging area in Cheshire, England, in the middle of the night—and in a sea of mud. Again, we had a seventy-two-hour quarantine on mail and phone calls.

We'd had a long, grueling day, and now, as we slithered about in the mud, trying to see something through the blackout and with the dampness penetrating to our very bones, our first impression was that "Merrie Olde England" wasn't so merry. Sleeping quarters were in long, cold, and dark Quonset huts, a wartime invention. Each one accommodated thirty nurses and was heated by three coke-burning potbellied stoves. Coke is notorious for not throwing the same heat that coal does, but we were lucky to even have coke—all essentials of living, including heat, were rationed in war-torn England. The only things in abundance were rain, mud, the penetrating cold, and Brussels sprouts. Almost immediately, everyone developed a cough that persisted for months—the infamous English hack. Bedding down at night in the frigid Quonset hut required dressing up rather than down, and we donned olive-drab, long woolen underwear, followed by wool overcoat liners, and wool socks, hats, and gloves. And woe unto the nurse who slept through her shift for feeding the heatless coke into the potbellied stoves!

I waited impatiently for the seventy-two-hour quarantine to be lifted. The bitter pangs of disappointment at my failed rendezvous with Harry were gnawing at me. As soon as mail and phone restrictions were lifted, I headed for the nearest pay phone (with my newly acquired English currency). This would be my last-ditch effort to send him a telegram, notifying him of my whereabouts, before his ship left the Mersey Docks in Liverpool. Surprisingly, my request to the operator to send a telegram was accepted. Mission accomplished! Now, I just had to wait and wonder if there would be a response.

Six weeks later, as our hospital unit was working out the kinks of our fully functioning hospital at Penley Hall in North Wales, Harry's response finally arrived. When I spotted that familiar handwriting among the other letters from home, I put his letter aside, to save the best for last and to savor it, over and over. My heart began to pound as I finally opened Harry's letter. As I started to read, the first sentence and subsequently, the entire letter, set my heart racing and my pulses pounding, not from symptoms of love, but panic, fear, and guilt.

I could hear Harry's icy tone as I read:

> "What in the world are you trying to do to me? Thanks to your two telegrams, one at sea and one on land, I am on the verge of being courtmartialed, and we are both under surveillance as possible spies for the enemy. Your first cable at sea was delivered directly to the admiral of the fleet, who summoned me immediately for an explanation. If the German submarines lurking in the area had picked up that message, it could have identified our position and destroyed the whole convoy. I eventually convinced the admiral that you meant no harm and were just trying to inform me of your whereabouts and didn't realize the consequences such an act could trigger."

Harry's explanation was accepted by the admiral with the admonition he was "*not to let it happen again.*" Unfortunately, it did happen again, when my second telegram was delivered to the admiral aboard the *Dorothea Dix* at the Mersey Docks in Liverpool. This time, I had made the unforgivable breach of security by identifying not only the name of the ship but also its location.

It took me weeks to recuperate from the cold tone of Harry's letter which cooled my ardor considerably. But I also harbored terrible feelings of guilt for being considered another Mata Hari. With the passage of time, I wasn't put in chains by the navy, nor was Harry court-martialled, and eventually, his letters regained their past warmth. I was delighted to receive the cartons of canned nuts and Goldenberg's Peanut Chews from his ship's store, each time his ship hit port somewhere in the British Isles. Months later, Harry did get a three-day leave to visit me on our hospital base and we had our long-delayed reunion.

Well remembered by the hospital staff from the telegram-sending episode in the mid-Atlantic, Harry received a warm welcome on the post, and the one naval uniform amid the hundreds of army uniforms prompted welcome cries of "The gravy's in the navy!"

Time and distance and new situations changed the tenor of our relationship for me over the next two years, though we remained the best of friends and corresponded just as frequently. When the war was over and I returned to my hometown in Connecticut, Harry visited frequently—and continued to do so, even after I became engaged to Mel, the man who was to become my husband. After his initial distrust of Harry's intentions, Mel learned to admire, respect, and cherish Harry's friendship. The two men had many mutual interests, including their professions. Harry eventually became "Uncle Harry" to our children and was accepted as a family member by all of our relatives. He was always "there" for us, sharing our joys and our sorrows. Harry died in 2002, leaving for posterity our warm memories of him, as well as a yellow cablegram that has a story to tell. ❧

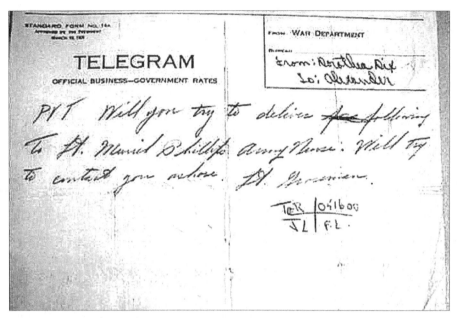

Telegram received in mid-ocean.

16th General Hospital nurses debarking Liverpool, England. (Associated Press photo from Army Signal Corps)

CHAPTER NINE

A RING OF TRUTH

IT WAS ONE OF THOSE *Believe It or Not* happenings that affected the lives of several people, the impact of which is still felt today, more than sixty years later.

The time was December 1943, during World War II, and I had made my farewell phone call home prior to departing for overseas duty—destination unknown—as an army nurse. Grateful that my mother was her usual no-nonsense, matter-of-fact self, I did detect breaks in her voice as she issued her parental admonitions to "Get plenty of sleep, try not to work too hard, and write as often as you can." Then, almost as if it was a postscript, she added, "Incidentally, Muriel, if you should ever get to England in your travels, Daddy has two aunts who emigrated to Manchester, England, from Russia about thirty years ago. They were both midwives, and their family name is Karengold, K-a-r-e-n-g-o-l-d. Try to find them."

Fat chance of that, I thought. Remember, we had been issued tropical clothing, and I was certain that meant we were headed for the Pacific Theater. I was unable to divulge this information, so I simply agreed to my mother's request, knowing full well that I wouldn't be crossing paths with these Karengold great-aunts.

On the fifth day at sea, when our tropical uniforms were replaced by cold weather clothing, I realized that Mom might not be so far off base after all. Twelve days after departing Boston Harbor, our ship docked at Liverpool, England.

Several weeks later, when our thousand-bed hospital in rural North Wales was operational, I began my quest to locate these two great-aunts in Manchester, which was only about fifty to sixty miles away. I sent a request to the Red Cross in that city, not expecting any positive response, as the aunts could have moved or even died in the thirty-year lapse since there had been news of them. My negative expectations were justified a week later, when the Red Cross acknowledged my request with the news that there were no Karengold families in their city directories. They did, however, have two Craingold families listed, and because there was some similarity between the names, they were enclosing the addresses of both families.

Except for the "gold" in both names, I didn't see *that* much similarity, but because I wanted to complete this mission, I did write to one of the names the Red Cross had sent. By return mail, I received a letter from a Myer Craingold that read as follows:

> Dear Leftenant Phillips: I was most interested to receive your letter and am responding by return post as I believe we may be the family you are searching for, even though my name is Craingold, and not Karengold. You may or may not be aware that with the influx of thousands of foreign troops now stationed in Great Britain, many imposters have feigned a blood relationship with the natives, either to exploit them for financial reasons or merely to find a home away from home.
>
> I do not believe that to be the case with you as there is a strong ring of truth to your letter and I would be greatly interested in further exploring the depth of any family relationship with you. For your information, the name of my mother and her sister was Karengold, but they felt by changing it to Craingold, they would be anglicizing it, to help them blend into their new homeland faster.

Bingo, Mom, I think we struck oil!

After an exchange of several letters, Myer Craingold and his wife, Gertrude, invited me to their home on my next weekend pass, and I set off for this visit filled with the excitement and uncertainty of meeting this newest branch of family. I was also loaded down with canned food supplies, which we were directed to do when visiting British families, as they had been on wartime rations since 1940. I discovered this wasn't a necessity as far as my second cousin Myer was concerned, because he was a pharmacist/oculist, whose clients often paid him in food items and delicacies not available to the general public.

I was met at the railroad station in Manchester by Pamela, the four-teen-year-old daughter, who approached me on the platform as I alighted from the train. Though the station was bustling with hordes of uniformed people, I happened to be the only female in the American army nurse uni-form, so Pam had no trouble in recognizing me. I learned many years later that when Gertrude sent Pam to the station to meet me she directed her to "walk on by if she doesn't look proper." I must have looked proper.

We boarded the bus that took us to the area closest to their home, about a half-hour's ride away. We drove through the heavily bombed-out business section of Manchester, which suddenly brought home to me what life must have been like the past few years, since the Battle of Britain began, with German planes raining death and destruction on them. Pam and I chatted continually throughout the bus trip, answering each other's ques-tions about our families, my life as an army nurse, and Pam's life as a stu-dent in this war-torn country. Soon, we were ascending the front steps of the Craingold home. It was an attached duplex, constructed of stone, in a neighborhood of similar residential homes. My inner excitement was at its peak as I realized I was about to meet my long-deceased father's first cous-in, Myer. Myer and Gertrude both greeted me with warm handshakes at the front door and then introduced me to their younger daughter, Shirley, a shy ten-year-old wearing an ear-to-ear grin. It was startling to realize the strong resemblance between my father and Myer, not only facially but in their similar builds of medium height and girth. Gertrude was shorter than Myer and had auburn hair and a rosy complexion; she exuded warmth and charm.

The Craingold home consisted of seven rooms on two levels. It was much smaller in size than the average American home, but well furnished, in what my mother would have deemed "good taste." As this was my first visit to an English home, everything was a revelation to me: afternoon tea and late dinners; using the knife in the right hand to help load the fork, which was held in the left hand; feather comforters on the beds rather than blankets; and my nemesis, the English water closet, or WC, a far cry from our American flush toilets. I came to dread trips to the WC, always fearful that the dark brown, water-filled box, suspended a few inches from the ceiling, would fall down on me if I yanked the pull-chain too hard. And yet, if it wasn't yanked strongly enough, there was no flushing action. My fears weren't groundless, though, as the first casualty among our nurses, two weeks after arriving in England, was a fractured arm, suffered when this brown box fell off its mooring near the ceiling and onto the sitting nurse. I don't think she received a Purple Heart for that injury.

I learned from Myer that both of my father's aunts, one of whom was Myer's mother, were still alive and living not too many miles away. There were numerous other relatives mentioned, too, and he promised to have them all in attendance on my next visit to their home. In discussions, not only with Myer and Gertrude but also with Pam and Shirley, I noted that they seemed so much more involved in cultural and academic pursuits than their American counterparts. They were all deeply interested in music, art, theater, etc. I felt intellectually inferior when these younger cousins discussed recent museum exhibits and symphonic programs they'd attended, programs conducted by eminent musicians whose names meant nothing to me.

On the other hand, they were fascinated to hear about my life in the army, from the professional angle to the general living conditions. They also were curious about the unknown family back in the States and the good life there, specifically New York City. Their eyes widened as I related how my widowed mother opened a dress shop to support her three children, and because clothing had long been rationed in England, they were delighted with my promises to have dresses and undergarments sent to them. Once appraised of their sizes, my mother was happy to oblige and continued to do so, long after the war ended. If there were food shortages in England, it certainly wasn't obvious over this weekend, as we were served delicious meals of roast beef and fresh salmon from Scotland, with vegetables other than the infernal brussel sprouts served daily in the Army Officers Mess. Myer must have bartered plenty the week of my arrival in Manchester.

Much too soon, the weekend came to a close, and on my departure I was soundly hugged by all and given books, stationery, and sweets. Throughout the train trip back to North Wales, I relived the events of the weekend, which already seemed like a wonderful dream. I mentally composed my letter home, detailing the visit with our newly discovered relations. Mission accomplished, Mom!

Today, Myer and Gertrude's children, grandchildren, and great-grand-children have close relationships with all our family. We send letters, call on the phone, exchange e-mail, and occasionally have personal visits, when the Brits come here or the Yanks go there. I have always been grateful that my letter to Myer, so many years ago, had a ring of truth to it. ❧

CHAPTER TEN

SPIT AND POLISH

SIXTY YEARS AGO I lived, breathed, and gloried in my profession as an army nurse, and life should have been 100 percent perfect. So what caused my cup of joy to curdle, rather than run over? It was the weekly showdown in the form of Friday morning inspections by the commanding officer of our thousand-bed hospital. I am aware that inspections are an integral part of institutional life, the military included, but the "spit and polish" in those days bordered on the ridiculous.

The patients had been primed all week to prepare them for Friday: "Don't moan"; "Don't groan"; "Don't complain"; "Don't thrash around and wrinkle your sheets." (The instructions almost could have included "Don't breathe.") Every inch of ward furniture—the beds, bedside tables, chairs, nurse's desk, etc.—was scrubbed beyond all reproach, as were the contents of the utility and treatment rooms, and lastly, the floors. Ah, the floors— they were the worst offenders and usually our Waterloo. In advance of the colonel's inspection, the floors were swept, scrubbed, and polished to such a high degree of gloss that our figures were mirrored in them. If, God for- bid, there was a bedside emergency in the minutes that preceded the visit from our esteemed commander, we wrapped newspapers around our feet so that we wouldn't sully the precious floor by walking on it.

As the clock moved toward twelve, the diminutive colonel—in full- dress uniform and wearing eyeglasses with Coke-bottle lenses—made his appearance, right on schedule and flanked by his aides and our chief nurse. All activity and talk ceased; the ward personnel and patients were called to attention. I stood at my desk, in strict attention, as the colonel returned my salute and began his trouble-finding journey through the length of the ward.

He wore white gloves and used them to sweep around beds and under mattresses—the gloves would clearly show any offending specks of dirt that the corpsmen might have missed on their cleaning detail. When this occurred, the colonel held up his hand to display the offending dirt. And he'd look accusingly at me, as I was the head nurse who'd allowed this.

In these same white-gloved hands, he also held a roll of toilet paper, so he could check for any smudges on the high-gloss floor. If the smudge could be removed with the toilet paper, the colonel would shoot me a penetrating glare that spoke a thousand words. If the smudge wasn't transferred to the paper, all was well—that meant that the smudge was caused by normal wear and tear. *Oh, let this farce be over with already!* I prayed.

Colonel Simpson stopped at a few bedsides to inquire about the patient's well-being and the quality of care received, but he really was more interested in finding dirt somewhere. As he passed an empty bed, he flipped a coin on it. Fortunately for us, the coin bounced. This indicated that there was no slack in the bed sheets.

The inspection tour finally was finished, and as the colonel and his entourage filed out the door, our chief nurse gave me a knowing glance that conveyed "I'll get back to you later, Lieutenant."

The inspection report never mentioned patient care; it seemed concerned with dirt smudges on white gloves and toilet paper.

This same spit-and-polish comedy was carried on, month after month, in our hospital in the States as well as in England—but the showdown became show-up when we move to Liège, Belgium.

Our tent hospital was far from complete when the Americans started a new offensive against the Germans, and we had to receive patients, ready or not. Many of the tents lacked cement floors, and we had no electricity or running water during the first few weeks of the offensive. Torrential rains made our hospital grounds a sea of mud, and we sloshed around in our tents, ankle-deep in mud and water. Flashlights and kerosene lanterns provided light, but it was still difficult to simultaneously give a morphine injection and hold a flashlight, so a corpsman had to be summoned to hold the flashlight.

Inundated as we were with patients suffering severe injuries, spit and polish took a backseat at this time, although the colonel did pay an unannounced visit, accompanied by only one aide, toward the end of our second week of operations. This certainly could not be considered an inspection; he was "just checking on conditions." After standing at attention momentarily, the colonel told us to resume our duties, and he plowed through the mud down the length of the tent.

I stifled a fit of laughter as I realized the colonel wasn't wearing his white gloves or carrying his roll of toilet paper, which he really could have used to wipe the mud off his boots. My unspoken thoughts? *Lots of dirt here, Colonel. What are you going to do about it?* ❧

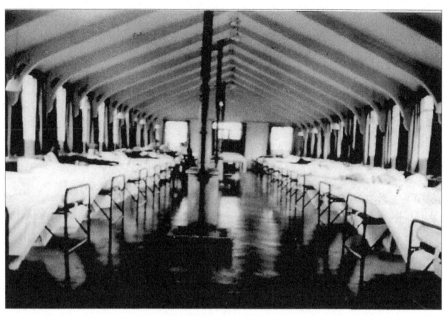

Floor before inspection at our North Wales hospital.

Passing in review before brass in Chester, England. Muriel is the platoon leader saluting the reviewing officer.

CHAPTER ELEVEN

WHAT GOES 'ROUND

BRIDPORT, IN DORSET, ENGLAND was the last place on my mind in April 2004. That's when I received a letter from a friend who had just returned from her annual visit to England. She wrote that the city of Bridport was celebrating the sixtieth anniversary of D-Day in June and was looking for foreign servicemen and servicewomen who had spent time there. City officials were anxious to learn of the memories the service people had of Bridport. Even better, my friend wrote, if there were any photos from that period, the daily *Bridport & Lyme Regis News* would print them. "I know you were there at some point before crossing the Channel," she wrote, "so I hope you will contact [the city officials], and if you do have pictures [to share], they promise to return them."

Did I have pictures? Over four dozen were culled from my army photo album. As the originals were too precious for me to risk losing them, my spouse beautifully reproduced them for the newspaper archives. As for memories … how could I forget?

We had been operating our army hospital in North Wales, caring for the D-Day casualties, when orders suddenly arrived early one Sunday afternoon to prepare to evacuate our hospital and grounds in two hours. We were to sail for Normandy, France. A new hospital unit would move in immediately to take over the care of the patients and to take up residence in the cement-block huts that we nurses had occupied.

This included their also taking over the expensive English bicycles we had all purchased months ago which were left in the bike racks next to each hut. The newcomers also would get to enjoy the fruits of our labors in the vegetable garden that we nurses in Hut 10 had planted weeks earlier—the radishes were now "radishing" and the lettuce was "lettucing." I hoped that whoever inherited my bed would appreciate the adjacent beautiful dressing table and bench I had painstakingly constructed from orange crates and skirted with red-dyed Curity diapers. It afforded me the luxury of feeling like a civilian for the few minutes I sat there daily, combing my hair or applying lipstick.

In exactly two hours we were loaded on to trucks, which took us to the railroad station, where we boarded the train that carried us through the night to southern England. We arrived in the small coastal city of Bridport at 8 a.m. We milled aimlessly around the railroad station, tired and hungry. No one expected us, and there was no place to go. Eventually, orders came from somewhere, and we were herded together and marched to Downe Hall, a deserted castle on the outskirts of town. The castle, which must have been empty for many months, was stripped of everything—except for the cockroaches and rats that roamed the place freely. One hundred nurses were easily housed in this mammoth structure, and within a week, it bore the inevitable signs of human occupancy: female underwear, having been laundered in our helmets, was draped from most windows and balconies. The fifty male medical and dental officers were housed at Mountebank, a nearby mansion that was part of the Downe Hall estate.

Typical of the unofficial army policy of "hurry up and wait," we did not board a ship for France the day we arrived, nor did we board a ship that week— or that month. Instead, we spent the month of July in our castle at Bridport, the hottest July in England on record. As anxious as we were to get to France and our eventual destination in Belgium, where we could do the nursing we came overseas to do, it was a wonderful respite from hospital routine to be so close to the beach in Bridport. Each day we marched the one mile to the rocky beach at West Bay, spread our blankets, and sunbathed, read, or played cards—and the hardy had a quick dip in the frigid ocean.

On one of our daily beach treks, I stopped to talk to a gentleman and his wife who were always working in their flower garden as we passed by. Shortly after that, the couple—Admiral and Mrs. Edwards—invited me and my roommate, Evelyn, to visit with them. When they learned that we missed the amenities of a bathtub and hot running water that we hadn't enjoyed in months, they insisted that we come to their home as frequently as we desired to use their bathtub. We were happy to accept their offer but, not wanting to exploit their generosity, we limited our visits to twice a week. The soak in their tub was heavenly. We always arrived with little gifts of canned foods from our mess sergeant—not that cans of Spam, beef stew, or powdered eggs were sumptuous gifts, but in this war-torn country, any food was accepted with gratitude.

We took many photos of the Edwards, their home and gardens, and their three grandchildren—six-year-old brother and sister twins and an eight-year-old sister, who displayed obvious affection for their grandparents. These photos recorded for posterity our relationship with the Edwards family, and many of these photos were among the twenty I sent to the newspaper in time for their D-Day celebration, along with my recollections of our stay in Bridport. This information was gratefully received and acknowledged by the newspaper staff preparing their special series coinciding with the 60th anniversary of D-Day, June 6, 1944. One full page was headlined "Memories of war hospital in town" and carried the reproduced photos from my album and my memories of Bridport, which included the wedding of one of our Hut No. 10 nurses to her Air Force lieutenant fiancé.

Following the ceremony at a lovely small chapel in town, the wedding reception had been held at a now cleaned-up Downe Hall, and I'd caught the bride's bouquet, thrown from a second-floor balcony and recorded photographically.

The newspaper editor sent me many copies of that edition, along with more letters of appreciation. I was happy to have been helpful in their search for veterans who had been there and was pleased that I'd been able to add to their collection of memories. The real thrill, though, arrived a week later—a letter, along with photographs of the three Edwards grandchildren, now aged seventy and seventy-six. The female twin wrote:

> You recently sent some photographs of 'Admiral' Edwards to the Bridport newspaper which were copied and sent on to me. I'm one of the children in the photo, the 'Admiral' was my grandfather. I can understand the title, Granddad Pops, as we called him, had been to sea on the old sailing ships, the windjammers. The promotion to such an elevated rank was

honorary and I'm sure the Americans had something to do
with it. He died in 1960, aged 87. Your photographs must be
at least 65 years old, it's wonderful to see them again. I hope
you don't mind me taking the liberty of contacting you, but
this has evoked such happy memories of my childhood.

When I responded to her very gracious letter, I issued an invitation
to the three siblings to visit with us if they ever came to Florida, so that I
could reciprocate the many kindnesses of their grandparents—and we did
have two bathtubs with hot, running water. ❧

CHAPTER TWELVE

VIVE LA FRANCE

A few weeks after the D-Day invasion of Normandy, our army hospital unit was en route to France from England. A former luxury liner, now converted to troop transport was our transportation across the English Channel. The staterooms allotted to the nurses were heavily infested with thousands of flat, bloodsucking insects known as bedbugs, so we fled to the upper deck, where we spent the next three nights sleeping on the bare deck.

By day two, the ship's larder was empty, except for stale bread covered with green mold. Prepared for all contingencies, we did have our boxes of K-rations, but unless one was *really* hungry, it was comparable to eating dry dog food. This voyage across the Channel normally took two to three hours, but because the Channel was still blocked with the wreckage of sunken ships and downed planes from D-Day, four days elapsed before Utah Beach hove into view.

We prepared to disembark as the ship dropped anchor and were soon climbing over the ship's railing, laden down with all our gear piled around our backs and shoulders. Once over the railing, we made our way down the precariously swaying rope ladder that lurched ominously with each wave that hit the ship. We were helped into the waiting LCT, a flat-bottomed landing craft, which headed for the beach when every bit of standing space was occupied by a body. Two hundred feet from shore, our LCT grounded, and we were advised to wade to shore, where trucks were waiting to take us inland to the site that would be our home for the next few weeks.

Bumping our way over the pot-holed Normandy countryside roads, our gay chatter ceased as we viewed the bombed-out villages, where the foul smell of death and decay still permeated the air. It was a rarity to see a house or building that had escaped the bombings unscathed.

Night fell, and our conveyances lumbered on endlessly, until—finally —the trucks abruptly stopped.

"All out, Lieutenants," said our truck driver. "We have a problem, and that problem is that we are lost. You will have to spend the night here. We'll be back for you first thing tomorrow."

But where was "here"?

As it turned out, "here" was a cow pasture—still inhabited by cows! But if the cows were here, that meant there were no mines in this field; therefore, it was safe for the nurses. Our visions of Paris, French perfume, flush toilets, and bathtubs with hot water, dissipated with the business of trying to find a level spot on the ground for stretching out for the night, without encountering any cows or stepping in cow droppings. We were unable to use flashlights, as enemy planes still invaded our airspace, and complete blackout had to be observed. Bloodcurdling shrieks from the first nurses to venture into the pasture pinpointed areas of fresh cow manure to avoid.

It was, indeed, a night to remember, sleeping under the stars with a herd of French cows that were certainly not constipated. I often wondered if the intrusion into their domain by American aliens changed the quality of their milk that week. ❧

In a Normandy cow pasture, doing laundry in a steel helmet; note laundry hanging out to dry on the tent ropes.

Chow time; no mess tents available.

Morning ablutions. Muriel's long GI underwear and
laundry drying in the background.

CHAPTER THIRTEEN

A TIME REMEMBERED

WHOEVER COINED THE ADAGE about "all work and no play makes Johnny a dull boy" had it wrong. All work and no play doesn't just make you dull; it can kill you. We army nurses, in Liège, Belgium, in the winter of '44 and '45, learned early on that we needed the release that "play time" afforded us, to maximize our efficiency as nurses in our work time. If not for this release, we might have ended up the same as some of our patients, called "Section 8's" in those days—psychiatric cases, unable to cope with the stress of war.

Now, sixty years later, as we ready for bed at 9:30 p.m., completely exhausted from a day in retirement, I marvel at the vitality and energy that my fellow nurses and I had so many years ago. We could put in a twelve-hour day caring for our battle casualties, under the most adverse working conditions, and yet find the strength to hop on a nurse-filled truck to dance away the evening at a nearby tank, infantry, or air corps Officers' Club. The club might be in a tent in a cow pasture or in a building in the city, but there were lights, music, male and female companionship, and booze. The days of drinking one Cuba Libre and considering it a drinking orgy were over. Now, most of us were seasoned drinkers, and it helped.

When we first arrived in Belgium, our tent hospital was still under construction across the Meuse River, five miles out of Liège, so we were sent to work at an existing American hospital in an old hilltop armory-like building. Temporary housing was found for the nurses in a four-story building a few blocks away, in the heart of the city. Every day and night we walked up the hill to the hospital and worked long hours, caring for casualties, mostly from the Battle of Aachen. Aachen was the nearest German city, eighteen miles away, and had been heavily mined and booby-trapped. As an operating room nurse, it seemed to me that almost every patient who was brought in had at least one extremity amputated. These casualties were heavier and more severe than any we had yet seen.

As an Armistice Day "gift," Hitler began sending his V-1 flying bombs (known as buzz bombs or robot bombs) into Liège to destroy the rail system and supply depots. Each bomb carried 2,000 pounds of explosives. You couldn't see them at first, you could just hear the putt-putt-puttering sound of its motor and then as you looked, you'd see a moving black dot that gradually began to look like a flying cross. In the nighttime sky, tongues of flame could be seen issuing from the end of it. As the bomb drew closer and the noise of its motor became louder, you'd start holding your breath as you mentally urged the motor of that bomb to keep running, because if the motor shut off before the bomb was overhead, it would plunge to earth at a 45 degree angle, with a horrible whining whistle, destroying everything in its path on the ground for hundreds of feet. Its concussion could be felt miles away.

If the motor of the bomb was still running as it passed overhead, then it was safe to resume breathing, that is, until they came out with a bomb that really fooled us, for the bomb had passed overhead and we had resumed breathing, but then, the bomb made an abrupt u-turn and headed back in our direction. The bombs came every fifteen minutes, twenty-four hours a day and they came for the next two and a half months. With direct hits, the destruction included flying glass and collapsing buildings, to say nothing of human casualties.

We had just gotten back to our quarters from a night-duty shift, at about 10 a.m., when the hospital received a direct hit from a buzz bomb, killing patients and hospital personnel. Some bodies were thrown fifty to seventy-five feet by the explosion; others were found hanging over rafters on the ceiling, and those who were still alive died before their bodies could be extricated from the wreckage. Fortunately, none of our own hospital staff were on duty there at the time, though a few were there as patients and survived the bombing, sustaining minor injuries.

We anxiously awaited the completion of our tent hospital, five miles away at Fayenbois, away from the collapsing buildings and flying glass. But no sooner did we move out to Fayenbois than the buzz bombs started dropping in our countrified area—and now they were coming over sometimes three at a time and from three different directions. Because of the new American offensive which started November 16th, and having to receive casualties without the benefit of tent floors, running water and electricity, compounded by weeks of pouring rain, we had to forego normal hospital protocol and improvise. The inadequate light from kerosene lanterns and flashlights had to suffice for medicating patients and doing dressings. Every tent leaked and it took all our ingenuity to keep the patients and their beds from becoming inundated.

With inches of mud for flooring our feet were completely waterlogged by the time we got off duty. Until we were issued waterproofed combat boots, we were forced to "appropriate" boots from patients who didn't survive.

We worked, slept, ate, and visited the latrine to the sound of buzz bombs, either flying over or about to drop and we never wanted to be caught in the latrine tent with four layers of pants around our ankles when one was dropping: combat pants, pant liners, long underwear and panties. Before even venturing into the tent, we would always pause at the doorway first and scan the skies for any incoming objects , then rush in and do what we had to do and rush out, still pulling up our outer layer of pants.

We soon learned that tent hospitals were not invulnerable; over the next two and a half months, our hospital was hit three times by buzz bombs, injuring or killing hospital personnel and patients. The GI Joes, as we referred to our patients, didn't like the buzz bombs and said they'd rather be back at the front lines, where it was comparatively quiet some of the time. They were always happy to be evacuated to hospitals in England or France, away from "Buzz Bomb Alley," which is what they called the Liège area. We were continually admitting and evacuating hundreds of patients a day under the triage system and our beds never cooled off.

Our hospital was an experiment by the War Department that wanted to put a general hospital in tents as close to the fighting lines as possible, using the triage system, where priority for treatment depended upon the severity of the patient's injuries. If the patient's injuries were extremely severe, requiring long hours of surgery and many months for recuperation, the patient received enough care to make him as comfortable and pain -free as possible and within a few hours, was evacuated to a general hospital in England, France or the States. If the injuries were such that the patient could be treated medically and surgically and returned to duty within a few weeks then he stayed with us for treatment and rehabilitation.

Our operating rooms were going twenty-four hours a day as we cared not only for our own battle casualties but for the Belgian civilians as well who were injured by buzz bombs .And these buzz bomb injuries were horrendous for the flying glass shards generated by exploding buildings penetrated deep inside the body and were extremely painful and difficult to retrieve.

For many of our patients, we were the first American women they had seen in months or years, and this was even more exciting for them than sleeping in a bed with a mattress and sheets, which they had not experienced since leaving the States. I can remember one patient, so accustomed to his fox hole, he couldn't adjust to the luxury of a bed and I'd come on duty in the morning to find him curled up fox hole style on the cement floor under his bed. The American soldiers were so grateful for us just being there, thanking us profusely for the slightest task we performed for their comfort, sometimes grabbing our hands and kissing them, and they worried more about our safety than their own. As harrowing as our existence was, it was still a very satisfying one because we were doing what we came overseas to do.

And we still had our social life when off duty, whether it was visiting friends at another post or just being in our own Officers' Club tent, dancing to the jukebox, writing letters, playing cards, or singing. Old songs, new songs, parodies ridiculing army brass—we sang wherever we were. Someone would raise his voice in song, and soon everyone had joined in. We'd exchange the latest rumors of the day—and rumors were always rampant, especially about troop movements, the latest bomb hits, or an addition to our liquor ration. The Officers' Club tent was akin to being back home with family members. Indeed, we were one family, and we needed each other. So ingrained were our feelings of closeness to one another that we retained and cherished those friendships for years to come—and still do, to the present day.

Yes, the war was a wonderful experience that I wouldn't have missed. We worked hard, and we played hard, but we were so glad when it was over.

Two Songs Frequently Sung by the Nurses:

ANC SONG (Army Nurse Corps)
Once there was a young girl who joined the ANC,
Soldiers were as nice to her, as nice as they could be.
First she met a shavetail fresh from OCT,
He wooed her and pursued her but too naïve was he.

Chorus:
Singing khaki and olive drab, brass and eagles too,
Soldiers will be soldiers, there's nothing they won't do.

Then she met a captain with fire in his eye.
He took her to his barracks and filled her full of rye.
He wanted to show her his etchings, but she was far too wise, For
she had seen the etchings of all the other guys.
Chorus

Then she met a major, who promised to be true,
But he had made the promise to wife and kiddies too.
Chorus

Then she met a colonel, who promised to raise her rank,
But when she didn't come across she found the rank was blank.
Chorus

And then she went overseas for glory and for fame,
But to her disappointment she found all men the same. Now the
moral of this story is plain as you can see,
Treat all men like children, but treat them tenderly.

BLESS THEM ALL

They say that in camp you will have a good time,
We've heard that all before.
You drink Coca-Colas and play the Victrolas,
But oh, how we'd like to do more!

Bless us all, bless us all,
The long and the short and the tall.
Now bless all the nurses for they rub your backs,
That's a lot more than you'll get from the WACs.

So we're saying good-bye to you all,
As gaily we answer the call.
No silk hose or girdles as we take the hurdles,
So cheer up my lads, love us all! ❧

CHAPTER FOURTEEN

THE COMMAND

"AS YOUR COLONEL and commanding officer, I demand that you immediately cease this uprising. I will not tolerate any more complaints and dissention among you nurses and any future trouble-makers will be transferred to other outfits. Headquarters wants us here in Liège. You have but one life to give for your country and should do so willingly. This is a command, and you will carry on!"

Eyes rolled as our runt of a near-sighted colonel invoked the historic words of Nathan Hale while addressing a gathering of about twenty nurses. Missing, however, was his usual roll of toilet paper and white gloves that he used in hospital inspections in the States and England. Some of us were sitting cross-legged on the floor, while the rest of us occupied whatever chairs were available on the fourth floor of the building that housed the hundred nurses of our hospital outfit. This building was located in the downtown business section of Liège, Belgium, and was a temporary residence for the nurses while our thousand-bed tent hospital was under construction in an apple orchard, five miles away in Fayenbois.

It was November of 1944, and we frightened, angry army nurses had requested a meeting with our colonel. For the past two weeks, Liège had been under constant bombardment by buzz bombs, and we nurses weren't too happy with living in this explosive environment. We realized when we volunteered for overseas duty that we might, at some point, be in dangerous situations, and now, our unfeeling commander was quick to point this out. Buildings were exploding around us, even as the colonel delivered his ultimatum, and we braced ourselves for the concussion as the noise of the explosions was heard.

What really got our goat, though, was the fact that the enlisted men and male officers, including our illustrious colonel, were living in tents at the tent hospital site in Fayenbois, where there were no collapsing buildings or flying glass. Fayenbois had not been the target for buzz bombs, and we wanted to be there, too, whether to sleep in tents, in a foxhole, or on the ground under an apple tree. We just wanted to be away from the dangers of living in a city under bombardment.

As a finale to this one-sided conversation, the colonel stated that the future nurses' residence was a sixteenth-century chateau, a short walk from the apple orchard that housed the hospital tents. The very first priority was to get the hospital in perfect operating order, and only then would the work begin of getting the long-vacant chateau in livable condition. Because a new army offensive had begun a few weeks earlier, it was estimated that it would be several weeks before the work on the hospital was completed. We listened with sinking hearts, each and every one of us feeling we'd probably be dead by then—that we were *expendable*.

The colonel's departure from our quarters elicited glum silence—the meeting had been a waste of time. With his command ringing in our ears to "carry on," those of us on night duty prepared to board the truck that would take us out to the peace and quiet of Fayenbois. Commuting to the hospital site was done by truck, which meant driving through the bombed-out, debris-strewn streets of Liège. Often, buildings were still falling and blocking the road as we drove by.

In order to reach the hospital site, the trucks had to cross the Meuse River on three different bridges, two of them pontoon bridges that replaced the permanent ones that had been bombed out. We dreaded going over the bridges, and each time we approached one, the truck driver stopped, dismounted the truck, and searched the sky for any flying bombs en route. They could be heard, sputtering along in the sky, long before they came into view—they resembled a small flying cross with flames issuing from one end and were more visible in a nighttime sky. If none was audible or visible, the driver high-tailed it back to his seat, and we went lickety-split over that bridge, trying to reach land before another bomb came winging along.

Obviously, everyone would rather have been hit by a flying bomb on dry land than over water, which led to spirited discussions in our four-story building about the best or worst floor on which to be when a bomb hit.

Bottom-floor enthusiasts felt there was a chance of survival by running outside while the top-floor proponents were plunging to the bottom. Top-floor enthusiasts were more philosophical, reasoning, "If you're going to get hit, do it fast, and get it over with, so you don't have to worry about being dug out at the bottom of a pile of debris." No doubt, their feelings were influenced by the experience of working in a nearby army hospital that had received a direct hit two weeks previously, which had been a gruesome calamity for patients and staff. No consensus of this controversial topic—top floor or bottom floor—was ever taken.

At our muddy hospital site, we worked our twelve-hour shifts in tents that not only lacked cement floors, running water, and electricity, but that also lacked basic hospital equipment. Travel time wasted precious hours, as we'd leave our Liège quarters at 5 p.m. for the night shift, and return—wet, bedraggled, and tired—at 9:30 or 10 a.m. the next day. Caring for the wounded kept us too occupied during the night hours to dwell on the colonel's pronouncements, and it was only after the next day's mid-morning return to our quarters, when we were again faced with the buzz bomb problem, that his words would echo in our ears.

It was shortly after noon, the day after our "meeting" with the colonel, when our fitful sleep was interrupted by happy exclamations: "Wake up! We're moving to tents in Fayenbois today! Start packing!" Had Headquarters gotten wind of the mini-insurrection, or had our commanding officer developed a little backbone overnight? We never learned the answer, nor did we question the decision.

So, we moved to Fayenbois to live in tents for a month until the chateau was habitable. But wouldn't you know? As soon as we arrived there, so, too, did the buzz bombs arrive, scoring direct hits on our hospital three times within the next two and a half months.

Liège was still getting plastered as were we in the suburbs, just as frequently, twenty-four hours a day. It was during this period that "Buzz Bomb Alley" became a feared destination for wounded servicemen. Our little colonel, who was so proficient at issuing commands, was a mere, impotent, human mortal under the buzz bomb onslaught. ❧

Muriel in front of a pillbox in downtown Liège; pillbox familiar to all troops en route to the front.

Hospital tents destroyed by exploding buzz bomb concussion; only the tent stakes remain.

Sixteenth-century chateau occupied as living quarters by the nurses.

Pontoon bridge over the Meuse River.

CHAPTER FIFTEEN

TWO PHOTOGRAPHS

IF A PICTURE IS WORTH a thousand words, these World War II photographs from my album have quite a story to tell. They appear to be of two people in different places and time, but for the record, both photos are of the same person, taken approximately seven weeks apart.

One is a sepia-toned head and shoulders portrait of an attractive young woman, taken by professional photographer Jacques Reynaud, whose name was imprinted in the lower right-hand corner of the photo. The subject, with tilted head, eyes gazing off into the distance, seems to be wearing an off-the-shoulder black lace gown, though only the top fringes of the lace can be seen. A black lace snood topped with a satin bow controls the mass of wavy brunette hair that's swept upwards behind her ears. Her dreamy, unfocused eyes, slightly rounded cheeks, and mouth in contented repose on the semi-profiled face present a portrait that hints of allure and perhaps romance.

If the reader has picked up on the glamorous aspect of this photo, then my mission was successful, for that was my intention. I was looking for glamour and femininity on the day I hitched a ride on one of our motor-depot trucks making the five-mile run into Liège for our hospital supplies. Two years of wearing olive-drab uniforms—including the past year of overseas duty wearing olive-drab combat pants, olive-drab long underwear, and olive-drab wool shirts—could make any woman feel unfeminine after a while. High combat boots that eclipsed a shapely ankle and constantly wearing a steel helmet that loused up any attempt at a decent hairdo didn't help the feminine angle either.

I was dropped off at my destination by the compliant GI truck driver, who was happy to oblige off-duty nurses on their forays into Liège.

Hurrying into the photography studio, I didn't stop to admire the many portrait photos in the storefront windows; I had studied them many times before. Monsieur Reynaud had no other clients at the time and was happy to oblige my request for a "feminine" photo. From my army-issue shoulder bag, I extracted a black lace snood, purchased during my one-day pass to Paris, and fitted my hair into it, with the bow sitting at a jaunty angle atop my head.

Monsieur Reynaud held up a black lace drape and indicated that I should unbutton the top buttons of my olive-drab wool shirt and pull it off my shoulders, as well as the olive-drab undershirt and bra straps. He then draped the piece of lace across my chest and shoulders as I sat before a full-size dressing table mirror. From the shoulders up, I truly looked feminine, almost like a socialite one would see in the rotogravure section of the *New York Times*.

I was then situated before a blank screen, facing the tripod-mounted camera. After fixing my head in a tilted position, Monsieur Reynaud raised his hand, said "Regardez".and disappeared under the curtained back of the camera. After two or three clicks, his head emerged from the curtain, and he approached me to tilt my head in another position; then he repeated the preceding steps for final picture-taking.

I returned one week later for the processed photo and was delighted with the end result. The portrait spelled "glamour" for me; it was a far cry from the grungy olive-drab-clad female I was in reality. This photo was one of my prized possessions throughout the war; and I carefully stashed it in my Valpak. Whenever the days and nights seemed unending, I'd take the photograph from its safe repository and reassure myself that someday, the war and destruction would be over.

The second photo from my album is in direct contrast to my glamour photo; it shows me in full work uniform: combat pants and boots, woolen gloves, steel helmet, and tanker jacket (given to me by a former patient and warmer than the combat jackets issued to the nurses). Hospital tents can be seen in the background, as well as traces of a past snowfall. Above the tents, in the far background, are the rooftops and chimneys of Belgian homes that were located on the perimeter of our hospital grounds, which had once been an apple orchard.

Much had transpired in the weeks since my glamour photo. Our hospital had been subject to constant bombardment by German buzz bombs; we had sustained two hits that resulted in loss of life (patient as well as hospital personnel), and now we were in the throes of the Battle of the Bulge, which had begun one week before my roommate took this Kodak snapshot.

German troops had broken through Allied lines along the Belgian/German border and were now ten miles from Liège—much too close for comfort. We nurses had been briefed on which emergency items to pack in the event of capture by the enemy. We knew we had rights under the Geneva Convention, but we assumed the Krauts would ignore this—our hospital tents had been bombed and strafed that week, despite the red crosses clearly outlined on the tent roofs. We had also received survivors from the Malmedy Massacre, where surrendering troops had been killed and atrocities committed, which demonstrated the blatant German disregard of the Geneva Conventions.

This second photo shows my dark-circled eyes, slimmer cheek line, and wan smile attempted for the photographer, reflecting the longer work shifts and my caring for the never-ending arrival of new battle casualties, as well as coping with the buzz bomb barrage and the stress generated by the proximity of the approaching German army. Suspended from my wrist by a leather thong, my right hand holds a blackjack that an ambulatory patient constructed for me,— a ten-inch length of hosing packed with lead sinkers. His instructions were to "slam the blackjack across the face of an approaching Kraut and aim for the eyes."

In the left jacket pocket you can see the outline of a switchblade knife that another patient insisted I keep in my pocket at all times. His instructions were to plunge the knife into the belly of a would-be captor, turn it, and then "Run like hell."

The photos have said their piece and are now reposing in my photo album of the war. I enjoy the "glamour" portrait for the sake of vanity—it's documented proof that I was once young, unblemished, and unwrinkled—but I take pride in my "work" photo, for it demonstrates that I did the job that I went overseas to do. ❧

Glamour photograph of Muriel.

Photo taken during Battle of the Bulge; Muriel holding blackjack in her right hand and outline of spring-blade knife is seen in the left pocket.

CHAPTER SIXTEEN

BATTLE OF THE BULGE, PART I

CHRISTMAS SEASON is a time for being merry, they say, but for those of us serving in the army in Liège, Belgium during World War II, Christmas was anything but merry.

The Battle of the Bulge had started on December 16, when German General von Rundstedt made his famous counterattack into Belgium from two different areas on the German/Belgian border simultaneously, creating a bulge or wedge, forty five miles wide and sixty miles deep into Belgium. In the southern portion of this bulge, was the small crossroads town of Bastogne in the Ardennes Forest region, looking very much like the spokes of a wheel on the map because of the many roads intersecting it, seven of them paved roads. The Germans had to get control of this town because its paved roads would provide easier access for their heavy mechanized vehicles to reach Belgium's major highways. It was here where American troops, 11,000 alone, from the 101st. Airborne Division, outnumbered and outgunned, were completely surrounded by Germans and given an ultimatum to surrender within two hours.

General Anthony McAuliffe, the acting American Commander, gained instantaneous lifetime fame with his one word reply to that ultimatum, and that one word was "Nuts." The German officer who delivered the ultimatum and spoke a perfect English, was perplexed and asked General McAuliffe's aide, "What is the meaning of this word 'Nuts'? General McAuliffe's aide replied: "It means, Go to Hell!"

Fifty-four short miles from Bastogne, was Liège, where our tent hospital was located. The German plan was to head up to Liège, cross the Meuse River there, head for Brussels, which they would bypass, and then on to Antwerp where they could easily capture the seaport and cut off all allied shipping, which meant no supplies, not only for the Americans but the British and Canadians as well.

About 25 miles southeast of Liège was the small town of Malmedy, site of the infamous Malmedy Massacre, where about 140-150 Americans were herded into a nearby field and though their arms were raised in the upright position of surrender, they were ruthlessly gunned down or clubbed to death or shot point-blank into the head. Many of them had their fingers and hands cut off, not just so the Germans could get their rings and watches, but more importantly, their warm winter gloves which the Germans lacked. This was the most brutally cold winter with the most snow and ice the Belgians had seen in over fifty years, with temperatures often plunging to thirty degrees below zero or more. Not all the Americans died under the German onslaught and under cover of darkness about forty of them who were still alive were helped by the Belgians or made it on their own to nearby American hospitals.

The Americans were completely demoralized by the German breakthrough and the entire U.S. Army was in a turmoil. Our anti-aircraft shot at our planes; our planes fired on our infantry—you've heard of *friendly fire*? Thousands of Americans were slaughtered, thousands were captured and thousands more were pushed back. German paratroopers, dressed in American uniforms, were dropped to infiltrate American lines and other paratroopers draped in white sheets were dropped on snow covered areas.

This was the situation when one week before Christmas, a sudden heavy, dense fog fell over all of Belgium, creating an eerie, gray, silent landscape and the only sounds we could hear were the muffled sounds of buzz bombs dropping. This fog was so thick, you couldn't see five feet ahead of you, yet the German tanks and infantry were able to move forward on the ground, but our planes couldn't get off the ground to bomb them, and the Germans headed steadily towards Liège.

At this point in time, our general hospital of 1,000 beds, was functioning as an evacuation hospital as we were one of the closest hospitals to the fighting lines, and the casualties poured in without having been treated first at a field or evacuation hospital which were much smaller and always closer to the fighting lines than a general hospital. They came with their bearded gray faces, muddied, bloodied, uniforms torn, sometimes they were just wrapped in a blanket and so many of them had the blackened, blistered feet of Trench Foot, which often ended in amputation. We had to have a special tent for our Trench Foot cases because once gangrene set in, the stench from the putrefying flesh sickened our other patients.

The injuries of our patients were indescribably horrible and we nurses had to put a tight lid on our emotions as we treated these mutilated bodies. Instead, we'd be very nonchalant: "Hi Soldier, what part of the States are you from?" And this was a good question to ask them for they all loved talking about their home town.

"Well, don't you worry, by the time you get back to that town of yours, you'll be fixed up as good as new." We told a lot of white lies but we had to give them hope.

We listened to the daily news reports of German advances with sinking hearts as the Germans got closer and closer to Liège. Two days before Christmas, as my roommate and I came off night duty, we decided to open our Christmas packages from home that morning because in two days time, by Christmas Day, we'd probably be dead. If we weren't killed by the buzz bombs, then we'd be captured and most likely killed by the Germans, and if anyone was going to enjoy those packages, it was going to be us. So here we were, sitting on our cot beds in our little fifth floor chateau bedroom at 8 a.m., opening the lovingly wrapped gifts from home and eating the home-made goodies that we washed down with our ration of French champagne. We each consumed a whole magnum of champagne that morning and had the best sleep that day that we had had in weeks. If the entire German army had marched through that little chateau bedroom, we would have been oblivious.

By the next day, December 24, the Germans were ten miles from Liège and had already dropped some paratroopers dressed in American uniforms into Liège. Most of the American hospitals in the area had already evacuated to Luxembourg or France and we felt like sitting ducks, hoping and waiting for orders to evacuate also which never came. Instead, we nurses were ordered to pack our musette bags with the warmest clothing we had and any first aid supplies in the event we were captured by the Germans, and to be prepared to move out with ten minutes notice.

Typically female, the first item to go in those musette bags, was the French perfume we had all purchased in Paris several months earlier, and this was followed by our cigarette ration, for a pack of American cigarettes could go a long way for bartering in war-torn Europe. And we were scared! I, especially, because of that "H" for "Hebrew" on my dog tags, the very ones Hitler wanted to annihilate. We knew from our Malmedy Massacre survivor patients that Hitler had no regard for the Geneva conventions.

Our patients were furious that American women were so far up front and when orders did come through that day to evacuate our sickest bed patients to the rear, they begged us to change places with them. It was at this point in time when my patients, who were concerned about my welfare, plied me with the gifts of the blackjack and spring blade knife with instructions for properly using them. ❧

CHAPTER SEVENTEEN

BATTLE OF THE BULGE, PART II

AS OUR PATIENTS were being evacuated, the fog that lay over all of Belgium for the past week began lifting and by nighttime, had completely dissipated and a full moon arose. This moon was so full and bright it lit up our hospital area with an almost daytime light and the painted red crosses on our tents were clearly outlined in this light.

I was on night duty in my surgical shock tent when sometime before 8 p.m., I heard the sound of a plane overhead, a sound we hadn't heard in the past week, due to the fog that had grounded all planes. I knew from the sound of the motor it wasn't one of our planes, (we learned early on to distinguish the sound of German planes from ours) and I stepped outside the tent to take a look. I was greeted by the most beautiful sight of what seemed like hundreds of red flares dropping through the nighttime sky and I stood there momentarily mesmerized by this 4th of July-like display. As I stood there, enjoying the sight, the plane that had dropped these flares began flying lower, back and forth over our hospital tents and nearby enlisted men's tents, dropping anti-personnel bombs and strafing the tents.

I dashed back into my tent where my patients were already putting on their steel helmets and told them to get under their beds. Fortunately, all my patients were ambulatory, as the sickest bed patients had been evacuated earlier that day. I found an empty bed and scrambled under it also, letting out a screech as I did so. My corpsman, who was at the other end of the tent, called out anxiously, "Lieutenant, were you hit?"

"No," I called back in a disgusted voice, "only by a loaded duck." In hospital lingo, a loaded duck was a *full urinal.* My patients laughed uproariously at this and it helped dispel some of the fear and tension we had all felt a few minutes before.

As the German plane continued flying back and forth across our hospital tents and enlisted men's tents, strafing and dropping his explosives, the anti-aircraft battery behind our hospital opened up and began shooting at this plane but they kept missing it and instead we had flak coming through our tents that we surely didn't need, and the plane eventually flew off into the night. Many patients and hospital personnel were wounded or killed; forty-seven of our enlisted men were injured, some seriously, and two of them killed outright. Our entire day crew came back on duty to help out in the operating rooms or surgical tents, wherever needed, working throughout the night and well into the next day. It was a night of horror no one will ever forget.

We later learned that this same plane attacked other American hospitals in the Liège area that night and was the same one that came back to our hospital again on New Year's Eve. He miscalculated however, and attacked in error, the POW compound attached to our hospital, killing one POW and wounding seventeen more, whom we ended up caring for.

Going off night duty that morning with a couple of other nurses, we straggled down the path to the nurses' quarters, too empty and spent to even talk, as each of us silently reviewed the scenes of horror from the previous night in our own minds. A nurse coming on duty greeted us midway in the path with a muted "Merry Christmas." It sounded absolutely ludicrous, we didn't even know what day it was, and it seemed to hit our funny bones simultaneously, for the three of us stood there in the path, bent over with hysterical laughter for a few minutes, and it was a good catharsis for our very somber moods.

Christmas Day dawned bright and clear, the sun was out for the first time in over a week and of course, the buzz bombs were out on their fifteen minute missions as they had been during the fog-bound week, but our planes were out for the first time in over a week. And so were the German planes, and we watched as they engaged our planes in dog fights not far from our hospital area, as spent machine gun bullets fell around us, and we saw flaming planes spiraling to the ground as we silently prayed they were German planes, not ours. The Chapel tent was overflowing that day but more time was spent in ducking than in praying.

Christmas week was a nightmare, with German planes coming over every night, (we called them "Bed Check Charlie"), to drop their paratroopers dressed in American uniforms, to infiltrate every American base. These paratroopers spoke a perfect English, with no trace of German accent, and they had been thoroughly briefed on American slang. One subject they hadn't been taught though, was that of American sports and when challenged by guards, as they attempted to infiltrate an American base, they couldn't answer such questions as: "Who won the World Series?" Or, "Who is the pitcher for the Dodgers or the Yankees?" Another question that could nab them was: "What shoe size do you wear?" And if they replied "Size 44," we knew we had them.

That same week of Christmas, the Prisoner of War (POW) compound that was attached to our hospital was searched and the POWs were found to have a huge supply of knives and guns they were planning to use in a breakout against us. During the few months the POWs had been working at our hospital, they were always very subservient and anxious to please as they went about performing their menial but necessary chores that freed up our own enlisted men for the more important tasks of helping care for our wounded soldiers. The POWs carried litters, shoveled snow, replenished coal buckets and cleaned latrines, and they were happy to be out of the fighting and to have a warm bed to sleep in and three square meals a day. However, once the German breakthrough began, they became very arrogant and surly and it was their very arrogance that prompted the search of their compound.

As Christmas week drew to a close, more of our planes were seen in the sky and soon they outnumbered the German planes. The next two weeks, we saw huge, constant waves of our planes, thousands of them by day, and those of the Royal Air Force at night as they flew on their missions to destroy the advancing German army and it was the most heartwarming sight and sound in the world, to see them and hear them. Thousands of German were captured, thousands more surrendered, and we felt the tides of war were turning in our favor. As our ground troops swept into Germany, they mopped up pockets of resistance and destroyed buzz bomb nests.

By January 25, 1945, the Battle of the Bulge was officially over. In this six week period about 19,000 Americans had been killed, 47,000 wounded and about 21,000 Missing in Action or taken as Prisoners of War. Fifty-three of our hospital staff received Purple Hearts, three received Purple Hearts with Oak Leaf Clusters, having been wounded more than once and two had been killed outright. Though there were many more battles to be fought before the Germans surrendered on May 8 and we were kept busy caring for the casualties of those battles, without the threat of being captured by the Germans or killed by buzz bomb, our lives were peaceful and content as we did the job we came overseas to do. ❧

Hospital tents after a heavy snowfall; note the icicles.

CHAPTER EIGHTEEN

DELAYED MAIL

July 13, 1945

Dear Mr. & Mrs. Novak:

This is the letter I should have written to you six months ago rather than foisting an unpleasant, heartbreaking task on my mother. But I hope you can understand how raw it was for me at the time, besides the factor of censorship when I could not reveal all the details to you, which I knew you would want. Now that the war in Europe is over and our hospital unit has moved back to France, I believe I will not be violating any security rules at this point, by telling you what really happened.

The Battle of the Bulge was raging in the midst of the coldest winter with the most snow Belgium had seen in fifty years, and the German army was ten miles away from our tent hospital in Liège, Belgium. Buzz bombs coming over every fifteen minutes didn't lighten the situation either. Coming off my twelve-hour night duty shift, I was at breakfast in the mess tent when I was approached by a fellow nurse who worked in the post-op tent.

"Phil," she began, addressing me by my nick name, "one of my patients is from your home town of Meriden, Connecticut, and I know you will want to see him. He's pretty much banged up but conscious." I was given his name, that of your son Frank, and told where to find his bed.

Working together as a family for almost two years, we nurses had heard many stories about each other's roots, and their hometown names were familiar to us. To find a patient here in war-torn Europe from one's hometown was like finding a long-lost relative. Though I didn't recognize Frank's name, I was sure we would have mutual friends or some common meeting ground, and I anticipated going on duty early that evening so I could stop off first and visit with him.

To say that Frank was "pretty much banged up" was putting it mildly, and if the War Department hadn't informed you of the total extent of his injuries, I will tell you that they were severe enough so he could never resume any kind of normal lifestyle again. I approached Frank's bedside, where he appeared to be sleeping, and called his name softly. His one eye, not bandaged, in an otherwise unblemished twenty-year-old face, opened immediately, and he registered surprise at this unknown person calling his name. I identified myself immediately as a nurse, also from Meriden, and his face lit up with a smile a yard wide. I knew he was as happy to see me as I was to see him, someone from my home on the other side of the ocean, thousands of miles away.

For the next three days, I visited with Frank before going on duty at night and in the morning when I went off duty. Though he came from the east side of town and I came from the west, and we had no mutual friends at all, there was still that bond of Meriden that we shared. We had both attended Meriden High School, so we compared mental pictures of the teachers we liked or disliked; we talked about the local landmarks that every native-born Meridenite was familiar with, like Hubbard Park; West Peak Mountain; the railroad running through the center of town; the crazy traffic tower at Main and Colony, etc. Even better, Frank did remember that his mom was a customer in my mom's dress shop so that made us almost blood relatives. We didn't discuss Frank's injuries, or my fears for his future life, missing an arm, leg, and eye, plus internal injuries, but just enjoyed the present .Oh, it was so good for both of us to rehash those memories of our town and forget about the war for a few minutes.

On Christmas Eve, that lone German plane flew over our hospital tents, dropping anti-personnel bombs, and strafing the tents, which tore like paper on the impact of the missiles fired. None of my patients were injured though other tents sustained severe loss of life, and I feared for the tent Frank was in. After a horrendous night when all day shift staff had been called back on duty to help care for the casualties, I hurried to Frank's tent and was horrified to find several empty beds, his among them. Besides my feelings of loss for your young son, I did feel a sense of relief that he wouldn't be subjected to years of a life, if you can call it that, in a VA hospital still filled with the human remnants of World War I.

I wanted you to take comfort in your loss from the fact that Frank didn't die on a bloody battlefield or in a foxhole, but was in a bed with a mattress and clean sheets. He was being medicated around the clock so he suffered no pain, and received the best medical attention available at the time. Conditions were pretty rough for the next couple of weeks and when I finally got to send a letter home, I told my mother about Frank and asked her to call you. I knew you would want to know the above facts about the circumstances of his death and the care he had received. I only learned months later that my mother's phone call, three weeks after Frank's death, was the first inkling you had that your son was gone, and I have no idea when you finally did hear from the War Department.

I do look forward to meeting you in person when I get back to the States, as my mother wrote that you were anxious to meet me. I hope these few details about Frank's last days will help—I know, just being able to talk to him about "home" was helpful for me also at a bad time.

Sincerely,

Muriel

CHAPTER NINETEEN

LETTERS HOME

INTRODUCTION

THE FOLLOWING PAGES are excerpts from letters sent home to my mother, sister, and brother during WW II, which were saved by my mother, though there are five months of letters that are missing, from December 1944 through April1945. The November 26, l944, letter and the one from October 31, l945, were returned to me about forty years later by the cousins to whom they had been sent. The missing letters would have covered our life and emotions in the Battle of the Bulge time period, leading to the defeat of the German army.

There are certain terms and abbreviations employed in my letters:

GIs—The enlisted men (derived from "government issue")

PMs—Afternoons off duty

DS—Detached service, duty with other hospitals.

ETO—European Theater of Operations

CBI—China, Burma, India Theater of Operations, where we expected to be sent once the war in Europe was over

D-Day—June 6, 1944, the day the Americans stormed the French coast-line to engage the Germans in battle

V-E Day—May 8, 1945, when the Germans surrendered

V-J Day—September 2, 1945, when Japan surrendered

K-rations—Cracker Jack-like box that held small cans of chicken, tuna fish, or ham, crackers and cheese, and a hard candy or cookie; used in emergencies when no mess kitchen was available (e.g., traveling, tent living, etc.)

C-rations—Hot canned foods, used when a mess tent was set up

Points—Forty-five points were needed to be eligible for returning home when the war in Europe was over; dependent on the number of campaign medals received and months spent overseas.

There were many weeks of detached service, when we did not function as a hospital, as with the times in North Wales, when we were waiting for our hospital to be built, or the many weeks in Normandy or Paris, when we awaited the routing of the Germans from Liège. If we weren't sent on detached service, we were given leaves to travel to other points of interest—London, or Scotland, and later in the war, Paris, French Riviera, and Switzerland. It was always a treat to "feel like a nurse" again after our weeks of inactivity.

The last two letters express the general despondency at the delays in sailing home once Japan surrendered, and there was nothing else on our minds but getting home.

LETTERS HOME

DEC. 31, 1943 SOMEWHERE AT SEA. Dear Mom: Happy New Year anyhow—that's about all I'm allowed to write, almost. Am feeling fine but think the next pleasure cruise I take will be by train.

JAN. 10, 1944 ENGLAND. Here I am on dry land but after studying the topography and geography of this country, you can imagine how dry we are. We are located in what we have named "Ye Olde Duste Bine" and the label on the door says"1/12 Officer Living." Pretty soon we're going to cross out "living" and put "Drowned in Dust" instead. These huts are better than tents and we even have a floor and roof thrown in, though they're both on the sunken side.… What this weather (they call it a slight dew here) does to my hair, I shall leave to your imagination.… There is such a complete blackout here you can't see your finger in front of your nose and you can believe me when I say no one bothers to get dressed to wallow through the mud at night to get to the latrine—you just use your helmets.

JAN. 11. Having a fine time trying to understand the customs, speech and money system of the English. I went through hell and high water trying to use one of their telephones today, operators are very courteous and they can always spot newcomers to the country and get a kick out of it.… These English trains sure are funny-looking contraptions and have all the comforts of home, almost. They are built in compartments, like separate coaches, 6 or 8 people in one and have this very old-fashioned ornate upholstery, with a mirror above the seats and pictures of famous spots around England and hotel advertisements. We had fruit and candy we had brought with us from the ship and threw it to the English children, who were overjoyed.

JAN. 16. We're living temporarily with the 304th Station Hospital until our own hospital is complete. Went shopping yesterday in Wrexham and had a lot of fun seeing how the English live. Everybody commutes by bicycle, even riding around the hospital grounds so we all put in orders for bicycles, which when complete with flashlights, repair equipment, baskets, etc. come to 11 pounds (about $44). The countryside is beautiful and all the hills are green, even at this time of year. The cottages are quaint and picturesque, the people very friendly but very apologetic for existing conditions in this country and are always reminding us why their homes need a coat of paint or why they have one set of clothing to wear.

FEB. 12. Last night we went into the town of Chester to attend Friday night services for both servicemen and women and civilians and they were practically like Friday night services in the states, at least the English Jews don't talk Hebrew with an English accent. Most of us went on account of the dinner they serve. Most English are very orthodox and everything is in Hebrew but we thoroughly enjoyed the little sermon by an English chaplain (Jewish) who is the youngest rabbi I've ever seen, handsome brute, and speaks beautifully. The dinner consisted of tomato soup, fish (stunk), Brussels Sprouts, (stunk), mashed potatoes (OK), tart and coffee for dessert.

FEB. 16. Went to Chester yesterday and visited the Chester Cathedral, which is very famous and built in the 12th century. The town in itself is one of the oldest in England and there are many historical points of interest as well as beautiful spots. There is a wall that runs around the city which was used as a fortress centuries ago, so we walked along this wall and really saw a good part of the city and the River Dee. We had tea in one of the more famous hotels there and it was so much fun. You have tea and bread and butter cut very thin, and a little jam, etc. Also a sliver of a plain cake. In prewar days you could ordinarily get scones and crumpets and trifle, but now, you're lucky if you can get slivers of bread and butter.

Everyone has tea anywhere between 3:30 and 5 p.m. and dinners in restaurants and hotels are served after 7:30 pm. And of course, you just can't go into a restaurant or hotel for dinner without having had reservations there. We went exploring and decided not to stay at the hotel for dinner so finally ended up in The Black Swan Hotel, and such a place! Something like Ye Greasye Spoone style, but you must expect that. So we had brawn, which is the meat from the pig's head, jellied, and is supposed to taste like our Spam, and we had chips (French fries), bread and butter and tea. Then we had to travel back about 8:30 p.m.—incidentally we couldn't do any shopping as the stores are all closed Wednesday to save on fuel.… We went into the pub till it closed at 10 and drank more of this English Stout, which is a form of their beer and makes you go like hell.… These English autos are like our baby Austins and you feel as tho your rear end is going to drag on the ground, they are built so low, but they are very powerful and can get up a good speed.

FEB. 20. Yesterday we went to Liverpool and had the most interesting and enjoyable day. We got into Liverpool about 2 p.m. and immediately went to the biggest and most modern hotel there and made reservations for dinner that night. I suppose they were very fortunate 'cause all the other buildings for miles around just ain't no more—gosh, it must have been awful when they were being blitzed. Well, from the hotel we decided to go to the Liverpool Philharmonic concert and were lucky to get box seats at the last minute, and right down in front. It was simply superb. The soloist was wonderful, very well-known over here by the name of Maggie Teyte and the orchestra was conducted by Dr. Malcolm Sargent. The concert hall also escaped the blitz and it was simply beautiful—a small-scale music hall. It was very modernistic, soft carpets and cushioned seats and we enjoyed it so much.... Being in Liverpool was almost like being in Boston—we saw some beautifully dressed women, which was a pleasure after the farmers we've seen around here, and there were loads of stores and even 2 Chinese restaurants.

As I was going to Manchester in the early A.M. I decided to stay over-night in Liverpool and was fortunate to get a room at this lovely hotel, and Mother, I nearly collapsed when I saw this huge room with the most wonderful bed with sheets and 2 pillows and pillow case and a satin comforter. There were full-length mirrors, and dressing table, chiffonier, lounging chair, etc. No private john, though there was a wash stand, but the john was down the hall. At night you put your shoes outside the door and someone cleans them for you.

We made for the bar which opened at 6 and made sure we were first in line, as they are all sold out in 15 minutes. We met up with some Amer-ican naval officers and drank rum and orange, tastes like hair tonic. At 7:30 we went up to this big dining room, almost like the Copley Plaza, with table cloths and linen napkins—ah, heavenly! Had hors d'oeuvres, rolls, roast pigeon (about 1 tablespoon of it), mashed potatoes, carrots and the eternal Brussels Sprouts. Had cheese and rolls and coffee and brandy for desert—oh Mother, it was so wonderful to sit back and relax and just feel like a civilian again. That place and the concert were worth coming to England for. Couldn't wait to get in to that delicious bed, with bed lamps, telephone, bed turned down—ah luxury! In the A.M. they woke me at 7 and brought me breakfast in bed—quite the fashion over here—sausage, ham, roll and toast, marmalade and coffee. Oh, it was perfect and whatever I spent was worth it, and in the States it would have cost 10 times as much. For the room and breakfast it cost 15 shillings, equivalent to $3—isn't that wonderful?

FEB. 28. EDINBURGH, SCOTLAND. I shall try to give you an account of each day's happening while on leave. Left at 9 a.m. and rode till 8:15 tonight, the train being 2 hours late. It was a beautiful day, bright and clear but cold, as it had snowed for the past 2 days, so we weren't sorry we had to lug our paraphernalia with us as gas mask, musette bags, helmets, etc., 'cause the added bulk kept us warm. We had a compartment to ourselves, 5 of us on the train and had a wonderful time all afternoon trying to figure out how many generations of bedbugs were lodged in those green plaid plush seats. The first couple of stations we stopped at, we'd dash out, buy cups of hot tea and meat cakes and eat them from one station to another.... The scenery was simply gorgeous all the way up and I think I'm going to love Scotland. The lowlands were covered with snow and the peaks blending in with the blue sky was a never to be forgotten sight. Then in the valleys the sheep were grazing in the greenest grass I've ever seen. The train didn't make many stops, fortunately for us, 'cause none of the stations have big signs out with the name of the town on it and no conductor comes through volunteering any information. Honestly, you could take a bath in these compartments and no one would disturb you. Passed several pretty little towns and we named each one we came to, as Birdcage-on-the-Rillera, Birdturd-on-the-Hudson, Pesthole-by-the-Sea, etc.

Pulled in tonight and went to the Red Cross to have them get hotel reservations for us, and you should see the place we're in tonight! Well, before my trip to Liverpool this would have been very magnificent but as we really intend to do the town up right, we want to be nearer the nightclubs and shopping district and we want private baths, no matter what we pay. Tomorrow we go on a search and we'll find it.

MARCH 2. GLASGOW. We never found it. We searched the whole city of Edinburgh but the hotels were full so we stayed where we were. The beds were soft and the rooms large and comfortable but not a bit of heat and I froze so much I didn't sleep 3 hours a night the whole 5 nights we were there. However, even the swankiest hotels didn't have heat, though most of them have gas heaters in the room and by putting in a shilling every 4 hours you get some heat and its better than nothing.... Edinburgh was almost like NY to us and their main shopping district is along one of the loveliest streets I've ever seen, Princess Street. The shops were all so modern and it was a pleasure to shop in them—not that we could buy much—you need coupons for almost everything.

At noon the bars opened up and from 12 noon to midnite we drank Scotch that day, it just flowed like water (we met the right people).... Oh what a wonderful time we had—millions of air corps officers and infantry and other Americans would join us and we were just one bunch of foreigners from the States, all stinkin' from drinkin'. Took 1 hour out for lunch and ate at the Brown Derby—not the real McCoy, and had Toad-in-the-Hole for lunch. The names are cockeyed and the cooking is even worse but when you're hungry, you know.

Wednesday we went up to the Edinburgh Castle and saw where Mary Queen of Scots lived for a while and all the others you read about in the history books. It started to snow like hell while we were there so we couldn't walk the royal mile to the Palace.... Had a real American Coca-Cola at the Red Cross that afternoon and were we thrilled! ... Today Hazel and I parted from the other kids and came to Glasgow, and I really like this city though most people don't. Not as beautiful as Edinburgh though there are more modern shops.... We got in about noon and were going out to Loch Lomond but it was so cold and the hotel we had reservations for had no heat, and the Red Cross said there was nothing to see at this time of year so we stayed in the city at the Red Cross and had heat.

We shopped at the American PX here and bought some peanuts—I ate a whole can right off. The people here are so much more modern than the English, dress better (naturally, as they haven't had to contend with what the British have) but they even have American plumbing systems. We get a kick out of the Scotch officers in their plaid kilts, and speaking of plaids, I'm coming back to Scotland after the war and buy them out.... Went to the movies and saw "Cry Havoc," very good. Tomorrow we're going to the art galleries and other places of interest here at Charing Cross.... I'm definitely coming to Scotland again as I've fallen in love with the whole country. The scenery is so lovely and the houses are so picturesque and this is such a pleasant change from battered war-torn England, you almost forget there's a war on.

MARCH 6. ENGLAND. It was a pleasure to come back from leave to find 23 letters, stacks of newspapers and my 2nd package from home with Kleenex, God bless the guy who invented it, and the wonderful chocolate covered peanuts and the safety pins. The kids howl every time I get a package or letter from Mother and some safety pins or common pins drop out.... We had a nice trip from Glasgow to Liverpool; there were 4 officers in the compartment with Hazel and me, all English and full of the devil. They kept us supplied with hot tea as the train was so cold—no heat at all—and sandwiches and kept us in stitches the whole time. You can keep your tea cups right in the train 'cause all these places are owned by the railroad concern and they pick up the cups at the last stop.

MARCH 10. No, I'm not doing any nursing yet but as you say, once we start there won't be any let up.... yes, our relatives are really grand and though I haven't had a chance to go out there again, I hear from them and call frequently. Will try to get out for Passover holiday. Was able to get Gertrude a couple of Maiden-Form bras from the PX in Glasgow which she had missed very much and also my 6 weekly ration of 2 pair of rayon stockings. They need so many coupons even to buy handkerchiefs over here so stockings are practically impossible for them to get more than a few times a year.... The past few nights have been as warm and balmy as a summer night, full orange moon, millions of stars and as light as day out. Last night I went out with Harold, the captain from this other outfit, and went up to his club and their jukebox had some wonderful records. Then we went to his hut with his 4 other drunken roommates, all well known doctors, rather businesslike during the day but at night they're worse than any bunch of school boys. We had scrambled eggs (powdered), toast and coffee and even popped corn in a tin can on the stove. One of them got hold of some duck eggs and so we poached them in vermouth. I was exhausted from laughing when we finally rode home on our bikes about 2 a.m.

Sammy will be coming back from detached service on the 19th and will I be glad! Have spent more time on these stinkin' English pay phones trying to talk to him. He'd call me and I'd have to call back and more darned trouble. By the time you get through yelling back and forth "I can't hear you," "Speak louder!" "What did you say?" the operator would cut in and say our time was up.... This morning for breakfast, we had real fried eggs and big juicy oranges and toast, so you can see that there's a big improvement in our mess since we opened our own camp.... Our diapers, which we have dyed red for curtains, are a great success and make our hut look so cute. Really should write the Curity people and tell them how useful their product is.

MARCH 17. Last night Sammy and I (he's the dentist I go out with in our outfit) went to an English dance held in some little hall near here and I laughed my head off the whole time 'cause this whole affair was different from any of our dances in the States. Whole families go, from the babies to the grandparents, and these big fat women get up and dance with each other and 10-year-old boys are lugging their grandmothers around. The whole place reeks of horse manure cause all the farmers are there and I don't think bathtubs are very popular in this country. Only the wealthy can afford them out in the sticks and sometimes they can't get them or haven't the plumbing system if they do have the money. There was a trumpeter there about 80 years old who had a bright red toupee perched on his head, and it was parted right in the middle and waved on each side, and every time he'd get hot on a jazz number, the toupee would bounce up and down and once it even slid off. I always thought they glued them on but apparently he perspired so much the glue must have melted or else he just planks it on and expects the forces of gravity to hold it in place.

MARCH 27. Real spring and summer weather of late and we're having a wonderful time outdoors, sunbathing, 15 and 20 mile bike rides, road hikes and planting our garden and fixing our front lawn. Have planted a border of flowers and it looks lovely. Had a dressing table made from a packing box and by dying some diapers a pretty shade of green to match my lamp shade, I have the prettiest ruffled skirt and table cover for it. Also upholstered a chair with the same stuff and used a bath towel for seat padding and just can't wait to get up in the morning now so I can sit at my dressing table and put my face on…. As I sit here I can look outside our front door, kept open all the time now, and can see the officers playing volley ball in the field back of their huts and they're all yelling away like a pack of kids, dressed in shorts and shoes. It's 7 p.m. but the sun is still throwing some heat and it's a big red ball of fire now. It gets cold at night though, and we are still allowed to have fires at night.

MARCH 30. I'm feeling fine and haven't so much as sneezed or blown my nose for the past 3 weeks so I guess I'm really acclimatized now. Then too, we're all much healthier with all our drills, hikes, and strenuous calisthenics and bicycling.

MARCH 31. I have some more requests to make of you. Hope you got my letter asking for a couple of bras and also to send me a couple of slips. If you threw out the ones I sent home, please go out and buy me one, and buy one frilly one with lace or something, just so it's feminine looking. Now that spring is here we're putting on our seersucker uniforms tomorrow to celebrate Easter and to surprise the boys. Never thought the day would come when those stupid bags would be morale building…. Am all out of food so anytime you feel like sending packages out, crackers, potato chips, peanuts and any canned stuff will be welcome.

APRIL 2. Have already written you about the two boxes I received last week and yesterday and today I received a box from you, the one with the cookies and Kleenex and the one with the cocoa and peanut butter, cherries and tomato juice. God bless you, my family—you don't know what you're doing for piling the calories on us and keeping up our faith in the home front. The cookies arrived in good shape, some were broken, but they were so delicious and fresh, and they were all gone by this morning. The girls said to tell you the cookies and marmalade were the best they ever tasted. The canned goods you sent are swell but we're saving them for a day when rations get low again, though lately we've been getting good food and plenty of it.

Yesterday the four of us went to one of the larger cities and shopped and had a wonderful time buying more garden seeds, bicycle tools, books, cards and I even got a hatchet. When I walked through the streets with that hatchet in my hand, the people all stared so and you could just picture them thinking "My, these American army nurses sure are being trained in all kinds of work." But it will help me in constructing a bureau and table and also chopping up kindling. Slept till 1 p.m. today and then Sammy came over to the hut and we had a late breakfast while the other kids did their correspondence and week's ironing. He did some difficult carpentry work for us and fixed all our flashlights, and I sewed on his insignia, so tit for tat.

APRIL 6. As of this month we're going to discard our zoot suits and don our seersucker uniforms. Of course, now that spring is here, we'll probably wish we were back outdoors drilling and hiking instead of being cooped up indoors.

Wonder what it will be like to be a nurse again.

APRIL 10. My uniform from Dayton, Ohio, that I bought last July, arrived today and really is beautiful, though the jacket is a little too long and will have to be altered. Today I'm so exhausted after 8 hours of hard labor in the operating room and this tired feeling reminds me of the good old days when I was a nurse. It was swell to get into uniform though, and all the doctors were so surprised every time we'd ride by on our bikes with our dark green capes and seer-sucker caps to match our brown and white striped uniforms, They'd yell "Gee, look at the nurses!" Unpacked and scrubbed instruments and basins from 8 to 5 and were my feet ever tired, but it's only the beginning.

Sammy and one of the doctors from his hut came for breakfast and we had a real feast in our hut. One of the girls goes with a farmer so we had a dozen eggs she hauled in the previous night and we got some bacon from the mess hall and had the tomato juice you sent me. So we had toast and butter also swiped from the mess, bacon and eggs cooked in our mess kits and Nescafé. More fun! For desert we had some Fanny Farmer candies one of the kids got from home and some cookies. After that Sammy spent about an hour and a half cleaning and polishing my bike and also polished my shoes for me—he doesn't think I do a good job on my shoes, so why should I complain? We went bike riding in the p.m. and took pictures which will take 6-8 weeks to be developed as they have to go to the base censor.

Fri. night went out with a cute captain from Base headquarters. At one of the pubs we met a farmer who gave us a dozen and a half eggs so we walked out to his shack in the hills and he had his wife cook them for us. Their home was typical of the farm houses of the poor folks around here—tiny, combined living and dining room and kitchen with ceilings so low we practically hit our heads when we stood up, and of course, the usual aroma of horse manure. Don't worry about me staying over here after the war—I'll take Meriden plumbing to all the sights England has to offer any day.

APRIL 16. Have to clean up our hut for a big inspection tomorrow and this one is going to be a humdinger. Half of the army officers in the ETO are inspectors I guess, and just go from post to post looking for things to find fault with. By gosh, no matter how perfect you may be, they'll always find something wrong. Have to salute them indoors, outdoors, everywhere except the latrine. So when we see brass on the post we usually turn around and go in another direction so they can't tell us our salute is at a 47 degree angle instead of 45.

APRIL 21. My letters will probably continue to arrive irregularly, not only because of the mail system, but also because now that we're working, I have less time. As for England being the worst place for asthma, no need to worry 'cause I haven't even had a cold for 2 months and feel even better than back in the states. I guess our training program has built me up pretty well and now that I'm acclimated to the dampness, it doesn't bother me at all. Sleep like a log, no insomnia and eat like a horse.

This week we have millions of visiting firemen running all over the post— inspectors, and we have to be on our toes continually 'cause they are so strict. You can't accomplish much work on duty 'cause when a strange officer comes through, you take it for granted that he's an inspector, drop everything, stand at attention, the charge nurse salutes, gives him her name, rank and position and then follows him around the place while he looks for trouble. As the colonel told me last night, we are not in the ETO but the ETI—European Theatre of Inspections.

APRIL 23. Today being a beautiful sunshiny Sunday, I'm now taking care of my correspondence, lying on a blanket on our side lawn. Due to the fact that I'm working in the O.R., I'll be having every other weekend off to compensate for having to be on call at night. Yesterday I received your package with the toilet paper, Kleenex, zipper, pins, etc., and thanks so much. Even though there's a war on, you would have died laughing if you saw the commotion here in camp about a half hour ago, all over a dog. One of the girls next door was taking her dog out for a ride in a basket on her bike when he jumped out and was run over by a big truck. She called the post here and they sent down an ambulance and 2 doctors and brought the dog back and gave him enough attention to warrant him being the King of England. He's alive with no broken bones but has a prolapsed rectum and the poor thing is lying in his box now, all worn out. Everyone in the camp has been here to see him and they talk in hushed voices just as though he was a real patient. One of the veterinarians from another outfit is on his way down to visit him. The latest pet in the nurses area is a baby fox and is he adorable—now—though I'd hate to be around in a couple of years. Can't get the goat I was bargaining for so think I'll drop the issue.

Did I tell you I received the chocolate bars and gum last week? Boy, they sure are wonderful and I still have them due to the fact that I'm abstaining for a couple of weeks till I lose some weight.

APRIL 26. Just got the package with 2 rolls of T.P. so I'm all set for the duration I guess—that stuff is very valuable for winning friends and influencing people around here. Am not working too hard as our O.R. was the last part to get set up and we're still busy making supplies etc. Wish you could see this set up, your eyes would really pop out, cause you could never imagine anything as elaborate as this. Of course there are a good many makeshift appliances but the real necessary gear is gorgeous.

My social life is booming and I have dropped the medics in favor of the Quartermaster, Infantry and Artillery. After going with the medics so long, these men seem so peppy and full of life and less on the wolfish side. Of course, when they move out, we'll probably have to revert back to the medics but we'll worry about that when the time comes. The countryside is more beautiful than ever now and even the weather is ideal. Ah me, I have spring fever and my fancies are turning to what they've been thinking of all winter. Met a cute dentist last night from Forest Hills—me and my affinity for dentists again.

APRIL 28. Last night we went to an Engineer's dance and had a swell time. Coming home from the dance the truck drivers lost their way so we rode all over England till 3:45 a.m. when we finally rolled into camp. Net result, our whole hut overslept one hour this a.m. Had a busy day in the O.R. and was on the go constantly, running from one case to another and was so tired when I got off duty I didn't even bother going to supper.

MAY 2. Just returned from Manchester, got a sudden 24 hour leave, the first in two months so of course, went to see our relatives even though I had quite a time before I saw them. The train was 2 hours late as usual and as they had tickets for the theatre and didn't think I was coming, went on ahead to the theatre and so I went out with Myer's assistant in the shop who took care of me beautifully until they got home. We hit every hotel bar in the city, had a great roast beef dinner at one of the hotels and drank double scotches till it was coming out of our ears. He was a handsome guy all right, and everywhere we went we'd bump into his friends who insisted on buying a drink for the "Yankee nurse." Anyhow, by the time we got back to the Craingolds, I was as high as a kite. Honestly, they are so grand to me and I really feel like one of the family. Already all the other relatives are fighting with each other for the privilege of having me visit them, and were they ever mad when I couldn't get to see them. After all, I only had a few hours and had to be back at 1 p.m. today. As it was, I was AWOL for 5 hours, haven't heard about it yet.

Sunday was one of the most beautiful days we've had yet and 3 couples of us went on a bike ride and picnic to a gorgeous lake about 6½ miles from here. We took pictures, went wading in the water, fed the swans and ate like pigs. Today when I got into the village near camp and was walking up the street, a cute officer stopped me and said he just had to talk to me 'cause I was the first American girl he had seen since he's been over here, and that happens so frequently. Only usually it's the enlisted men who will stop us and just pump our hands up and down and say hungrily, "Gee, it sure is like heaven to see an American girl." Well, if we do nothing else in this men's army, we're keeping up the morale pretty well.

MAY 28. Today was one of my Sundays off for the month and it was a broiling scorcher day, the 3rd real hot day we've had so far. So I slept all morning, got in my bathing suit and took it easy on the back lawn all afternoon. Now at 8 p.m. the sun is still hot and I'm like a broiled lobster. The rest of the kids in the hut had PM's and were all out in their bathing suits and it almost looked like Long Beach. All we needed was an ice cream cone, an ocean and some sand, and it would have been the real McCoy. We'll be living in tents before too long and I'm going to hate giving up my dressing table and bicycle. Will have to start sending home a lot of clothes that aren't practical for a rugged life and I hate to part with my housecoats too.

JUNE 26. Received both of your letters of June 14 within the past week but just didn't get around to answering for reasons #1: I was a busy girl part of the time and #2: I was a tired girl the rest of the time. I'm sorry you were so worried you wrote you had to go to Dr. Stippich for an adjustment. Why, you just have an enlarged imagination like mine at times, 'cause we hardly know there's a war going on and if it weren't for the nature of our work and the hours we put in some times, we may as well be back in the states.

JULY 2. It's raining again for a change, as a matter of fact it rained almost all week, but it's an old story with us by now. Had some time off the other afternoon so Elaine Nigro—one of my Cambridge classmates and I went to visit another of our classmates at a General Hospital about 35 miles from here. By dint of our thumbs and army uniform, we got there eventually via 2½ ton trucks, weapon carriers and jeeps. Had a swell visit and as we were about to hitch our way back we spied our chaplain visiting the chaplain on that post, so we got a ride home too, as each chaplain has his own jeep now. I'll probably be sending home a money order or bond one of these days cause my cash has been piling up month after month as there's no place to spend it.

SEPT. 10. NORMANDY, FRANCE. It is 3 p.m. on a windy but sunny Sunday afternoon and for the first time in over 2 weeks we've had no rain for the past 8 hours. Yesterday in a freakish, almost hurricane like rain storm, there were hail stones as big as lima beans, and per usual it started when we were all in the chow line and we all got a good pelting. Today the kids are at their bedding rolls to find the terrific damage the rain and dampness caused and everything in them is mildewed. It is so cold here it doesn't seem possible a month ago we were sunbathing—even two weeks ago but I guess winter is setting in early. We wear so many clothes to bed we can't even turn around and the air is so biting at night we have to sleep with our heads under the blankets.

Still very little mail coming through but I got 2 packages from you the past couple of days—one with cookies, salmon and peanut butter and one with Kleenex, cookies and prunes. Needless to say everything was wonderful and the prunes are as effective as ever. Even the stinking bees which are out in full force today after 2 weeks hibernation, like the prunes, and I hope they all die of dysentery.

The bees love chewing gum and nibble right through the paper to get at the stuff. Oh yes, also received all the pkgs. of gum you sent.

Am so glad you made me take that old blue bathrobe of Grandma's with me—I wear it to bed every night and it sure is warm, wrap my feet and legs up in it. It's so long since I've worn a girdle, I probably won't fit into the ones I have. I don't know how I'll ever get along without my fancy olive drab wool underwear, but I can't wait to try it anyhow. If I stay here much longer and have to wash my hair in chlorinated water I'll be a real blonde by the time I get home. We have a loudspeaker in our mess tent and at chow time we get music with our meals and you have no idea how wonderful it is. Even heard my favorite Warsaw Concerto today and was ready to swoon. Gosh, a little while ago one of the girls created an uproar in camp by waving around an empty coca cola bottle which she brought back as a souvenir from some other camp where someone got hold of a real bottle of coca cola and everyone here had to hold it and smell it, and in general just acted like a bunch of nuts.

SEPT. 14. I'm on detached service now with another hospital and we're getting plenty of work and I'm tired. These tent hospitals are really something— never would have believed it possible back in the states. The hours are long and all this talk about 8 hour shifts is a lot of bull 'cause the work is never done when it keeps coming in all the time. You really have to hand it to these girls who sometimes work right around the clock and not a peep out of them. Boy, if I ever go back to nursing, please kick me hard. I can't see what I'm writing, it's so dark in here but can't let this good paper go to waste.

My French comes in handy, even working in the hospital, what with the civilian employees and some patients so I'm now official interpreter for the operating room staff. Wish I could tell you something about the work, etc. but I can't so you'll have to wait till I get back. Well, what's new at home—are women still wearing dresses and high heels or is that all a figment of my imagination?—just can't imagine any female in anything but pants and helmets. Well, I'm glad I'm working even though I'm kinda tired.

Heard a couple of days ago that my pilot friend was missing but it may not be true—at least I'm hoping he'll turn up again 'cause he was one sweet fellow. That's why it doesn't pay to tangle up with the Air Corps, but as far as that goes, any branch of the service, especially in the combat zones. Well, I think I'll climb out of my combat suit into another one and a set of long G.I. underwear and grab a few hours' sleep.

SEPT. 17. Well, here it is Sunday night and I'm recuperating on my luxurious cot after a day's work. I've just had a nice hot bath out of my helmet after stealing the hot water from our mess line where we wash our mess kits and I'm feeling 100% refreshed. Some of the men are going to services tonight and even though it is such an important holiday, I think the Lord will forgive me if I'm too comfortable to walk a mile down and back to where services are being held at another outfit. There's going to be a movie on this post tonight, "Gaslight" which I'll probably go to unless I fall asleep.

Two hours later—just got back from the movie and it was wonderful though full of suspense. And it seems that at all the breathtaking parts the film would either break or it would be time to change the reel. Besides a radio, we now have a gasoline lamp and though it's not a very bright light, we take turns keeping it at our end of the tent and tonight it's my turn and I'm making the most of it. Am having a lovely time chewing on a sour green apple, almost as good as Fanny Farmer chocolates. See how well I can talk things into myself. We went to a dance last night and I met some officer there who is in the same regiment as that colonel I was going with back in England and is a Brig. General now and quite the guy over here.

SEPT. 20. As for me, I do feel that after the war I won't want to do any nursing again, 'cause I'm getting my share over here after all those weeks of loafing. I'd like to look at whole people for a change and not just patched up fragments of them. As to the nature of our work I can't divulge it as it's a military secret, and I spend my spare time sleeping.

We have stew a-plenty these days, had it 8 times last week but once in a while we get a run of good food like chicken, steak, eggs and oranges, all in the same week and it's wonderful. Cripes, it's dark in here even with one lantern going and I'm practically sitting on top of it.

SEPT. 23. Not much to write about, but the weather has turned a little warmer, thank God! Did get a chance to attend services one morning for a little while so got my New Year's religion in. Went on a shopping spree this a.m. to a fair sized town that wasn't too badly damaged but my shopping was confined to postcards and a bottle of ink as their stuff is all crap and expensive. Very soon I'll be able to get some perfume, and I'll try to send some home. Some kids I know got Chanel #5 in Paris and very cheaply, seeing as how a few packages of cigarettes accomplishes wonders over here. They also have real silk stockings and nylons for $15 and up a pair. They have beautiful lingerie, all handmade too with lace for 2000 francs and up, equivalent to $40 a piece. Some things like cheese and bread are very cheap and delicious too but you need coupons for that stuff. I did manage to get a 2 lb. round cheese for 60 francs which would probably cost about $4.50 at home-and it's delicious. I've been eating that all week 'cause I'm getting tired of stew and dehydrated cabbage, which is forever repeating.

While visiting one of these towns here, we had a chance to see a French funeral, small-town style and it was really very picturesque. A very ornate and beautifully decorated coffin, resting on poles and covered by a raised canopy, all decked out with wreaths of flowers was carried by 4 people— 4 teen age boys, as it was a child who had died. They were all dressed up fit to kill, and in back of them marched a couple of little girls, decked out like a Xmas tree, bearing more flowers and something that looked like a diploma or birth certificate. Then in back of them marched all the women of the family dressed in solid black, with sheer black veils which reached down to their waists, and they were followed by a few men dressed in mourning clothes. They paraded through the streets like that and all traffic stopped for them. The people on the sidewalk all stopped walking and just looked, till they went by. It's supposed to be bad luck to cross the street in front of a funeral procession, so we, too, had to wait.

A couple of hours later. It's pouring like hell again, for a change and I'm trying to finish this by flashlight. In 6 weeks' time here in France, I've decided this country is even wetter than England, but maybe it's just the season. Anyhow, the fog at night beats any I've seen in England, the mist starts forming over the fields just before dark and soon it's so thick you can't see a foot in front of yourself. Tonight we're supposed to have "Dirty Hour" which we have once a week religiously and everybody tells all the dirty jokes and songs they've ever heard. Anybody who hears any stories or jokes during the week has to save them up for "Dirty Hour."

So that keeps the conversation clean all week long. Then of course at "Dirty Hour," our tent is besieged by gals from all the other tents who are too lazy to start their own. This is all for now so will hit the hay. Whenever you do happen to send out a package, some prunes would be gratefully accepted by one who has the reverse of the backdoor trots.

SEPT. 27. Whether or not you've been getting my letters, I don't know, but just in case you miss up on them for a week or two, don't worry as I may not be able to write for a while. I'm back from D.S. now, came back a few days ago and then went on D.S. at another hospital, but again, I'm back in our cow pasture. Haven't received any mail in about two weeks. They say there are thousands of mail bags waiting to be sorted out, so some day when the war stops long enough to get the mail sorted, I'll probably get some letters from you. Got a couple of packages today, candy from Rhoda with butter crunch which was the best thing I've tasted in months, peanuts and chocolates. I thought you'd be glad to know I attended services last night and tonight and they were really nice. They were held in a tent in a nearby outfit which was jammed to capacity with soldiers, nurses, Red Cross workers and patients. Tonight they had a big dinner at the conclusion, and it was very nice—canned chicken and crumb cake.

The services weren't like anything you'd ever see back home in that no one was dressed in their best clothing and we all attended dressed in our combat suits and helmets. However the spirit among the men was more sincere than anything I've ever seen and the speakers were good, so it was very worthwhile.

I've been having a helluva time trying to shake a full colonel off my tail who I met about a week and a half ago and has been pestering the life out of me since. He's only about 60 years old but oh my, he has such young ideas. He simply won't take any hints so I'm glad now I won't have to see him any more. I always brought one of the other girls with me and he was getting suspicious—such an old goat. I swear he's positively senile. 2 minutes after we met it was "Darling" and "Precious" and how beautiful

I am. Well, anyhow, I got a gasoline lantern from him which I've wanted desperately, floor covering which will cover a whole tent when we set up, candy and little souvenirs. Had some good meals at his post, on real dishes, drank champagne till it came out of my ears but I was too sober to suit him. Cripes Mom, would you have a helluva time over here with these old goats.—want to swap places?

According to the newspapers, everyone at home seems very optimistic about us all being home soon, but little do they know! And the war isn't over yet. I expect to work harder than ever before, and don't expect lousy old hemorrhoid cases either, though it would be nice if that was all we got.

OCT. 2. PARIS, FRANCE. Well, I've seen Paris and I can die happy now. Mother, after this war is over, don't spend your money on a trip to England but go to Paris instead 'cause it's like something out of this world. Maybe it means more to us having lived in cow pastures so long and this glimpse of civilization is really thrilling. The women are so beautiful, so smartly dressed, all wearing fur pieces and fur coats and the most gorgeous hats you've ever seen. The streets are the widest in the world I believe, and much lovelier than our Fifth Ave. because there is more space and everything isn't so crowded.

When we were being loaded on to trucks in front of the station, they gathered around in mobs and saluted and cheered and were genuinely glad to see us. I have more darned addresses of people to look up, that I just met on the street. The sidewalk cafés were all open and it was just like the movies. Of course we saw some parts that were affected by the war, but the beautiful buildings and historic monuments were untouched.

We had quite a trip down from Normandy and I can't wait to hit the hay because I'm exhausted. The train—well we had a lot of fun and passed the days away by playing bridge, gin rummy, reading and eating all day and all night too. There weren't any sleeping accommodations so we slept in our chairs, two in a seat with all our luggage piled under and over and around us. The first night I tried sleeping in the aisle but I was blocking traffic, so I didn't bother any more. The second night I took a sedative and got a couple of hours sleep.

Before we left our cow pasture in Normandy I picked a lot of apples so we ate them along with our K-Rations. As I spent a lot of time on the train hanging out the window I made some good hauls from the G.I.'s we passed along the way and the French people. One day I got a big box of

10 in 1 rations which serves 10 people and had canned roast beef, canned butter and jam, and also got a big can of tuna fish and a loaf of bread, a handful of small onions and a big bouquet of flowers. The second day when we were out stretching our legs, I met a French soldier who gave me 3 quarts of cider, a loaf of bread 3 feet long, a big basket full of tomatoes, onions and carrots, and did we have a feed! We smelled like horses the whole time from those onions but they were wonderful.

Water facilities on the train just weren't and we couldn't wash at all or change clothes either, and were a filthy looking mess when we arrived. Never thought I'd be devouring onions and chunks of bread on my way to Paris but in the army, anything goes. One of the best surprises of all is that we're now temporarily billeted in an old French chateau with millions of rooms and have double decker beds and *real* straw mattresses. My gosh, when we saw these we practically cried for joy. There are real toilets here and I've never seen such ornate things in my life—beautiful flowers painted all over them—no doubt to inspire one.

I might have known all this was too good to be true, a mattress, a toilet and no more tent, 'cause tomorrow I go on detached service again with another hospital and just hope they don't live in tents.

OCT. 3. Can you picture me sitting in a lovely maple bed with springs and box mattress, between clean sheets and a reading lamp at my elbow and soft colored rugs on the floor. I'm on D.S. now and start work tomorrow in the operating room. This hospital was a French one previous to being taken over by the Germans and is the most gorgeous thing I've ever seen. The buildings are all modern design with every convenience imaginable and the gardens outside are like something out of this world. Just hope we stay long enough to really see Paris, especially since we got paid yesterday and I have 2 months salary to spend. The kids say you can spend it in 2 minutes flat cause the prices are high. Did you know there are subways and elevators in Paris, running out to the suburbs? I should really take a bath now—no hot water but they have bathtubs and real toilets that work.

As soon as I got here today I took all the clothes off my back and gave them to one of the French maids who clean the quarters, and she's going to press my uniform and wash my clothes. It seemed so good to hang clothes away in a cupboard and lay our underwear on shelves. We were just told the quarters we are occupying are the ones that the prostitutes for the Jerries occupied—no wonder they're so nice. Boy, they treat their women all right—guess I missed my vocation.

OCT. 13. LIÈGE, BELGIUM. It's about 8:30 p.m. and I just got off duty and am in bed now resting my dogs which are barking furiously. We leave here at 6 a.m. and get back any time from 8 p.m. on, and my feet get out of practice when I don't work continually. Yes, everyone at home was far too optimistic about the outcome and it won't be over for some time yet. And the fighting is really fierce too. God, sometimes I'm glad I'm a nurse and can be of some help and other times it's so sickening I'd give my bottom dollar to be in some other profession. Gee, we used to think we were busy when we were back in England but we didn't know a damned thing about anything then. The things you do seem to be humanly impossible sometimes but in the army there's no such word as impossible and you just go ahead and do things more or less automatically while some inner force keeps pushing you on. We're lucky, I suppose, to be on D.S. cause once we get our own place, we'll have more responsibility and will have to work even longer hours.

No matter how cold our quarters may be, it's still home to come home to at night and nothing looks or feels better than my little canvas cot. A couple of days ago I visited our hospital site which will be ready soon and we won't have to live in tents this winter, though the hospital, officers and E.M.'s will all be in tents. We're going to live in a huge 16th century chateau surrounded by a moat with a drawbridge and all. Some of the bedrooms are enormous high-ceiling affairs with fireplaces, and they'll probably stick about 10 girls in the rooms and then on each floor the rooms get smaller till you get right up to the garret where there's room for no more than 2 people in a room. It will be my luck to get stuck up there.

Well anyhow, they've promised us heat this winter as there's plenty of coal in Belgium and there are a couple of bath tubs. It will be better than tents I think, and we'll surely need a lot of heat cause these chateaux with their stone staircases and floors are like ice.

You've probably read in the newspapers how the French treated the collaborators, and here in Belgium the treatment is pretty much the same. It's a fairly common sight to see a lot of people dragging a man or woman through the streets after they've shaved off their hair and painted swastikas all over their face and head. Sometimes they strip them completely and make them go through the streets that way.

We got our liquor rations for the month yesterday—a quart of scotch and a pint of gin and though I'd like to drink about half the scotch I don't dare 'cause I can't sleep it off in the morning, and you never know when you'll be called out so you have to keep your wits about you. Hope to hear that some mail comes soon and some of those packages. We've eaten nothing but hash since we arrived and it sure gets monotonous, but after the noon meal we had today our hash tonight tasted good, cause there wasn't any food left and we had cold dehydrated potatoes and lukewarm tea—ugh! Who knows, maybe I'll lose weight yet—I sure can stand it.

NOV. 26. Never in my year overseas have I put in such a hectic life as I have the past few weeks and I'm afraid if the buzz bombs continue annoying us the way they have, I won't have to worry about any post war plans. We've been lucky so far, having had some narrow squeaks, but it can't last. It's the most awful feeling in the world when you hear the motor of the bomb stop almost above you and then wait a few seconds for the explosion. I'd rather have it all at once and get it over with, but then, Hitler never consulted me. Incidentally, keep this mum, won't you, as I wouldn't want my mother or Ruth to worry though frankly, I'm scared silly and for the first time in my life I've lost my appetite.

I'm on night duty in our tent hospital which is in a sea of mud, and with the continual rain for the past 2½ weeks, it will never dry out. The work has been hard and the hours long but I really feel satisfied now because we're doing the stuff we came overseas for, and they really need us. Our quarters are in the heart of a city, some miles from here, so we have to commute each night—leaving there at 5:00 p.m. and getting back at 10 the next morning—and we're supposed to sleep. Sleep, however, is out of the question when buildings all around us are being bombed and each time they get it, the force practically knocks us out of bed. Well, c'est la guerre but I wish to hell it was over.

Gee, I've been sitting down for 15 minutes now without having to get up and that's really something 'cause some nights I don't sit down at all. I have charge of two big shock tents where all the seriously wounded are kept, so as a rule I'm kept occupied all night—so well occupied, I can't stop to worry about buzz bombs when they go over. Besides, it wouldn't do to show the patients how scared I am either, 'cause they haven't any particular love for them, themselves.

APRIL 10, 1945. Am having a beautiful time for myself tonight—just stepped out of the fire bucket and am clean as a whistle, did all my washing and the radio is working like a charm. It has been a beautiful day today and just a little while ago everyone in our chateau had their noses stuck out the windows and all the officers ran out of their tents to see a most beautiful sight. For miles around, as far as the eye could see, our planes were on their way home, and there isn't a prettier sight than them in the sunset. From my window now, I can look right down into town and see the reflection of the sun setting on the Meuse and it all looks so peaceful, it's hard to realize that it hasn't always been this way.

Had a nice day yesterday—some of the girls were hitching to Cologne and Duren so I went as far as Aachen with them. We hitched a ride on a couple of gasoline trucks and as soon as I got to Aachen, I hitched an ambulance ride right to the outfit where I had my date. We spent a nice day together and then last night we drove back here and stayed at our club for a couple of hours. Am going to his dance there on Sat. night. We still don't know whether we're coming or going as far as the CBI is concerned, and every day the story is different, however, you can make up your mind it will be at least another year before I do get home.

The civilian maids who work here do all my ironing, washing and sewing—I don't do any except socks, bras, etc. and I've gotten so lazy I won't even sew a button on myself. Oh boy, just wait till we move again and don't have our maids and we sleep in the same clothes for weeks at a time, so I'll make the most of it now.

JULY 12, CHALONS-SUR-MARNE, FRANCE. The snapshot of me en route to the Riviera which you said looked like a bowl of flowers on my head, was practically that, without the bowl. Every time the train stopped the soldiers would rush out and pick a few flowers, and I stuck them in my hair till finally I had so many, it looked just like a hat and everyone got a big kick out of it, so one of the army photographers took a couple of pictures of me with it.

Our scare of the CBI a couple of weeks ago has quieted down and everyone reassures us continually that we won't have to go, but I'm still skeptical. Anyhow, we're making the most of life around here and leading sort of a peaceful existence. There are plenty of dates, 2-3 calls a night but there's nothing to do except go to our club and drink or go to their clubs and drink. Reims is very dead and there's nothing in Chalons, so the only thing to do on our day off is either spend 6 hours traveling to and from Paris or stay in bed all day. I hitched into Reims a couple of days ago on a coal truck, an oil truck and a jeep and had lunch there with one of my friends who's stationed there, did some window shopping and hitched back. It's gotten awfully hot again, but the stables I work in are cool so we're pretty comfortable. We're not working hard, in that we don't put in any overtime on duty but we're kept busy with all the soldiers from the redeployment camps and a lot of sick Krauts—must have at least 600 of them here. You'd die if you saw some of these specimen of the super duper race, haven't seen anything yet closely resembling a real man. The ages range from 14 years to 67 among my patients and except for the very youngest, most of them look at least 20 years older than they actually are.

AUGUST 5. Guess things at home must be as dull as they are here and this war seems to drag along for everyone. Haven't heard anything more about the CBI so for the present feel as though we'll be left here, and will remain as the outfit is scheduled to stay till next May. How we'll ever last that long, I don't know 'cause everyone hates this place so. As for these bronze stars, there's nothing too much attached to them except that we get 5 points for each one. Everyone in the outfit who was present the dates of the various campaigns got one, so it's no credit to me. We got one star for the Battle of Northern France, Battle of the Rhineland and the Battle of the Ardennes. We missed out on the Normandy stars by one week when there was still plenty of air combat going on, but what the hell!

We feel we really earned the Ardennes star but they skipped up by not giving us one for the buzz bombs. Hell we can't even get promoted, so without a 1st in the eyes of the world you're no good. It was over 2 months ago we had our interviews and if we stayed in Liège, they would have been through in a month, but now having moved, they'll probably never come through, and I'll get home as a 2nd Lt., my bars just a little more tarnished.

Later on—Just got back from a picnic with a gang of nurses and fellows and had a swell time, went surfboard riding though I usually toppled off. Some of the fellows brought a big barge down from Germany so we rode up and down the river on that. We fished but not the kind of fishing one usually does. They threw cans of TNT in the water and the explosion killed all the fish, and we'd just swim in and get them as they rose to the surface. Then we had a big bonfire and cooked the fish. Had fried chicken and dozens of bottles of iced champagne—very good time and repeat performance tomorrow night.

AUG. 12. Nothing at all to write about but am on duty and killing time, waiting for the doctor to start rounds. Well, from the looks of things, it's all over now—and so what! We'll probably still have to stay over here till next spring but we surely won't have to go to the CBI. Not much celebrating around here which is very unusual, but I think most people are too fed up by this time to bother.

I have a good chance of taking a 3 month secretarial course in Manchester, England but gosh, I'd hate like hell to be over there and have our outfit go home so don't think I'll bother signing for it. On the other hand, if I should want to take some courses when I get out of the army, I always can under the G.I. Bill of Rights. I'll probably start sending home a lot of clothes soon, though most of this G.I. underwear I'm going to give away.

SEPT. 14. Just got back from an exciting and fantastic one week leave in Switzerland with Johnny, one of the other nurses in our outfit. The Swiss Alps were awesome, Lake Geneva at Vevey, beautiful and fashionable and the small villages of Zermatt and Kandersteg were charming, all places I'd love to revisit as a civilian. It's a pristine country, seemingly untouched by war like the rest of battle-scarred Europe, and the people were friendly but very reserved. Johnny's fiancé, an RAF pilot who was stationed in Egypt flew unexpectedly to the Swiss Leave Center at Mulhouse on the French/Swiss border, determined to get married. There was such a flurry of activity and excitement as the American Red Cross workers scrounged for material to make a wedding gown and ended up making it from sugar sacks. I'll bet she was the only bride ever, whose wedding gown bore the inscription down the back that read: "Through the Courtesy of the Swiss Leave Center and the American Sugar Refining Co."

OCT. 30. MOURMALON, FRANCE. This is just another one of my notes 'cause there's still nothing to say except that things look blacker than ever, and it really looks as though we're stuck here for the rest of the winter. Everyone is so discouraged and nothing short of a miracle will get us home before Xmas. There are over 2,000 nurses in this particular area and no one is moving anywhere. The men in our outfit are at Marseille, expecting to sail any day, and we were supposed to follow them down. However, the latest is we'll be sailing from Le Havre whenever we do sail but all our heavy luggage is at Marseille, and as every item has to be declared before we sail, they'll have to send it back up and that should take a couple of months.

Nurses with 45 points have gone home while nurses with over 100 points are still here, so you can't go by this point system at all 'cause it's snafued up. They're giving out leaves and passes again which is a bad sign 'cause when an outfit is almost ready to go home, all leaves are cancelled. It's bad enough staying here but there's no mail for over a month, and it's going to be a pretty lousy Xmas here from the looks of things.

Well, I guess no matter how quiet a Xmas it will be, it will still be better than last Xmas so it's still something to be thankful for. I'm lucky too in that one of the fellows I used to know in Liège is down here at one of the camps and takes me out every day in his own jeep, and we go all over the countryside so it makes the time fly by more pleasantly. Everyone else here is going nuts cause most of their friends have gone home or don't have transportation to get here, and all they do is go to the movies or stay in bed and read. This isn't a very cheerful letter but no one feels very cheerful around here 'cause there's nothing to be cheerful about.

OCT. 31. To Cousin Pam. Yes, we're still here but on the last lap of the journey, I hope. Today we got alerted and are leaving tomorrow noon on a boat train from Le Havre and are scheduled to sail on the Vulcania, an old tourist boat on Nov. 3.

Honestly Pam, this has got to be it 'cause we just can't stand any more disappointments, but I really think this is it. Gosh, we're so excited now—for the first time, and I'm just too incoherent to write. Will write as soon as I get home so keep your fingers crossed for me. Give my love to everyone and remember, we haven't seen the last of each other yet. ❧

Dressed formal for a one-day pass in Paris; Muriel is on the extreme left, facing the camera.

PART THREE

POST-WAR

CHAPTER TWENTY

THE FUTURE IS NOW

THE TAXI PULLED UP in front of the brick house, which I had often despaired of ever seeing again. I quickly paid the fare and ran the length of the front walk to my mother's outstretched arms, while the taxi driver followed with my Valpak, which he planked down on the cement porch floor. Too late to warn him, we heard the crackle of broken glass, followed by the aroma of wine emanating from the bag. "Damn it!" I wailed, "Those are the three bottles of champagne I carried back from France to celebrate!" They survived the trip across the Atlantic and getting carted from pillar to post at Fort Dix, getting my army discharge, and now this had to happen on our front doorstep. Well, on examination, it wasn't a total loss—only two bottles were broken.

There I was, back in civilization again, and it was wonderful to be back home for good, in familiar surroundings, with family and friends hovering. Seven years had elapsed since I left my Meriden, Connecticut home for nurses training in a Cambridge, Massachusetts hospital and my commission in the Army Nurse Corps on graduation. The last two years of my army service had been spent overseas in England, France, and Belgium, with buzz bombs and strafings included. With an ocean separating me from my home, the two years seemed like ten.

After the initial excitement and euphoria of being home subsided, I was filled with a strange unrest, still half in the army and yet out of it. For so many years, in nurses training and in the army, my life was programmed for me into time allotted for work, eating, sleeping, and recreation, with no major decisions to make. It was a cocoon-like existence, where I was insulated from the outside world, just following the rules that were set out. I could only think and talk about my immediate environment, which the outside world didn't penetrate. And I loved every bit of it; it was the best—and the worst—time of my life.

Suddenly, there were no rules to follow, no schedules to adhere to; I was a free agent. Being a civilian wasn't what I thought it would be. Shopping for groceries was strange, getting accustomed to the food stamps and the plastic bags you had to knead to put color into the white margarine. Transportation was nil, for we had no car, and none were available at the auto dealerships for the next year, and then you had to be on a waiting list. Everyone seemed to know about the latest invention that I was just hearing about—television—and when I viewed it for the first time I felt like a female Rip van Winkle.

While overseas, we yearned for the time when we could wear colorful dresses and high heels, and now that the time was here, I felt like a stranger inhabiting my own body. I didn't look like "me" in a dress. Each time a troopship landed in New York or Boston, all I needed was a phone call, and I was off to meet returning classmates or army buddies—and always in my olive-drab uniform. The reunions were a time for reminiscing, usually in a hotel lounge or bar, and the more alcohol consumed, the more nostalgic the reunion became. I missed the camaraderie of the women who had been my roommates, hut mates, and tent mates for the past several years. I also missed the social life the army had provided, with a different date for every night in the week, if I so desired.

Back in Meriden, I had to get back "in circulation," which took months, as the servicemen were still returning and trying to adjust also. When I did date, the evening would be spent rehashing the war, which was a mental catharsis for me and for my dates. The veterans were the only ones who spoke my language. Most people would say "I know the war was rough for you, and you don't want to talk about it," so I didn't talk. The war was over; it was time to get on with our lives.

Getting on with my life wasn't so easy, as I realized when I ducked under a table at the sound of a champagne cork popping and then burst into tears. A sudden clap of thunder or door slamming created the same situation, always ending in tears, a luxury we weren't allowed at work overseas. Nurses weren't supposed to cry when caring for a young, permanently maimed body; we just exuded an aura of serenity and confidence to mask our feelings of horror. Our emotions had been bottled up for the duration. The only tears I openly shed were the same ones the thousands of returning troops shed on the morning our ship slowly glided past that beautiful Statue of Liberty.

I had hoped that travel would dissipate my feelings of unrest, insecurity, and being a stranger in a once-familiar land, but it didn't help, because I always had to go home again. Going home meant facing a dwindling bank account and making plans for the future, which meant going back to work. Though nursing was the profession that I had gloried in and found so fulfilling and gratifying while in the army, at this point in time I wanted no part of civilian nursing. The American GI was the best, most uncomplaining patient in the world, one who would suffer in silence rather than "bother" the nurse by asking for medication if he thought we were too busy. And he was grateful for the slightest attention given him, happy to be alive, between clean white sheets for the first time in months, and most of all, cared for by American women, the first he had seen since leaving the States. The gratitude of our servicemen, their acceptance of pain, and their concern for the guy in the next bed wasn't too readily found in civilian hospitals, at least, not before my army experience.

What was I to do now? How much longer should I accept my mother's largesse? She went to work every day; it was time I followed suit. To further add to my feelings of inadequacy, the town *yentas* didn't hesitate to inquire why, with all the men available, I hadn't brought home a doctor husband—or any husband, for that matter. Up until this point, marriage was the farthest thing from my mind, but suddenly, they planted a seed. While in the army, it was fun dating them all and feeling that marriage was for when I *was* old enough or for when Mr. Right would come along. Now, at twenty-five, maybe I was old enough; and maybe I was going to linger on the vine because there weren't any eligible candidates around. There was no chemistry whatsoever with the men I was seeing, and the specter of being what was called an "old maid" in those days mingled unpleasantly with my muddled concerns about getting back to work.

I came of age as I realized, *the future is now.* 🐾

CHAPTER TWENTY-ONE

THE NAME IS THE GAME

MONEY WAS BURNING a hole in my pocket. What does one do with separation pay after serving three years in the Army Nurse Corps in World War II? You spend it on luxury items you would never have considered purchasing before the war. Yes, I spent it all.

Purchase No. 1 was a Persian Lamb coat, known in the those days as a "Jewish raincoat." Persian Lamb wasn't in the same category as mink, but it was on a par with sheared beaver and much more durable. It was a very respectable fur that could take rain and snow well, it lasted forever, and it was popular with the Jewish women in New York.

Purchase No. 2, which emptied the till, was a fourteen-day cruise to Miami, Nassau, and Havana. Finances did not allow for a private stateroom, but after my years in nursing school and the army, the meaning of privacy was unknown to me. Sharing a stateroom now with another female was just an extension of my former life.

Upon boarding the cruise ship in New York Harbor, I made my way through the celebrating throngs to my assigned room. My roommate for the next two weeks was on her knees, unpacking her luggage. She was a pixie-like creature with a thatch of short jet-black hair and bangs that reached to her eyebrows. (To this day she swears she never had bangs, but I remember what I saw.) Fully extended, she barely reached my shoulders.

I was totally unprepared for her thick southern drawl that oozed like molasses. "Hah, ahm Betty Benson, and ahm from Lexington, Kintuckeh." Gesturing toward a cluttered corner of the sardine-can-sized stateroom, she informed me, "Ah hope mah easel and paints won't git in youah way. Ahm a painter."

I assured her there was no problem, being accustomed to years of sharing living space, and introduced myself. "I'm Muriel Phillips from Meriden, Connecticut, newly discharged from the Army Nurse Corps."

Betty's wide-set black eyes danced joyfully as she threw her arms around my waist, exclaiming, "Oh, ahm so glad for three things! Ahm so glad youah young, youah not a *nigra*, and youah not a *Jew!*"

I was stunned. Over the years I had experienced a few mild anti-Semitic remarks from people unaware I was Jewish, because my surname, Phillips, "didn't sound Jewish." Thoughts raced through my head. *Should I tell her I'm Jewish and then have to live with someone who dislikes Jews for the next two weeks? Should I ask for a new stateroom? No, they said the ship was filled. Should I keep quiet and ignore the remark so we can live in peace?* I made a quick decision in favor of keeping the peace, though I had guilt feelings about not acknowledging my religious faith.

We soon settled into a very pleasant shipboard camaraderie. It was good to have a companion for the shipboard activities, especially at mealtimes. During the day, Betty would set up her easel on deck to paint or sketch, and she proved herself to be a very accomplished artist. Admiring crowds surrounded her, and I enjoyed her notoriety as an artist. At night after dinner, we would go to the ballroom and wait to be asked to dance by the men, who were outnumbered ten to one by the women.

On our first night at sea, I was asked to dance by one of three New York plumbers who were traveling together. They had left their wives and children at home in search of sun and relaxation, and dancing was part of their relaxation regime. I couldn't understand how their wives tolerated staying at home with the kids while Daddy-O frolicked at sea. The Three Plumbers, however, did seem devoted to their families and were quick to display their photographs and to purchase gift items for them in the ship's store. They were wonderful dancers, and I was happy that I didn't have to join the wallflowers lining the walls of the ballroom, wistfully eyeing the women fortunate enough to have a dancing partner.

On the third day at sea, we rounded Cape Hatteras, an area notorious for rough seas, and I was miserably seasick. Early in the morning, I ventured up on deck, hoping the sea breezes would help the nausea and dizziness, but I learned the hard way that one does not vomit into the wind.

The next twenty-four hours were spent in my bunk, alternately heaving or sleeping, while Betty hovered about like a mother hen. At some point during the day, the Three Plumbers appeared at our stateroom to inquire about my absence the previous night. I was aware of Betty standing at the door, saying, "Murrill is doing just fahn, thank you foh coming." Betty never pronounced my name right; it was always "Murrill, not "Mur-i-el."

Shaky but alive the next day, I went up on deck and was greeted enthusiastically by the Three Plumbers. Their demeanor turned serious, though, when all three asked, "You know what your roommate is? She's a lesbian."

A lesbian! I had heard that word but had never seen one. (Being able to identify a lesbian was not part of our nursing school curriculum.) "Oh, my God, what do I do?"

"Just don't let her get too friendly" was their reply.

Now I know why she climbed up to my bunk each night to plant a good-night kiss on my mouth. I didn't like it but thought she was just an affectionate person. Ten more days of the trip suddenly loomed like a big black cloud. What should I do to ward off any more affectionate overtures? Ha! I had the solution.

Despite my weakened condition, I literally flew back to the stateroom, where Betty was packing her art supplies for a painting session on deck. I faced her and took a breath. "Betty, you know what? I'm a Jew." I thought that would keep me safe from any advances.

Bewilderment clouded Betty's face. "But youah so nice, and you don't have horns."

"Of course I don't have horns," I retorted. "Since when do Jews have horns?"

Tears were now running down Betty's face, and she seemed truly distressed. "Oh, Murrill, youah the first Jew ah ever met, and in Kintuckeh we always heard that Jews had horns."

I accepted Betty's profuse apologies, but to ensure my safety, I was deliberately very cool to her for the next few days. Fifty years ago, the terms "lesbian" and "homosexual" were usually whispered, and our distorted ideas of them were just as outrageous as the idea of Jews having horns.

Betty's penitence and sadness at my rejection of her friendship wore me down, and by the end of the voyage, we had resumed our earlier camaraderie. Upon departing the ship, we exchanged addresses, never realizing our paths would cross again as quickly as they did.

Because the employment field in my hometown was extremely narrow, I went to New York, where I found work immediately in the office of an eminent orthopedist. Betty's art studio was in New York, and we would meet frequently for lunch or dinner. She was always interested in hearing about my current boyfriends, and they enjoyed her company and visiting her studio with me.

To this day, we keep in touch. She is still painting prodigiously at the age of eighty-seven, and her portraits and landscapes command large sums. For the past two years she was involved in caring for her companion of fifty years, who withered away with Alzheimer's disease. Betty simply said, "She would do the same for me."

I have always been grateful that I didn't terminate our friendship, so many years ago. ❧

CHAPTER TWENTY-TWO

PREJUDICE AND PRIDE

I REALIZED IN MY FIRST FIVE MINUTES on duty that I should have adhered to my vow, made months before while still in the army, to never do civilian bedside nursing. After caring for the great American soldier, no other type of patient could fill the bill. I recalled my superintendent of nurses, who constantly harped on money being "dirty, filthy lucre" and that we "should never let money influence our nursing decisions." Unfortunately, my almost-defunct bank account was sadly in need of an infusion of this "dirty, filthy lucre," and the quickest way to replenish the coffers was to take some private-duty cases for a few weeks.

The Wednesday before Easter, I was called by the agency to report for day duty at the home of a ninety-year-old woman who was recuperating from pneumonia. At that age, I thought, most people expire from pneumonia, so this woman must have the constitution of an ox. She wasn't confined to bed at this point, but because of her advanced years, the family physician wanted her vital signs checked daily and reported to him. Having no means of transportation, I hiked the three miles across town, all uphill, to the imposing three-story residence of Mrs. Serena Townsend and her two maiden-lady companions, distant cousins of the long deceased Mr. Townsend. I was greeted at the door by one of the cousins, Miss Jane, whose first words were, "My goodness, we haven't had a young one like you in this house for at least five years." That should have warned me. I was then ushered through this dark mausoleum of a home, with shades drawn to prevent the furniture from fading, into the kitchen, where Miss Jane motioned for me to hang my coat on the wall cloak rack.

"Have a seat," she said, "and we'll talk while Mrs. Townsend is sleeping. As soon as she wakes, she'll ring her bell, and you can meet her then."

For the next half hour, I was regaled with the history of Mrs. Townsend, whose forebears came over on the *Mayflower*; her great-great-grandfather Isaac Curtis had been one of the founders of this town; her great-grandfather had built this home, and numerous streets and buildings in town were named after her father and grandfather. My fleeting thought at this recital was that it was a shame Mrs. Townsend couldn't have married a man named Curtis to perpetuate the glory of the name. Of course, Mr. Townsend had been president of a bank, not to diminish his importance. And Mrs. Townsend and her mother had both been presidents of the DAR, so, as Miss Jane pointed out, this was a very illustrious family.

Miss Martha entered the room just then, and as we were introduced, the ringing of a bell cut short all talk, and the three of us headed for what I learned later was the back staircase (or servant's staircase), which opened into the kitchen. Mrs. Townsend's bedroom was a large corner room on the second floor, well lighted by two large windows, unlike the gloom of the rest of the house, and a doorway led from her room to an adjacent bathroom. Even though she was sitting in bed, I could tell she was tall. She also was gaunt, with an austere expression on her craggy face. Her hawk-like nose was her prominent feature, and it overshadowed her thin, bloodless lips. Sparse strands of white hair hung from her pink scalp, and with her blue-veined hands that resembled claws, she looked more like a witch than a human being.

"Serena, this is your nurse, Miss Phillips," crooned Miss Jane, "and she is here to take good care of you."

"I don't need a nurse," growled Mrs. Townsend, "and the only reason that doctor wants me to have one is so he can keep me alive and send me bills so he can live in style." She certainly didn't seem to be *that* sick, and I regretted again taking on a private-duty case, because this woman was the direct antithesis of my wonderful, grateful GI patients. "I'll tell you right now what the rules are, Miss Phillips," she told me, "and you keep them in mind. You are to use the back staircase at all times, as the help is not allowed to use the central stairway. You are not to waste electricity, and make sure you put lights out when you aren't in the room. And make sure you don't waste water—people of your generation are wastrels. And Miss Jane will cook my meals as she always has, though you may as well earn your keep and carry the tray upstairs for her."

Thus began my first day working for the town blueblood. She was able to sit up in the straight-back upholstered chair between the windows, where she would look out at the lines of traffic and bemoan the fact that automobiles made so much noise; it was a disgrace they were ever invented. When this house was built, it was in a beautiful, fashionable neighborhood, which the advent of automobiles had changed, and now this commercial highway outside her window was despicable. I didn't dare disagree with anything Mrs. Townsend said. For the most part, I just nodded my head as if in agreement.

At lunchtime, Miss Jane announced I was to come down to the kitchen and have lunch with her and the handyman, Edward, who had been the family retainer for about fifty years and did the driving and odd jobs around the house. Miss Martha would be on call upstairs while we ate. I was asked how I wanted my eggs cooked, and when I replied that I liked them scrambled, Miss Jane replied, "Well, that's good because that's just what I'm having." She then evenly divided the one scrambled egg she had made in the frying pan, putting half on her plate and half on mine, along with a piece of toast. Edward did "hard, physical labor," according to Miss Jane, so he merited a whole cheese sandwich for his lunch. *Frugality is fine, but let's not overdo it,* I thought. And I knew that I'd be bringing my own sandwich the following day.

After lunch I walked with Mrs. Townsend around her room and the upstairs hallway, a pace behind her, as I was warned, "I'm perfectly capable of walking on my own, so keep your hands off me." Each time I went into the bathroom to get wash water for her, I was again reminded, "You're wasting water, shut it off *now*." I asked if I could read to her, but she glared at me and replied she wasn't blind yet and was capable of doing her own reading. If I left her room for a few minutes so she wouldn't feel as if she were under constant surveillance, she yelled after me, "Nurse! You're not getting paid to waste time!" She did allow me to give her a back rub when she moved back to her bed after a couple of hours of being up and around in her room, and it was the only time she had no complaint. Actually, I took it as a compliment when she sniffed, "Well, I'm glad to see they taught you something worthwhile in your nursing school."

In four days, that was the first personal remark she had made to me, for up until then, I had been just an unwanted nonentity. I couldn't wait for this case to be finished but felt I was committed to stick it out until her physician canceled the order for an RN. Just before I went off duty on Saturday afternoon, Miss Martha asked if I would be coming in to work the next day, Easter Sunday. I replied that I most certainly would be there, as it was not *my* holiday, and it would be work as usual for me.

On Sunday morning, as I deposited Mrs. Townsend's breakfast tray on her bedside table, both Miss Jane and Miss Martha appeared at the door, dressed festively in coats, hats, and gloves. "Well, Serena, we're off to church now for the Easter service, so we'll see you later," said Miss Martha as she and Miss Jane turned to leave.

A bombshell was dropped when Mrs. Townsend shrieked, "You're not going to leave me alone with this Christ killer on Easter Sunday, are you?" The cousins gasped, and stood speechless, as if rooted to the spot, and for the first few seconds, I was speechless, too. Visions of my superintendent of nurses intoning "Nurses do not leave their post" swam before my eyes— but not for more than five seconds, when my pride spoke up for me.

"No, they aren't leaving you alone, because this 'Christ killer' is going home, and they are stuck with you." I picked up my coat and purse, said good-bye to the still-speechless ladies, walked down the central stairway for the first and last time, and out the front door.

I didn't mind losing out on four days' salary; it was worth it to be out of that atmosphere, and as I began my three-mile trek home, it was all downhill, and I was free and exultant. ❧

CHAPTER TWENTY-THREE

SMALL WORLD

IF EVER HE WERE DIVESTED of his macho trappings of sartorial splendor—namely, the tailor-made uniform of a U.S. Army Air Force major—Bill probably would have resembled a clump of cooked, long, white spaghetti standing on end. He was tall, skinny and so light skinned, I would later tease him about his bar-room pallor, which contrasted greatly with his twinkling deep-set brown eyes and thick mane of wavy dark brown hair.

It was the winter of 1944-45, and Bill's air force outfit, stationed in Liège, Belgium, had requested "the pleasure of the company of a truckload of off-duty nurses" to attend a dance at their Officers' Club. The Battle of the Bulge was almost over, with the Nazis being pushed back into Germany, and everyone was in a celebratory mood. As I sat at the table of nurses, waiting to be asked to dance, I noticed Bill standing at the bar, assuming a debonair pose. He leaned on one elbow and brought a drink to his lips with his free hand, while he gazed out over the sea of nurses' expectant faces. When he headed toward our table, I averted my eyes, not wanting to seem too eager. I did notice, though, that his mere act of walking exhibited such fluidity of motion, he seemed to have elastic joints and ball bearings in his feet. I suppose this accounted for his being such a superb dancer.

We whirled and dipped and swirled to the music and kicked up our heels as we jitterbugged. As he led me through intricate dance steps, I felt as light as thistle down floating on gentle air currents, and I didn't want the music to end. As I later reported to my roommate, Evelyn, "He's the best dancer ever!"

Not only was he an excellent dancer, but he also was an accomplished drinker, as I found out over the next several months, so much so, that I realized it was a good thing that he was in administration and not one of the "fly boys," as we nurses called our favorite P-38 pilots. Bill was a real party animal and always found the best officers' mess or bistro that served a black-market steak and had a jukebox for dancing. After my third or fourth date with Bill, I reported to Evelyn that besides being such a wonderful dancer, Bill was also a gentleman and that he respected me.

Evelyn seemed incredulous. "You mean you haven't necked with him yet?"

"No," I responded. "He pecks my cheek as he leaves me at the door, and it's a real relief to find someone who is such fun and not a wolf."

"Give him time," snorted Evelyn, a disillusioned divorcée.

So we drank, dined, and danced in Belgium until the war in Europe was over, and our hospital outfit moved back to a sleepy little town in France, about fifty-five miles from Reims, the champagne capital. Within two weeks of our arrival in France, Bill's air force group moved to Reims. It was natural, then, that on my overnights twice a month at the R&R chateau for female officers, Bill and I would resume our pattern of drinking, dining, and dancing. But we also enjoyed exploring the historical sites of interest in that city, and there were plenty, like the magnificent Reims Cathedral or the champagne cellars, where we imbibed generous samples of their famous product. As the weeks and months passed, I still received my peck on the cheek at the door, for which I was grateful, as I had absolutely no romantic interest in Bill whatsoever. I tried conjuring up some feeling like love for him, but I was emotionally blank in that respect. So I was surprised—but glad—that he didn't demand more of our relationship. I was interested in a carefree, fun existence, and I had it.

A year and a half later, with the war over in Europe and Japan, I was working as a civilian nurse in an orthopedic office in Manhattan and sharing a two-room Westside hotel apartment with my girlfriend, Fran. We were leading the kind of existence every single young woman dreamed of in that era: an interesting job; going to movies, theater, museums, nightclubs, restaurants; and plenty of men, back from the service, for dating. Into this scene none other than Bill showed up, a minor executive for a national hospital fund. His office was about ten blocks from mine, and he had an Upper Eastside apartment, naturally, as Eastside apartments were more fashionable than Westside apartments, and Bill was very status oriented.

He gloried in being recognized by the head waiters in the restaurants and nightclubs we frequented. He was impeccably dressed in his tailor-made suits, which probably cost him a month's salary or more, and he enjoyed seeing me well dressed.

We picked up our relationship where we'd left off in Belgium and France, drinking, dining, and dancing, and we explored Manhattan to its fullest. We didn't venture out of the city, as Bill had no car, but in the city, there was no need for a car. On two different occasions, by train and bus, we ventured to the Pocono Mountains, where his elderly parents owned and operated a small country club and nine-hole golf course. This had been closed during the war years, and Bill was helping his father in the reopening operations. I had never seen that part of the country and was happy to accede when Bill forwarded his parents' invitation for me to come, not realizing what lay behind the invitation.

I was warmly welcomed by Bill's parents—almost too warmly, for on the second visit I realized they had more romantic ideas about our relationship than Bill or I had. When his mother showed me the fund-raising tablecloth she was working on for her synagogue, where names of their children, spouses, and grandchildren were embroidered, I panicked when I saw my name entwined with Bill's. Apparently, his letters home from overseas, telling them about the Jewish nurse he had dated, and then his seeing me again in New York had made it a fait accompli as far as they were concerned. They wanted nothing more than to see Bill married. I felt like an utter impostor, and en route to New York, I informed Bill that he had better start breaking the news gently to his parents that there was no marriage on the horizon. I had other ideas—Mel had come back into my life after a fifteen-year hiatus.

When we were ten-year-olds in Connecticut, he and his mother often came to visit a relative who lived next door to us, Cousin Ann. Mel would be sent to our home to stave off boredom while the adults visited. I had not heard of or thought of him in years, until I met Ann on one of my frequent visits home. She informed me that Mel, a dentist now, had just been discharged from the navy and was living in New York with his parents. She urged me to call him, as she knew he would want to see me. That one phone call to Mel decided my fate for the rest of my life.

He had grown to be a tall, good-looking adult, with his blue eyes and full lips. He had slightly protruding front teeth, brown wavy hair, and a well-built physique that didn't require the need for the custom-made suits Bill wore to camouflage his skinny torso. I sensed an immediate rapport with Mel, and he was intrigued by my army experiences and questioned me by the hour about my life as an army nurse. We discussed military tactics, various battles, and the generals who had commanded those armies. I was "different" from the type of women he had been dating, and in no time, we had a serious romance brewing, especially after his first kiss, which was no mere peck on the cheek.

Mel and I often met on the same cross-town bus as he went to his dental office on First Avenue, and I went to my orthopedic office on Fifth Avenue, across from Central Park. He would meet me in the park at a designated bench at lunchtime, toting a half gallon of ice cream and two spoons for our lunch, and we ate it all. Besides the war, we also discussed politics, current events, music, and books, and I was always relieved to note that our views ran pretty much in the same vein. He even got me involved in joining his Jewish War Veterans post, where he edited the monthly newspaper and was responsible for a front-page photograph and article about my army nurse experiences.

As with Bill, Mel and I drank, danced, dined, and explored local points of interest, and as he did have frequent access to a car, we weren't confined to Manhattan alone. I will say the dancing wasn't the same as it had been with Bill. I did not feel as light as thistle down when dancing with Mel, and he complained that dancing with me was like driving a truck, but we both knew our relationship had more important issues to it than dancing.

Bill realized that I was seeing a lot of one certain person when I declined his invitations for dinner or theater, and he named this unknown creature "Gargantua." It became common for Bill to remark, "I suppose you're going out with Gargantua tonight." When I informed Mel of Bill's name for him, Mel immediately dubbed Bill "Dracula," and on the occasions when I had to turn down Mel's invitations because of a previous commitment to Bill, Mel would reply, "You're probably going out with Dracula." So between Gargantua and Dracula and a few others in between, those two years in Manhattan were a great time in my life—and it culminated in my marriage to Gargantua in August of 1949. Dracula took the news philosophically, as he had seen it coming, and he wished me well and promised to keep in touch, which we did by mail, though infrequently, for several years.

Upon our marriage, Mel and I moved to Wappingers Falls, about sixty-five miles north of Manhattan, where he had established a dental practice three months earlier. A few months later, Mel came home from the office with regards for me from Bill, passed on by an Italian patient, Nick, who owned and operated a local hotel. Nick was also a magician who appeared in New York nightclubs. According to Mel, the conversation went as follows:

"Hey, Doc, I meeta da friend of your wifa, Bill, who coma to da magic show at nightclub in New York, and wenna I say I liva Wappingers Falls, he coma to me after da show to say his old girlfriend liva Wappingers Falls. I tella him you my dentista, and he say for me to say hello."

The world was surely getting smaller, with Bill's presence in Belgium, France, Manhattan, and now, surfacing by word of mouth, in Wappingers Falls!

Several weeks later, Mel re-enacted another of Nick's office conversations, which was the following:

"Hey, Doc, very good ting your wifa marry you and not Bill, very good ting. Bill and his friend, bigga, strong, good-looking guy, coma my magic show tree, four time, and one night after da show, he tella me coma his apartment for drink, so I go wid him and friend, Don. Nice-a apartment dey got, bigga living room, bigga bedroom, and bigga double bed dey sleep in. Very good ting your wifa marry wid you, Doc."

Yeah, I was glad, too, that I'd married Doc. This explained the nightly peck on the cheek, showing me off at air force dances, the visit to the Poconos to meet the parents, etc. I was the convenient vehicle for him to maintain respectability and acceptance in a world not yet willing or ready to accept him for the man that he was. Neither of us suffered, though, for we both enjoyed the relationship while it lasted. I did see Bill about twenty years later, when my college daughter, Suzy, accompanied me to Manhattan for cocktails with Bill, who hadn't changed at all—still the accomplished drinker, debonair, well-dressed, and charming. Suzy enjoyed meeting this man from her mother's past, but she remarked later that she, too, was glad I'd married Doc. ❧

CHAPTER TWENTY-FOUR

DISDAINED, REJECTED, ACCEPTED

I RANG THE DOORBELL of their eighth-floor apartment in happy antic-ipation of spending a day with Mel, exploring Long Island. His mother and stepfather had requested that Mel drive them out to Long Island, so they could visit with Mel's married stepsister and her family, and Mel had asked me to accompany him. After dropping them off, we'd have the car to ourselves for the entire day, until it was time to pick up his folks again and return them to their Manhattan apartment. There was still a shortage of cars for sale in this immediate post-war period, and it was a treat for Mel to have one at his disposal so that he could take me to visit some of his favorite haunts.

The front door was flung open by Mel's mother, jolting me out of my brief reverie. Gone was her usual broad, welcoming smile, which had greeted me on previous visits. Instead, her facial expression was cold, grim, and forbidding. No "Hello, Muriel"; just "Come in," ordered in a dead voice. Then, "I'll tell Mel you're here." She ushered me into the large, softly lit foyer, furnished with comfortable upholstered chairs that flanked two mahogany tables on either side of the room. She didn't invite me to have a seat or even say "Sit," so I stood, wondering what in the world could have happened to precipitate this icy attitude.

A couple of minutes later, Mel, looking troubled, appeared in the doorway that led to the bedroom wing of the eight-room apartment. Oth-er doorways led off the foyer to the dining room, living room, and kitchen. "Why are you standing?" Mel asked. "You'd better have a seat, as this might take a few more minutes." He turned and headed back to the bedroom wing, and I knew from the sound of his footsteps that he was headed for the master bedroom, the farthest room off the foyer. Then I heard the agitated voice of his mother, followed by the cool, calm voice of his step-father and a few sharp words from Mel, but I couldn't distinguish any actual words.

There was no reading material in the foyer to distract me, nothing like the dog-eared magazines one would find in a physician's waiting room. I had no alternative but to sit and listen to the rise and fall of the voices emanating from the master bedroom. Suddenly, Mel's mother crossed the foyer and flounced through the doorway leading to the kitchen. With flared nostrils and tight, flattened lips, she gave me a disdainful glance, as if to say, "Something smells in here, and it's you." Following in her footsteps was her husband, trying to reason with her, and Mel bringing up in the rear, his face a veritable thundercloud.

For a few minutes, angry voices continued from the kitchen area, and then the parade of Mel's mother, stepfather, and Mel retraced their steps, from the kitchen doorway back through the foyer and into the bedroom wing. Another dirty, disdainful glance was directed at me in passing by Mel's mother. Now the pitch of the voices rose higher and then, most distinctly, I heard her utter the words: "I will not ride in the car with *that woman!*"

What in the world was going on? Who was she referring to, and why was everyone so upset? I didn't have long to wait for the answer. Mel rushed into the foyer, with flushed face, obviously angry, and motioned to me. "Get up. Let's go. *Now!*"

"But what about your parents?" I asked as he ushered me out the front door. "Aren't we going to drive them out to Long Island?" Mel rang for the elevator; it appeared almost instantly and reached the ground floor before Mel answered my question.

He ground out his response between clenched teeth. "No, we are not driving them out to Long Island, not today or any other day."

"Why?" I persisted. "You were so looking forward to having the car for the day. And what was your mother so mad about? She acted as if she was mad at me."

"She didn't want to drive in the car with you," Mel admitted, "so I told her I wouldn't drive them anywhere."

I was almost in a state of shock—to think that I was the one she referred to when she uttered those words that seared into my brain: "I will not ride in the car with that woman."

"Why has she changed her mind about me?" I queried, tears streaking down my face. "When I first came to New York, she was always so happy to see me and urged me to come for meals, and she even called me at my apartment. What did I do to have her hate me so?"

Mel put his arm through mine as we walked in the direction of the subway, He struggled to find the words. "Well, you see, when you first came to New York, I was dating Laura, the divorcee with the little girl. You remember my introducing you to her?" Of course I remembered, as I did the others he introduced me to at the Sunday afternoon tea dances at Leon and Eddie's. "My mother was sure that I was serious about Laura," Mel continued, "and was trying to break it up, so when you arrived on the scene, she was happy as a lark to see you, because you were diverting my attention from Laura. You could do no wrong in her eyes—until she suddenly realized I was seeing only you. She has been after me to date the daughters of her mah-jongg and bridge friends from 'Long-guy-land,' who don't interest me in the least. You are the villain in her eyes now, not Laura."

Passersby looked at me in sympathy, as I was sobbing openly while we walked, and Mel tightened his arm protectively around me. I could still feel his mother's disdainful glances cutting through me, and this sense of rejection was something I had never felt before. "Don't worry about her," Mel soothed. "She won't stop me from seeing you, and in time, I'm sure she'll change her mind."

He was right. She did change her mind, after she realized that Mel and I were getting married, with or without her approval. Once it became a fait accompli, I was her daughter, not a mere daughter-in-law. Many years later, when we visited her in the nursing home, I was always greeted with "Here's my Muriel," and her broadest smiles were for me. ❧

CHAPTER TWENTY-FIVE

LIVING PROOF

OUR LANDLADY, Mrs. Spinelli, was not God's gift to humanity, for she was as ugly to behold as was her disposition—vile, vituperative, and vindictive. Her wide, dark-complexioned but ruddy face bore a perpetual scowl, and during fits of anger, which were frequent, her Mediterranean coloring became beet red. A peasant-type babushka covered most of her black hair, which was streaked with gray. The babushka tied under her chin and rested on layers of wattle that obscured what was meant to be a neck. Full bosomed, full bellied, and full hipped best described Mrs. Spinelli's short torso. It was always garbed in a dark print cotton housedress, covered by a smock, over which was worn a many-pocketed apron that concealed unknown objects.

If she had shoes, I never saw them, for bed slippers covered her feet as she waddled, several times a day, across the two driveways that separated our homes, usually starting in mid-morning. A summer kitchen was maintained in the basement of our house in which she did all her cooking, canning, and laundry. We knew she had a kitchen in her own white stucco house that was newer than the one she rented out to us, because we could see a gleaming linoleum floor when the back door to her home was opened. There were usually a few pairs of shoes lined up on the back porch—no one entered that house wearing shoes.

Our rental was a large four-room apartment on the first floor, and the O'Learys lived on the second floor. They warned us when we moved in, fresh from our honeymoon, to stay clear of Mrs. Spinelli and her fiery temper, as did the young couples who rented the three studio bungalows in back of our house. One of the couples was Mrs. Spinelli's youngest son, Jackie, and his bride, Ginny, who despised her mother-in-law, who had a penchant for barging in on them, day or night. Once they had the temerity to change the lock on their front door—for which she was given no key—open warfare existed between them. Mrs. Spinelli stood on her back porch, screaming epithets at them and shaking her fists whenever she saw them entering their car or bungalow; her face was always mottled with rage.

Our charming landlady's oldest son, Joe, who was about our age, lived with his parents; he operated an electrical appliance store in the front lower level of their home. Joe befriended us and occasionally dropped off a few fresh vegetables from the enormous vegetable garden in the rear of the property, which was his father's domain. Mr. Spinelli, a passive, bent figure in work clothes, smiled warmly at us in passing but never stopped to talk, as he spoke little English. He seemed burdened by the frequent verbal explosions emanating from his wife, which we heard all too clearly across the two driveways, and when she wasn't screaming at him, she was cursing her son Joe.

We were happy to limit our dealings with her to delivering the monthly rental check. And if we encountered her in the yard or basement, we'd get a nod of her head in response to our "hello," so we were grateful for our peaceful coexistence. The peace was shattered, though, when Joe presented us with an eight-week-old black-and-white Springer Spaniel puppy, which we took to our hearts immediately. We named him Pitz, a refined way of referring to his habit of piddling on the floors until he was housebroken, which seemed like forever. Pitz became a revered family member, accompanying us wherever we went. I loved walking into the village with Pitz on his leash, showing him off to strangers, who exclaimed over this cute, cuddly puppy. I felt very much like the proud mother of a newborn baby.

With spring weather upon us, I took Pitz outdoors to let him frolic on the lawn behind the house, where he explored every tree and bush, racing excitedly in and out among the shrubs. Frequently, the O'Learys descended their back staircase so they could pet him and sit with me on the back steps, enjoying his crazy antics. It was after one of these backyard sessions when Mrs. Spinelli, suddenly aware that we had a dog, made the laborious climb up the hill and five steps to our front door. She pushed the bell in for three long rings. I opened the door to find her standing there, panting, with bosom heaving, although I couldn't tell whether it was from the energy exerted in climbing or from anger. It was obvious, however, that she was *mad*.

"I see you gotta dog," she wheezed.

"Yes," I replied, "and he's completely housebroken."

"I don't care if he is or he ain't," she countered. "He gotta go."

"But there's nothing in our lease that says we can't have a dog," I pleaded, "and besides, your own son Joe gave him to us."

She thrust her face, now mottled red and purple with anger, up to mine, and as I stepped back slightly, she promised ominously, "I'll take care of him for that." As she turned to go, she snarled a parting, belligerent threat: "You get rid of that dog, or I'll do it for you."

Mel and I had no intention of "getting rid" of Pitz; we loved this frisky, lovable puppy that got his kicks from springing into our laps and bestowing satiny-smooth kisses on our hands and faces. For the first couple of weeks after the warning, we did not take him outdoors, and when we took Pitz on outings in the car, we made sure she wasn't cooking or laundering in the basement to avoid any encounter with her.

As time passed, we relaxed our vigil somewhat, as we'd had no more visits or threats from Mrs. Spinelli. I began letting Pitz out on the front lawn to play, tethered to a long leash, so I could pull him back if he should venture past the corner of the house and into her line of vision. This plan for Pitz getting his exercise seemed to work well for a week or more, until he kept us up most of one night with vomiting and diarrhea. I was in the veterinary office first thing in the morning, carrying my limp, barely conscious little puppy. George, the vet, who had become our friend in the four months since we became parents of a dog, advised me with a grave countenance to leave Pitz for treatment. I told him of Mrs. Spinelli's threat to "get rid" of Pitz, and George just nodded his head and said, "It's very possible he might have gotten into something poisonous."

That night, George called with the heartbreaking news that Pitz had died. We felt sure Mrs. Spinelli had something to do with his death, but we had no proof, so could not make any accusations. We mourned the loss of our little puppy, and each time I set eyes on his doggy bed or food and water dishes, a new wave of tears ran down my face, so we put his furnishings away until such time when we would be able to use them again for another Pitz.

This happened sooner rather than later, for two weeks after the death of Pitz, George called to say someone had dropped off a three-month-old black-and-white Springer Spaniel who closely resembled our Pitz. Were we interested? We rushed to his office and came home shortly after, carrying Pitz II. He looked and acted so much like his predecessor that we fell in love with him immediately and decided to continue with the same name.

We decided at this point to start looking for a home of our own, so we could escape this hostile atmosphere. There weren't too many homes that we liked that were available for purchase, so we decided to buy land and build our own home. I scoured the local countryside and soon found seven beautiful country acres, just a five-minute drive from Mel's office. My uncle Mike, an architect, drew up plans for the home we wanted. Soon after, we signed a contract with a local builder, who promised to have the house completed in three months, and he was true to his word. I was pregnant by now with our first child, so we needed the extra room our new home would provide, as well as the peace of mind for our dog—he would be able to run loose throughout our seven acres.

Until our home was built, I kept Pitz indoors and out of sight of Mrs. Spinelli, except for an occasional quick outing down the front steps, on leash, to root in the bushes for a few minutes like any normal dog. We were concerned, though, when her son Joe paid us a surreptitious visit one night after she had left the house to run some errands. He was a completely mature adult, but because his business operation took place in his mother's home, he was under her domination. She had forbidden him to have any contact with us since his transgression of giving us our first Pitz. Joe warned us that his mother was aware that we had another dog and was angry enough "to do something about it."

Joe's warning came a little too late, for two days later, Pitz II exhibited the same symptoms as his namesake and died at the vet's the following day. This time we demanded an autopsy, and yes, as we surmised, Pitz had ingested some poisoned meat. We immediately contacted the local sheriff and told him of the circumstances of the death of both dogs and requested that he investigate. The investigation didn't proceed very far, though, because when she was questioned by the sheriff, Mrs. Spinelli emphatically denied having anything to do with the deaths. And because neither we nor any of the other tenants had seen her putting out poisoned meat, we couldn't prove our point.

But the sheriff's visit did initiate an all-out war between us and our landlady. From that point on, she went out of her way to make our lives miserable, even expanding the battlefield by including the O'Learys, our friends, in her barrages. When I went outdoors to hang clothes on the clothesline, she would stand on her back porch and yell out to me, "You dirty Kike, why don't you go back to Jerusalem?" And when she saw the O'Learys, her cry became, "You dirty Micks, why don't you go back to Ireland?" At first I ignored her taunts, but eventually I retaliated: "And why don't you go back to Italy?" (We had too many Italian friends for me to use the derogatory term "Wop," though I was sorely tempted.)

The name calling was only the beginning. Her next step was to shut off the furnace in the basement so that we had no heat. Rather than giving her the satisfaction of complaining, Mel had a large kerosene heater installed in the living room which heated the apartment only minimally, though, and we had to wear heavy sweaters at all times when indoors. Our new home, well under construction, couldn't go up fast enough for us, and every day we visited the building site to check on the progress.

Shortly before the house was finished, in December, Mrs. Spinelli's latest warring tactic was to lock the garage doors so Mel couldn't park the car in the garage. It was at this point that we discovered that for the entire year that we had lived in the apartment, all of her electrical appliances in the summer kitchen—the stove, washing machine, and fluorescent lights—were on *our* electric meter.

Two weeks before we were scheduled to move into our new home, Mel finally had enough. I was plagued with morning sickness, intensified by the fumes from the kerosene heater, which wasn't throwing enough heat for comfort. He'd called to say he was on his way home for lunch, but I answered the phone in tears from my abject misery. He was so angry that when he arrived home to find the garage door locked, with Mrs. Spinelli working in her summer kitchen, he slammed the car into the garage doors. This effectively kept her prisoner inside—with the car flush up against the doors, she couldn't open them to get out.

And there she stayed, pounding on the cellar door to our apartment, screaming invectives, which we drowned out by turning up the volume on our radio, until Mel was ready to return to his office and backed the car away from the garage doors. This garage door incident did enough damage to the doors that we received a hefty bill for the repair from her lawyer, several months later. But at the time, we felt it was worth the expense to trap that hellcat in the basement and giving her a dose of her own nasty games.

Moving day was a happy day for both Mel and me. When the mover's truck rolled up the driveway and started loading our furniture, Mrs. Spinelli was back in position on the back porch, calling out her venomous taunts, and even berating the innocent men arranging our belongings in the truck. As we drove down the driveway for the last time, it was to the tune of her farewell to us: "Good riddance, you damned Kikes."

Our new home was heavenly, particularly after the months of living with tension and suffering from kerosene fumes and lack of sufficient heat for comfort. We reveled in the freedom and warmth. One of our first missions after the furniture was in place was to go to the SPCA and pick out our third Pitz, who remained alive and well, free to roam our seven acres, for the next fourteen years.

Several months later, I answered the front doorbell and was surprised to see Mrs. Spinelli's son Joe standing there. We had always been friends, despite his mother, but this wasn't a social call. It seems that his mother had been working early mornings for a chicken farmer, who had a huge egg route throughout the county, and her duties were to gather eggs and place them in boxes for delivery.

Ever devious, she stashed away enough eggs each day to start her own egg route locally, even having the gall to use her employer's boxes. He eventually realized there was a shortage of his eggs being sold and called the state police, who found several dozen cartons of eggs in Mrs. Spinelli's car.

As they were about to apprehend her, she demanded to go to the ladies room, where she smashed a few dozen eggs on the walls and ceilings and down the toilets. She had been secreting the eggs in the pockets of the various aprons she wore and would make frequent trips out to her car to deposit them in the boxes. The police were anxious to find out how long this business had been going on, and the purpose of Joe's visit, as he was working with the police, was to discover if we'd ever seen her carrying or transporting eggs, either in boxes or in her apron pockets. Unfortunately, we could not verify this complaint, as much as we would have enjoyed incriminating her. As we later found out, her only penalty was the loss of her job with the chicken farmer and the lucrative egg route that she'd apparently had for a few years.

As small as our town was, we never laid eyes on Mrs. Spinelli again, which was no loss. We were involved with the births of our children (Corky and Suzy), Mel's growing dental practice, and our social and community activities. Mel did learn from one of his patients, a bungalow tenant of Mrs. Spinelli's, that her gentle, patient husband had died, which was probably a welcome release for him, and that she was terminally ill with colon cancer. Though we wouldn't have wished it on her, we also felt no sympathy for her. It wasn't easy to forget the indignities we suffered from this woman, whose own family turned against her. I watched the obituary column for a while but never saw her name and soon forgot about it.

A few years later, I happened to meet Joe Spinelli in the drugstore and was informed that his mother had survived the cancer, against all odds. She was alive and well and still making the lives of her newest tenants—and Joe—miserable. She was living proof that only the good die young. 🙚

CHAPTER TWENTY-SIX

MATINEES

WEBSTER'S DICTIONARY defines the word *matinee* as "a daytime dramatic or musical performance." This was not the specific meaning Mel had in mind on a snowy afternoon in mid-January, a few weeks after we had moved into our spanking new, custom-built home in the woods.

After spending the first year of our marriage in a rented apartment, harassed continually by the tyrannical Mrs. Spinelli, we were enjoying the spaciousness, freedom, and privacy in our very own house. On days when Mel had extra time between appointments, he frequently came home for lunch, and we'd discuss future purchases of furniture to fill up the still-empty spaces or the spring landscaping he planned to do.

On this particular day, there were several blocks of open time in his appointment book for the afternoon, caused in part by cancellations due to a sudden mid-morning snowstorm and in part because even though his dental practice was growing rapidly, Mel was still "the new young dentist in town," and remained so for the next fifteen years. After a leisurely sandwich lunch, and with still three hours before he was due back in the office for a 4 p.m. patient, it seemed most expedient to fill those hours as Mel proposed: "How about a matinee?" I knew he wasn't referring to a musical or dramatic performance.

Far be it from me to be labeled as one of those women who have "headaches," so I acquiesced and followed him down the hallway, which separated the bedroom wing from the rest of the house, and into our bedroom, a few feet from the front door. The snow was swirling thickly and silently outside our bedroom windows, even obscuring the view of the trees bordering our property. We felt locked away from the outside world, wrapped in each other, and we certainly were not sleeping.

At some point, perhaps twenty to thirty minutes later, we were rudely interrupted by the ringing of the front doorbell, followed immediately by someone opening the front door and walking into the foyer adjacent to our open bedroom door. A female voice called out, "Yoo-hoo! I'm here, and I brought my sheets."

Mel leaped out of bed, grabbed his clothes off the chair, and darted into the bathroom, muttering angrily, "Who in hell is that?"

"How do I know?" I retorted. I headed for my clothes closet and gave the bedroom door a shove to obstruct the view of our bedroom from the eyes of the person standing just a few feet away. "I'll be right out," I called. As I rushed to put on my robe, I wondered why that voice sounded familiar. Still tying the belt of my robe, I stepped into the hallway to confront none other than Sadie Bisberg. Sadie was the wife of a Long Island dentist we had met recently. Although the Bisbergs were a full generation older than we, they pursued the relationship with us as fellow professionals on their frequent vacations and long weekends in their summer home, a few miles from us. Their two adult sons were much closer to our ages than the parents and probably more stimulating company. Very much aware of my flushed face, disheveled hairdo, and rumpled bedding that was clearly visible from the foyer, I stammered out a greeting to her, adding, "Mel had cancellations for this afternoon so we were taking a nap." She nodded, as if she really believed me, as I continued, "But what in the world brings you here in the midst of this snowstorm? I thought your place was closed for the winter."

"It is," she answered, "but I needed some summer clothes for a cruise we'll be taking next month, and I came here to get them. Of course, all the utilities are off at the house and when this blizzard started—and it really is a blizzard now—I knew I wouldn't be driving back to Long Island today. So, I brought my sheets and hope you'll put me up for the night."

Could I refuse? No. I hung her coat in the front hall closet and showed her into the guest room, where she proceeded to strip the bed of my newly laundered sheets and replace them with the ones she had bunched up under her arm. I backed out of the room, murmuring, "I'll get dressed now. You make yourself at home." I was completely mortified at having been caught in this situation, and as I quickly dressed and made up our bed, my thoughts ran in the vein of *Mel and his matinees! I could kill him!*

And where was he? Now showered and dressed, Mel took off for the office, with nary a greeting to Sadie, leaving me to entertain this uninvited guest.

I made us a cup of tea to help kill time until I could escape to the kitchen to prepare dinner. I was still in a state of shock; as she babbled away, I mentally rehashed her interruption of our tryst. I couldn't wait for her departure the next morning. Despite Mel's declarations ("You're married now; it's legal"), I flushed with embarrassment each time my thoughts veered in that direction, which they did for months afterward and on every future encounter with Sadie.

Sadie's unexpected snowstorm visit so traumatized me that it had a profound impact on the rest of my life. Early mornings? Yes. Night time? Yes. Matinees? *Never!* &

CHAPTER TWENTY-SEVEN

OUR ECUMENICAL ERA

I COULD SPOT THEM IMMEDIATELY upon entering the waiting room of Mel's dental office, for these young Augustinian novices, training for the priesthood, stood out among the other patients. This was at a point in time when the "clean-cut all-American boy" was no longer clean-cut looking; instead, he was unshaven, unshorn, and unkempt. Boys were sporting beards, pigtails, and headbands and wearing odd assortments of unmatched, unshapely clothing.

In contrast, the young novices—most were in their late teens and early twenties—were immaculate in their uniforms: black suit and tie, white shirt, black socks, and highly polished black shoes. They were clean shaven with well-trimmed haircuts—just reeking of cleanliness from all angles.

At the same time that many of our all-American boys were burning the American flag, moving to Canada, and denouncing the "Establishment," these idealistic young men, bent on attaining their dreams of priesthood, were polite and respectful, jumping to their feet when addressed by an elder, and responding with "Yes, ma'am" or "No, sir."

As dentist for the novitiate, Mel became familiar with the young novices over time, and he enjoyed regaling me with tidbits concerning their latest dental visits or those of the priests. He was especially anxious for me to meet the priest who was most responsible for the personal guardianship and welfare of the young men, Father Bill Peters. Mel enjoyed ideological and political discussions with the priest, at least to the abbreviated extent one could in a busy dental office.

Before long, Father Peters was invited to our home for more in-depth exchange of ideas on religion, psychology, and current events, and it was easy to understand Mel's liking for this charming, erudite individual, who could discourse most knowledgeably on any subject. He was a perfect Paul Newman look-alike, with a similar height and build. Were it not for his wire-frame eye-glasses and clerical collar, he could have easily been mistaken for the popular movie actor.

Father Bill was the ideal mentor, teacher, and caretaker of his young charges, as he was well fortified with several degrees in education, psychology, and religion. An inordinate amount of patience and a marvelous sense of humor were among his other attributes, and he was truly loved and respected as a father figure by the novices.

As our relationship with Father Bill deepened, we had the opportunity of meeting the other priests who were responsible for teaching and administration, as well as the four elderly nuns who shared the housekeeping, laundering, and cooking duties at the novitiate. The nuns had come from Italy, years before, but only one of them, Mother Angelina, spoke enough English to make herself understood.

Fortunately for us, the novitiate was located less than a mile from our home, and we frequently made the scenic walk through the fields, up to the top of the hill that overlooked the brick novitiate buildings below. The backdrop for these buildings was the magnificent, breathtaking expanse of the Hudson River, beautiful at every season, whether ice covered in the winter or plied with all manner of boats and ships in spring, summer, and fall. The Catskill Mountains loomed in the background, a craggy, uneven silhouette; a fitting, protective backdrop for the river that wound among the foothills.

Mel and I endeared ourselves to the novices one hot summer by offering a day's outing to the nine-acre lake on my in-law's property, six miles away. Except for medical or dental visits, the novices had not left the grounds of the novitiate in almost a year, so they were in sky-high spirits when the great day arrived. We had recruited six friends to provide transportation to and from Willow Lake for the twenty-eight young men, and when our cavalcade of seven cars rolled up the long, winding novitiate driveway, cheers rang out from the novices. They were now clad in shorts and T-shirts and laden with baseballs, bats, and gloves, swimming gear, tennis rackets, beach towels, and blankets for picnicking. The nuns, who had packed baskets brimming with food and drink, stood outside the dormitory building, waving to the boys and throwing kisses as they took off on their big adventure. Father Bill and another priest, Father Lynch, followed in the official novitiate car.

It was a never-to-be-forgotten day for the novices, whose voices rang out joyously across the usually serene lake. Now, the lake was alive and throbbing, as the young men enjoying a freedom of mind and body they had not experienced since beginning their training. They cavorted in the water, fished, and explored the lake, as well as playing baseball, hiking and racing. And they ate and ate and ate. As dusk fell, they gathered firewood to finish off the day with a campfire for roasting marshmallows, and their lusty voices were raised in songs they had learned years ago, in a different lifetime.

When our appointed chauffeurs arrived, the tired and sunburned but happy young men piled into the cars with their game equipment and empty food baskets, profuse in their thanks for this wonderful break-in-routine day. En route home, driving through the small sleeping town of Fishkill, I heard an awestruck, excited voice from the backseat cry, "Look! Neon lights!" A neon-lit Coca-Cola sign in a darkened store window was as dazzling as the lights of Time Square to these novices, who had been sequestered for months from what we would term normal, everyday life.

Because Father Bill was a frequent guest at our home, he and Mel addressed each other as "Mel" and "Bill," but I still felt strange about addressing him without prefixing "Father" to his name. After having his mother and sister for tea one weekend, I was shocked to hear that *they* addressed him as "Father Bill." I remonstrated with Mel later: "If his own mother and sister call him 'Father Bill,' don't you think you should?"

"He calls me Mel," my husband replied, "so I can call him Bill." And apparently, Bill didn't object, because the warm, family-like relationship grew, and we were frequently invited to the novitiate to share some of their holidays.

Their studies of the Old Testament coincided with our observance of Passover, which they also celebrated with a seder in which we were active participants. A couple of times when their class was very small (ten or fewer), they were invited to our home for the seder; otherwise, we went to the novitiate when there was a larger enrollment. How thrilling and memorable these seders were—Christians and Jews, each reading the story of Exodus from their individual prayer books!

Each year prior to the holiday, two or three students came to our home for instruction in the art of making matzoh balls, the traditional Jewish accompaniment with chicken soup. One year, about a week before Passover, I spied Mother Angelina while shopping in town, a bulging shopping bag on each arm.

"Hey, Mother Angelina!" I yelled. "Wait up; I have to talk to you." She greeted me with a smile and leaned forward to kiss me on both cheeks as I asked, "When are you going to send the boys, so I can show them how to make the matzoh balls?"

She shook her head. "Oh, no," she earnestly replied. "You coma our house and maka da matzoh ball. Lasta year dey maka da matzoh ball, beeg lika da futball, hard lika cement. Even da dogs no eat."

So, the afternoon preceding the first seder, my mother-in-law and I wound up in the huge novitiate kitchen, rolling and shaping 168 matzoh balls, allowing three balls for each of the fifty-six seder participants. Many of them were guests from a neighboring novitiate across the Hudson River. There were no matzoh balls left over that night for "da dogs" to eat.

Our rapport with the inhabitants of the novitiate continued but a couple of years later, the day came—much to our dismay—when, for lack of a sufficient numbers of applicants, the doors of the novitiate closed forever. It was the end of an era of warmth, camaraderie, and sharing with our friends of a different religious faith. It was our hope that we impacted their lives as positively as they impacted ours. ❧

CHAPTER TWENTY-EIGHT

BURGLARS WELCOME!

HE WAS TALL, DARK, AND HANDSOME and, like his Italian compatriots Caruso and Pavarotti, had a voice that could charm the wings off angels. Not only that, but he exuded warmth and sincerity when we first met him, and he seemed to have extensive experience in the installation of burglar alarms. There had been a rash of burglaries in the area and because our home was in the woods, concealed from the road and other neighbors, we thought it prudent to have an alarm system installed.

I wasn't aware of Carmine's operatic talents until I heard him singing my favorite arias as he worked in the basement, wiring the panel for our burglar alarm. I stood in the doorway to the basement and yelled down to him, "Carmine, where did you learn to sing like that?"

"Oh," wafted up his reply, "I studied opera here for years and then continued with my studies in Germany when I was serving in the Army."

"Well, why aren't you doing it professionally," I asked, "instead of installing burglar alarms?"

"I have to make a living and apparently, I'm better in electronics," he replied. "The opera companies aren't rushing to sign me to a contract."

We learned the hard way that Carmine should have stuck to opera, for as sincere as he was and eager to please, his alarm system seemed to have two functions: not working at all, or working overtime. The kitchen sensor was so sensitive that it would pick up a butterfly or bird flying past the dining room window and set off the alarm, which rang inside, outside, and on the police monitor. Even in the middle of the night, when birds and butterflies supposedly sleep, the alarm would go off, not only shocking us out of a sound sleep with its shrill careening sound but keeping me awake the rest of the night as well.

It was bad enough when we were home and the alarm went off without cause, but when we were away, whether for an hour or a week, it was quite common to pull into our driveway to find police cars—sometimes even fire trucks—parked there. (Once, two fire trucks from another county across the Hudson River actually answered the call.) Carmine always made his house calls immediately in response to our phone messages. He'd be very apologetic about the malfunction and each time had a different approach to repairing a system that refused to be repaired. We were embarrassed and apologetic, too, to the civil servants, the firemen, and police, who'd come out on a wild goose chase, and I wondered when we would end up like the boy who cried wolf. Some day, that alarm would go off, and no one would answer.

After putting up with Carmine's system for two years, the day came when we knew we'd had enough—when the burglars actually came to our home, our noisy, wailing, shrill alarm was silent. It went off apparently hours after the burglars had left with their loot, because the police arrived within eight minutes of receiving the alarm and discovered an electric clock pulled out of the wall that had stopped six hours earlier. The fact that the alarm went off at all was probably the usual malfunction caused by a butterfly or bird, or maybe just on general principles.

We had two children by this time, Curtis and Suzanne, and had taken them on a long-promised visit to Niagara Falls for three days, and on returning home, we were greeted at the front door by my mother-in-law—a surprise in itself, as she lived a good six miles away and did not drive. "What are you doing here?" I asked.

"You had burglars while you were gone," she replied, "and the police picked me up so that I could go through the house with them. They'll be back tomorrow to discuss it with you. And Muriel, you should see what those burglars did! They left their dirty black fingerprints all over the woodwork and cabinets in the dining room and living room!"

I must have had a look of consternation on my face as I anticipated the damage and loss. My mother-in-law, however, misread my look and was quick to reassure me. Very pleased with herself, she said: "You don't have to worry at all, because I cleaned up every one of their dirty fingerprints.

I took the can of Bon Ami and went through all the woodwork in every room, so you won't have that job."

When the police sergeant arrived the next day he quickly left, there being no reason for him to stay to get fingerprints that were no longer there. As he left the house, his parting words were: "The next time you get burglarized, please tell your mother-in-law not to wash off their fingerprints." ❧

CHAPTER TWENTY-NINE

THE HIRED HAND

HE REFERRED TO HIMSELF as "the hired hand," but his actions belied that title, as he was anything but servile. In his mind, the 116-acre estate belonged to him—he was the one who loved it with a fierce intensity; he was the one who mowed the lawns, raked the hay, mucked the stable, maintained all the buildings, and raised and lowered the flood levels of the lake. He was also the only one on the premises who could drive a car, so he was the right hand *and* the left hand for my in-laws. As far as he was concerned, however, their only reason for being was to sign his weekly pay-check and fork out the money needed to run Willow Lake.

They needed the estate like I need more wrinkles, but I can't com-plain too much about Ollie and his arrogance and his red-hot Norwegian temper—it was really my fault that they had to deal with him. Though he could be almost charming and affable at times, when everything ran smoothly, he was known more for his temper that engulfed everyone with-in hearing distance.

Shortly into our marriage, Mel and I had our home built out in the country. My Manhattan-dwelling in-laws, suddenly intrigued with country life, began appearing at our door on weekends—uninvited and with increasing regularity. I was so provoked when they showed up one weekend—when we already had *invited* guests and not enough beds for everyone—that I exploded at my mother-in-law. "If you like it so much up here, why don't you buy your own place?"

Surprisingly, she replied, "If you find us a place we like, we'll buy it."

I didn't need a second invitation to contact a real estate agent, and within a few short weeks, my in-laws were the proud and happy owners of Willow Lake, and they "inherited" Ollie as part of the deal.

They had fallen in love with the place at first sight, and indeed, Willow Lake was beautiful. Still, Mel and I wondered if two aging city-dwellers—his mother was in her late sixties; his father, his early seventies—needed a nineteen-room, four-story fieldstone mansion to rattle around in. I was just glad to have them settled in a place of their own, and we were especially grateful for the nine-acre lake on which the house was situated—great for swimming in the summer.

Willow Lake, nestled in the foothills of a mountain range in the Mid-Hudson Valley, had been given to Margaret Sanger, the birth-control advocate, as a wedding present by her husband, J. Noah Slee, in 1924. The grounds were magnificent three seasons of the year and charming when covered by winter snows. In spring, millions of daffodils bloomed all around the lake, which was ringed with flowering Japanese willow trees that dipped down into the lake. Exotic shrubs and trees, imported from many parts of the world, bloomed at this season, and it was truly breathtaking to view the French lilacs, the various species of rhododendron, the yellow splashes of forsythia, and the bowers of redbud trees and dogwood. The surrounding mountain range was reflected in the lake, and in the fall, the lake itself was ablaze with color.

My in-laws spent happy hours walking the grounds or sitting in Adirondack chairs overlooking the lake, just drinking in the beauty and serenity of the scene. Sometimes they rowed the boat around the lake or fished for the abundant bass in this little corner of paradise.

As you can imagine, with a place this size, Ollie was an absolute necessity, and did he ever know it! He was not only a jack-of-all-trades, but he also was a master of them all, so aside from an assistant to help with the mowing and plowing in the winter, he ran the estate almost single-handedly. He made all the decisions as to which repairs were to be done, which supplies had to be purchased, which gardens would be dug up, and which crops should be planted. There wasn't anything he couldn't repair, from a dead furnace to a recalcitrant tractor or truck, to a non-functioning washing machine or refrigerator. But if either of my in-laws had ideas that conflicted with Ollie's, too bad, because Ollie had the final say.

He would show up at the garage by 7 a.m. and could be found somewhere on the grounds until after dark each day. A baseball cap was perched on his head and a fat cigar was in the corner of his mouth as he went about his chores; he also wore a perpetual scowl. He was familiar with every foot of the property, and God help anyone who desecrated it! Typical of his feeling of possessiveness and need to control was a time after my father-in-law died, when my mother-in-law wanted to create a new flower garden. Ollie refused to dig one, so after he left at night, she dug and planted one herself. When Ollie discovered it the next day, he flew into a rage, slapped her face resoundingly, and pulled out all the little plants she had so painstakingly inserted.

Six miles away, I answered my phone to hear the almost incoherently sobbing voice of my mother-in-law; I quickly drove there to seek out the problem. Ollie was nowhere in sight, and she was in a state of shock, so I packed up some clothes and brought her back to our home. When Mel heard the news, he was furious and immediately called Ollie to sever his employ. Ollie didn't have to ask why he was fired, but neither did he apologize. For the next two days my mother-in-law barely spoke, but on the third day she picked up the phone, called Ollie, and told him to come pick her up and get on with his work. As long as she lived there, she knew that she needed Ollie, and he knew it, too. Eventually, the time came when my mother-in-law could no longer live there alone, and we had to sell Willow Lake. The movie producer who bought the property inherited Ollie, as Dad had inherited him years before, seemingly the sweetener each time to clinch a deal. Ollie worked for the new owner for several years before succumbing to a heart attack.

His wake was attended by all the townspeople, who came out of respect for his widow and daughters. He lay there in his open coffin, with the baseball cap on his head and a cigar in his hand. The scowl that had always dominated his features was replaced by a peaceful expression—it was so unlike him that he didn't resemble the Ollie we knew. As I left the funeral home, I overheard one man whisper to another, "I surely thought he'd outlive us all." 🐿

Manor house at Willow Lake.

Aerial photograph of Willow Lake.

CHAPTER THIRTY

A HOSTILE TAKEOVER

"UNFORTUNATELY, I can only confirm the previous diagnosis you received for your mother. Yes, she has Alzheimer's, and it is unsafe for her to be living alone. This insidious disease for which we have no cure, will take over the life that she knew."

With sinking hearts, Mel and I exchanged glances, thanked the doctor, and escorted my mother-in-law out to our car for the long trip home. We didn't realize it then, but her disease would take over all our lives, not just hers. Mel was her only child; therefore, her well-being was our responsibility.

The situation that prompted our physician visits occurred on Thanksgiving, a few weeks prior, as Mother helped me in the kitchen. I was peeling carrots over the sink when she thrust her forearm before my eyes and proudly said, "Look, Muriel, I still have all my summer tan." I was shocked to realize that what she called "tan" was the end product of several weeks (or perhaps months) of unwashed skin, and when I took her into the bathroom and applied soap and washcloth to the forearm, the "tan" disappeared. Rather than feeling shamed at this exposure, Mother only giggled.

For all the years I had been in this family, my mother-in-law was labeled "crazy clean," as it was her habit to take not one but two baths a day. She would vacuum and dust her eight-room New York apartment *before* her daily housekeeper arrived. When Mother smoked her cigarettes, she always carried an ashtray in one hand and a tissue for wiping the ashtray clean after she had dumped the dead butt and ashes into the toilet. Her same cleanliness phobia was part of her life with Dad at Willow Lake, and even after Dad died, Mother persisted in living alone at Willow Lake, doing the household cleaning herself and she spent long hours in the flower gardens that were her joy. Life was comparatively uncomplicated until the Thanksgiving Day episode.

Once the devastating diagnosis was made, Mother's Alzheimer's condition seemed to deteriorate overnight, and it was imperative to find a live-in companion quickly. That wasn't so easy to accomplish, as she adamantly refused to "have a baby-sitter" and didn't want any strangers living in her house. Finding the right type of person for the job was a monumental task, because most unemployed people at the time were on welfare and not interested in putting in time on a job when they could get paid by New York State for doing nothing. We needed someone with tact and understanding, who could handle Mother gently when she forgot to bathe or change her clothes. Mother always said that she "just took a bath this morning" or "just had my dress cleaned," though the odor and food stains proved otherwise. We learned to say, "Your doctor wants you to take daily baths because it is good for your circulation, which helps your memory." She was very much aware that her memory was poor and frequently mentioned that she must be going crazy; of course, we reassured her that we all forget things at times.

Several supposedly competent women were hired over the next few weeks, but none of them lasted for more than a day, as Mother fired them as soon as I had them installed at Willow Lake. I finally found a solution by telling Mother that we needed income in order for her to continue living there, and we'd found a lovely person who wanted to pay Mother rent to live in one of the bedrooms. Apparently, the fear of not being able to live in the home she loved convinced Mother to accept Georgina, though if she'd ever had an inkling Georgina was getting a salary rather than putting money into the coffers, Georgina would have been bounced like the others.

Playing games and telling "white lies" became part of our lives, as Mother resisted almost everything we tried to do for her. Typical of the games was the incident of buying Mother new corsets and bras that had to be fitted to her, as she had a very abundant bosom and full figure—these weren't items I could purchase for her and bring home. She insisted she didn't need new undergarments, though the ones she had were threadbare and held together by safety pins. I invented a fictitious contest sponsored by the Chamber of Commerce that I had supposedly won, and the prize was free corsets and bras from the lingerie shop. To authenticate the deal, I also had a letter from the store, inviting us to come in to collect the prize.

As time passed and Mother's condition worsened, we knew the time was fast approaching when we would have to sell Willow Lake and install her in smaller living quarters. Skyrocketing taxes, enormous heating bills from an antiquated furnace, and increased living expenses had us juggling bank accounts to pay the bills. When we would bring up the subject of finances, Mother's reply was always the same: "Dad said I could live here for the rest of my life." *That* she could remember, though she didn't know what day of the week it was. One observation I had to make in defense of her memory loss was that it made her a happier person. For most of her life she was known as a chronic complainer, and at this point in time, mercifully enough, she couldn't remember all the things she used to "bitch" about. She became placid and gentle, easily diverted, and went about humming and singing under her breath. At times she would revert back to her childhood and ask for her mommy and daddy, and when we took her driving, she amused herself by counting the cars on the road. Then, there were times when she seemed completely normal; we could recognize a lucid day by the number of her complaints.

The lucid days eventually came to an end, and Mother became more reclusive, often locking herself in her bedroom for hours, with no sounds of life emanating from the room. She ignored my pleas to let me in, as I stood outside her door, jiggling the doorknob and knocking. I was always fearful she might try to light a fire in the fireplace in her room, and on one occasion, when there had been dead silence for hours, I had Ollie mount a ladder outside her bedroom window so he could look into her room. There she was, calmly rearranging her bureau drawers, taking items from one drawer and placing them in another.

As the emergency phone calls from Georgina increased, coupled with the financial worries concerning the upkeep of Willow Lake, we realized that this hostile takeover of all our lives by Mother's disease must cease. The time had come; Willow Lake had to go. ❧

CHAPTER THIRTY-ONE

WILLOW LAKE GAMES

September 15, 1976

Dear Everyone:

I haven't written a letter to anyone for almost six months so I am making a report of my activities in multiple copies to save myself the time and energy of having to repeat myself for about 25 people whom I "owe." Hope you don't mind, I promise I won't do it again, but right now, it's the only way I can catch up.

To start with, we put Mel's mother's estate, Willow Lake, on the market the end of March as she just didn't have the money to pay the skyrocketing taxes and heating bills, salaries of her caretaker and hired men, and general upkeep of this aging mansion. Juggling bank accounts for two years, we had no alternative but to sell and it was a great emotional strain on us, the son and daughter-in-law, to reach the point psychologically, where we had to take the bull by the horns.

This house was Mother's whole life, her love and source of pride, and the fact that she lived alone in it for ten years after Dad died, must attest to her emotional tie to this nineteen room home on 116 acres in beautiful isolation at the base of a mountain range, which was reflected in the nine acre lake. Granted, some of the nineteen rooms were not lived in as they were attic rooms for storage, or wine, laundry and game rooms in the basement, but Mother knew and loved every nook and cranny of them all.

Breaking the news to her was more than difficult because she had been losing her memory gradually and it had deteriorated greatly this past year. It just didn't penetrate when we tried to tell her there was no money to operate Willow Lake, her one mantra was: "Dad said I could stay here the rest of my life." As good a businessman that Dad was, he did not have the foresight to plan on the aforementioned culprits as well as loss of income, an ancient heating system that could not be repaired and a leaking slate roof requiring the ministrations of a non-existing specialist.

We realized we had to come up with a more tangible reason for selling other than finances, something we could show her, and this turned out to be sawdust, the byproduct of termites. I concocted a letter using the logo of a local exterminating company, indicating the house was infested with termites, and then, our plan was to show Mother through the house, from attic to basement, to view for herself the piles of sawdust I had planted everywhere. According to the letter, the house had to be sprayed with poison chemicals which would harm all the furnishings, so she would have to move all her belongings out of the house for six to eight months till the fumes from the poisonous chemicals were dissipated. And of course, her homeowner's insurance policy would cover all costs. We felt this was the kindest way to get her out of the house, and then she would have hopes of moving back … always to be "soon." It was our expectation that with her poor memory, within six months she would stop asking to go back to Willow Lake.

Now that we had the plot cooked up, all we needed was a buyer, and believe me, we weren't inundated by them. Big mansions like Mother's are a white elephant on the market these days and when we got one serious offer in May, much less than the asking price, we were glad to accept it, with the closing date set for July 1.

The next project was to find an apartment suitable for Mother who is accustomed to living "big" and for several weeks I scoured our part of the county looking for one with 3 bedrooms for her and her caretaker. The 3rd bedroom was to use as a TV room, which she has always had. After a thorough search, I found the best complex to be the first I had looked at and only two minutes by car from our home. This complex was new, with 660 apartments, beautifully landscaped in a rural setting but with only twelve three-bedroom apartments, and very much in demand. We were lucky to be given first preference because the owner of the complex lived above the one available apartment and preferred two "nice, quiet old ladies" under him, rather than a family with a pack of kids.

So the apartment was mine with a down payment, and then I started holding my breath for the sale contract to be signed, as I didn't want to sign a year's rental lease until Willow Lake was actually sold. And I was still holding my breath when I put down payments on a new couch, carpeting, draperies and upholstery fabrics for renovating the frayed but familiar furniture. Everything was on hold till the actual signing of the contract on July 1, and until that date, I felt as though I was sitting atop a volcano.

Now was the time to break the news to Mother about the termites, which we did very gently one day (after a few sleepless nights) and we showed her the little piles of sawdust which made the story authentic, plus the letter from the exterminating company. Mother's reaction was of incredibility till we showed her the piles of sawdust, and then, it began to penetrate. But, for the next few weeks, for the rest of the time she lived there, we had to keep reminding her that she was moving due to termites, but that she would be moving back when the poisonous exterminating fumes had vanished.

The next step on my schedule was interviewing auctioneers who would be auctioning all the contents of Willow Lake that would not go to the new apartment. Inasmuch as Mother had been in the china and giftware business for years, her kitchen cabinets held the contents of seventeen sets of dishes, some of them having place settings for twenty-four rather than the usual twelve, and she had the finest of brands of china: Spode, Royal Worcester, Minton, Havilland, seven different patterns of Wedgewood. All these sets of dishes were in excellent condition, complete with demitasse cups and saucers, and matching vegetable dishes and platters that had the auctioneers drooling. They were all vying for the job and that was another decision I had to make, to get the one who had the best following and rep-utation. The restaurant-size kitchen with dozens of wall cabinets that held Mother's stash of dishes, was probably one of the determining factors for her purchase of Willow Lake.

Once the auctioneer decision was made and a date set for emptying the house, I began my daily transport of empty cartons I had been collecting for several weeks, to start the long and horrible task of packing. It took six cartons alone just to hold the contents of the breakfront, which was destined for the apartment. All the while Mother helped me pack her treasures, she repeatedly asked, "Why are we packing?" I would go over the story of the termites again and again, but I could have saved my breath. Oftentimes when I arrived there the following day, cartons had been unpacked and their contents hidden away.

July 1 arrived, the day when all of our efforts and planning of the past few months would culminate in the signing of the contract to sell the property to the purchaser, a New York movie producer. What should have been a routine one to two hour procedure, with all terms supposedly having been spelled out very amicably in advance, turned out to be a nightmare of a seven hour day that left us all drained and angry. The buyer waited till this day to present us with a list of his demands, some of which were: he wanted the station wagon which we had planned for Mother's use at the apartment; he wanted a particular set of Wedgewood china I had earmarked for one of our kids; he wanted the repair of a previously unseen, twelve inch long crack in the dining room wall under the casement window to be followed by painting the entire room and ceiling; he wanted the two living room Oriental rugs included in the sale price, which I had already been advised would bring in thousands of dollars at auction. These are only some of the ridiculous demands made and the only one that merited attention was the repair and painting of the dining room wall crack, without the entire wall and ceiling paint job requested.

At three different times during those bitter seven hours when we were accused of "nickel and diming" the buyer, our lawyer closed his file, packed it into his briefcase, stood up and announced that this sale could not proceed, motioning for us to get up and leave with him. Each time this happened, my heart plummeted to my feet as we moved reluctantly toward the door, to be stopped by the mollifying voice of the buyer's attorney: "Well, let's not be hasty, come back and we'll talk this over."

By day's end, the contract was signed with our guarantee to repair the cracked wall and to leave eight place settings of the Wedgewood china for the buyer, our only concessions. We left their lawyer's office victorious, in that our mission to sell was accomplished, but were completely devoid of all feelings of pleasure and relief that this procedure should have engendered. We still had to wait another week for the completion of an acreage survey, and only when this was done could I finalize the orders for everything that was on hold. A year's lease was signed to start on Aug. 1, and we scheduled Mother to move into her new apartment on Aug. 2.

I had been "playing games" with Mother the past couple of years to achieve results when she resisted changes to benefit her, like the imaginary lingerie contest I had won, in order to get her fitted to undergarments. And when she refused to have us hire a badly needed companion for her, this was accomplished by dint of the companion supposedly paying rent, rather than Mother paying her. The termite infestation was now added to the game playing, more lies for the good of the cause.

During the previous weeks when we were showing the house to real estate agents, prospective buyers and auctioneers anxious to land this job, we would have Georgie, the companion, take Mother out for a drive so she wouldn't question the appearance of strangers on her property. It was always my fear she would arrive home before their departure so I would usher them toward the front door long before they were ready to go. The first time I saw these unknown personages pawing through her treasures, poking into her cabinets, my stomach churned violently and I was overcome with terrible feelings of guilt.

The continual explanations, deception and game playing which had gone on for so long was beginning to take its toll on me. Living in a state of almost constant tension resulted in my voice becoming increasingly hoarse as the summer progressed and eventually I could only whisper and expectorate blood-tinged mucous. I was seen by a head and neck surgeon at Memorial Hospital in New York who, despite my protestations that this was the result of tension, scheduled me for laryngoscopy and biopsy under anesthesia the very week I was to move Mother into her new apartment. When I protested that the condition was tension induced and not a malignancy, the surgeon retorted "If so, then it's the worst case of tension I've ever seen."

We spirited Mother to Connecticut to be with my family for a few days to avoid the trauma of seeing a moving van load her belongings into a truck, and then friends and neighbors rallied around to get the apartment completely settled so that Mother could move into it twenty-four hours after her furniture was taken from Willow Lake. Dishes were washed and stacked in the lined kitchen cabinets, beds made, furniture polished and pictures hung, achieving that "lived in" look for this new home, in such a short span of time.

On August 2, the companion returned with Mother from her Connecticut sojourn and Mel escorted her into the lovely bright and colorful apartment while we held our breath, awaiting her reaction. "It's so beautiful," she stated, "I won't want to go back to my old place." So far, so good. Unfortunately, it was too good to last because two hours later she picked up her purse and announced, "Now take me home." So then began the retelling of the termite narrative, a foretaste of the coming weeks and months.

The following day was to be hospital admission day for me, but I found that during the one week of preparing to move Mother and the actual move, my voice became stronger with each day. I was examined by my physician who found that, miraculously, the previously inflamed and ulcerated vocal cords had improved about 90%, proving my diagnosis of tension as the causative factor. The exam under anesthesia and biopsy were cancelled, and I was to return for examination a month later. What a great reprieve at a critical time, when I needed every spare minute for disposing of the rest of the contents of the house!

Now with Mother settled in her apartment, I inventoried with the auctioneer, the remaining furniture and articles that had not been sent to the apartment. The date was set for auction in time to get the place emptied before the new owners took title to Willow Lake, less than 6 weeks away. The auctioneer was mainly interested in the large items that would bring the best prices, like furniture, paintings, Oriental rugs, crystal, the imported handmade banquet-size dining cloths, china and sterling silver. He wanted no part of the contents of drawers, closets, bookcases and bric-a-brac, so that was my job, to dispose of what was left in the nineteen rooms, which was plenty!

Though Mother and Dad had furnished Willow Lake completely on purchase, adding most of the contents of their eight-room New York apartment years later didn't exactly create a "sparsely furnished" home. This helped account for the presence of four vacuum cleaners, three sewing machines, three carpet sweepers, four sets of sterling silver flatware, two sterling tea sets, etc. I hired a very responsible young man with truck, Warren, the son of a friend, anxious to earn college tuition for the fall and prepared to work nine hours a day six days a week for the next several weeks. Each morning we would arrive with empty cartons gleaned from liquor stores and supermarkets, and starting in the attic, systematically worked our way down through the house to the basement, emptying every closet, every drawer, every bookcase. We unpacked dozens of cartons that had never been opened when Mother and Dad moved permanently out of their New York apartment so their contents had to be disposed of also.

Articles were sorted into four categories: category one was for small but expensive items the auctioneer would sell privately; category two was for me to put aside, sterling flatware sets and china for our kids as well as familiar sentimental objects and family picture albums; category three was for donating to The Salvation Army which included the entire contents of Mother's hotel-size linen closet, blankets, and clothing in good condition; category four was for garbage and this was the busiest category of all, that saw Warren making dozens of trips outdoors to his truck which he emptied at each day's end at the town dump. There were so many items that would have gotten good prices at a flea market or garage sale, but there was no time for that.

The large attic that ran the length of the house was lined from floor to ceiling with cartons, furniture, filled bureau drawers, and fully packed steamer trunks, all very organized and neat, with a wide passageway between the cartons and furniture, which made the job so much easier. There were cartons of magazines, dating back from 1924, tons of empty bottles, rolls of string, tied up stacks of paper bags, large rolls of plastic sheeting, mattresses and twin beds piled atop each other and bureaus left over from the previous dude ranch occupants. Mother never threw anything away, which accounted for her dead husband's extra set of dentures grinning up from a pantry drawer or for the fact that her waste baskets were always empty. One auctioneer he had been selling contents of estates, he had never seen one so loaded with "junk," but it was also the cleanest and most systematically placed junk.

A huge walk-in cedar closet was loaded with clothes and furs, dating back to the 1920's, all with coordinating hats, shoes and handbags. Any theatrical company or costumer would have treasured these items but again, time was of the essence and the entire contents of the cedar closet went into the garbage category. Mel had once offered to accompany me on Sundays when Warren did not work, but being his mother's son, and a sentimentalist, I knew much in the garbage category would end up in our own basement, so I refused his offer. As the rooms got emptier and emptier, my spirits rose higher and higher as I saw the end in sight.

My summer had been one of complete isolation from family and friends as I was too exhausted at night to even talk on the phone, and just wanted to crawl into bed as soon as possible. It was a red-letter day when the house was stripped bare of every vestige of the former occupant, cleaned for the new owners, and I walked out of the house for the last time. On September 10, the new owners took title and that same weekend the auction took place, just 9½ weeks from the day the contract was first signed.

I hope this will satisfactorily explain why you haven't heard from me all this time.

Love,

Muriel ❦

CHAPTER THIRTY-TWO

AFTERMATH

ONCE WILLOW LAKE WAS SOLD and Mother was established in her spacious new apartment, I was ready to rest on my laurels and recuperate from the lost six months of my life. That wasn't to be.

Even though we tried to establish the same daily living pattern that Mother had had in the past, my phone rang with crisis calls—one to three a day—from Georgie, the companion. I would immediately drop what I was doing and make the two-minute drive to Mother's apartment complex to defuse a situation. (I was grateful that the best apartment available for Mother was so close to our home.) As soon as I entered the apartment, Mother would make a beeline for the front hall closet, grab her coat and pocketbook, and hopefully ask, "Did you come to take me home?" Very patiently, I would review the spiel about the sawdust and termites responsible for her Willow Lake departure, and by then, the reason for my hurried visit had evaporated.

During the first couple of months, the emergencies were minor ones, like Mother refusing to eat, bathe, or take her medications, but as time went on, though she asked less about "going home," the crisis situations became more serious as her Alzheimer's disease progressed. It had been on the same plateau for a year and a half, and then suddenly, almost overnight, it plunged downward. Though the psychiatrist had predicted this, the sudden decline was shocking to behold. Medications were of no help, for they either depressed her to the point of extreme lethargy or agitated her to the point of violent bursts of anger and frustration.

There were numerous incidences of Mother's sneaking out of the apartment and getting lost in the huge maze of the apartment complex's buildings; fires were set from open gas jets in the kitchen; opened faucets flooded the flooring and carpeting; objects were thrown into the toilets, creating constant plumbing problems. At this particular time, Georgie declared that she wanted to retire so she could live with her sister in Virginia. Just what I needed!

The employment agencies were no help, as the unemployed seemed to only want to work for IBM, known for its liberal benefits and job permanence. And there was a lot to be desired in the caliber of the people who condescended to "try out the job" of caring for Mother. Within two weeks, I hired five caretakers; two left voluntarily because they didn't like the job, and I fired the others for sheer incompetence.

I decided to advertise in a Glens Falls, New York, newspaper, miles away on the border of Appalachia, where poverty was endemic. I hired Helen over the phone, sight unseen, the one woman who answered my ad. She sounded intelligent, seemed empathetic when I discussed Mother's problems, had a driver's license, and was as desperate for money as I was desperate to hire a caretaker. She lived with her daughter, unemployed son-in-law, and their four children in a four-room hovel (based on her description), and the idea of having her own bedroom and bath, a car to drive, meals, and a salary sounded heavenly to her. She arrived by train the next day, and I was just so grateful to have some relief from the growing problems of Mother's care that Helen looked beautiful to me, despite her shabby clothes, unkempt hairdo, and mouthful of empty spaces between the few brown and yellowed teeth she still had. (By the time she left our employment, Helen had a mouthful of new teeth with which she could chew, and she looked ten years younger, courtesy of Mel, my dentist husband.)

Helen accepted her duties with equanimity, was a careful driver, and seemed genuinely concerned for Mother's welfare, although as a housekeeper, she was as slovenly as they come. Beds were left unmade, soiled dishes were piled up in the sink, and the dust was thick on the furniture. The first time I arrived at the apartment as Helen and Mother were having lunch, I was horrified to see open cans of food on the table, the jagged lids sticking up, and spoons stuck deep into the cans. Helen wasn't aware of the purpose of the fine vegetable serving dishes and platters in the kitchen cabinets; it was much easier to eat directly from the can. On her first few grocery-shopping forays, her purchases consisted mainly of smoked meats—cold cuts, sausages, ham, hot dogs—an abundance of pastries, canned beans, peas, sardines, and bottled sodas. Fresh or frozen fruits and vegetables were not in her vocabulary, nor were cereals and dairy foods, like milk, eggs, and cheese. It was obviously incumbent upon me to do the grocery shopping to ensure Mother's healthy diet.

Helen coped with Mother's increasing Alzheimer's manifestations philosophically and dealt with her good-naturedly, but I worried that the apartment-complex owner, who lived directly over Mother, would ask her to vacate the apartment. As time went on, Mother became more excitable, oftentimes going out on her balcony to shriek at passersby or at the children playing below, or she would empty a teakettle full of water over the balcony to disperse the playing children. Her psychiatrist urged us to place her in a nursing home before she or anyone else was injured.

Mel and I realized that she needed more structured and professional nursing care but dreaded the idea of having to institutionalize her—we had visions of patients with blank, expressionless faces, tied into wheelchairs, lining the nursing home hallways, which smelled unpleasantly of urine. Still, with heavy heart, I started my search for a nursing home without the "institution feel" to it and was fortunate to learn of a private one just a few miles away, named "Hudson House" because of its one-mile proximity to the Hudson River. This was a twelve-patient, private, assisted-living and nursing home, owned and operated by a physician and two RNs, in a beautiful five-acre setting along a rural country road. The building itself had been part of a larger estate and was a large, white, colonial-style, two-story frame structure, shaded by massive maple and oak trees. Colorful flower gardens flanked the building on all sides, and the wide expanses of lawn were dotted at intervals with several comfortable padded lawn chairs. This looked more like a country gentleman's estate than a nursing home, and my spirits rose as I felt the general tranquil atmosphere here would have a calming influence on Mother.

The interior of the house was furnished like a private home, with soft couches and easy chairs, well-polished mahogany furniture, and colorful wall paintings and draperies, the antithesis to the institutional furnishings and atmosphere I had dreaded. The upstairs bedroom that would be Mother's, was the largest in the house, with windows overlooking the front and side lawns, and a bathroom to be shared by a next-door patient. The pre-requisite for patients being accepted here was that they be ambulatory and able to dress themselves, which covered Mother—so far. According to the nurse who showed me around, the majority of the patients here were diabetic or colostomy patients who needed dressings, medications, and shots in emergencies, when families were unable to cope with those situations. Also here were patients recuperating from fractures, who couldn't manipulate stairways in their own homes, and a couple of Alzheimer's patients, like Mother.

I brought Mel back to see the home the very same night, and he agreed that this place seemed ideal for Mother, and she would get the professional care and supervision she needed. It was close enough for us to visit frequently or to bring her to our home for a few hours for a change in her routine. We submitted her physician's recommendations and health records, paid the necessary fees, and set her admission date for a week later. This would give me the needed time for packing toilet articles and clothes she would be using here and to arrange to transport the two pieces of furniture that would fit into her bedroom: a favorite rocking chair and a small escritoire she enjoyed.

I moved Mother in two days later, rather than in one week, because Helen's daughter had emergency surgery, and Helen was needed back in Glens Falls to care for the four young grandchildren, the father having disappeared weeks earlier. I concentrated on packing up Mother's belongings to the accompaniment of her repeated question as she faced the open suitcases on the bed: "Where are we going?" I tried to explain to Mother that Helen had to go home and that she was going to live in a lovely house, with gardens she could work in, if she so desired, and there would be other people in this home for company. She wasn't impressed and insisted, "I like it here." At least she had forgotten about wanting to return to Willow Lake.

Our daughter, Suzy, had arrived home unexpectedly for a few days between college sessions and accompanied me as we drove Mother to her new home; she was unhappy that we were uprooting her beloved grandmother for the unknown. As we pulled up in the parking area of the well-kept grounds, Mother agreed that yes, this was a pretty place, and as we ushered her through the comfortable, attractive rooms, she smiled in appreciation. Once we got upstairs to her bedroom, however, and I started unpacking her clothes, she became apprehensive, wanting to know why I was hanging her dresses in *that* closet, and why I was putting her clothes in *those* drawers. She became more and more agitated as I continued unpacking. The accompanying nurse told Suzy and me that we should leave immediately and not come to visit for at least three days, though I could call daily to learn of Mother's progress in adjusting to her new environment. As Suzy and I hurried to the car, both heartsick, Mother's head appeared at her open bedroom window, and she frantically called out, "Suzy! Come and get me!" It was a horrible time, as we were both crying inwardly. Suzy shoved my shoulder, vehemently protesting, "Did you have to do that?"

Both Mel and I felt there was no alternative, unless I was to become a prisoner nurse by bringing his mother into our home and caring for her twenty-four hours a day. I didn't want that, nor did Mel want or expect me to do so. This past year of bearing the brunt of selling Willow Lake, emptying it out completely, and preparing the new home for Mother (where she lived for less than eleven months), plus all the employment problems with her companions, all took a toll on me, and I felt ready for some psychological counseling myself. Now I had one month in which to dispose of Mother's furniture and belongings, which I had so painstakingly planned for her enjoyment in the new apartment. We were lucky that our signed lease was only for one year.

My next-day phone call to Hudson House wasn't too encouraging, as the nurse reported that Mother had cried a good deal and was confused, but the following day's report was on a happier note. It seems that the large, expansive dining room reminded Mother of Willow Lake, and she was bent on removing the patient who was sitting in "her" chair at the head of the table; (that was where Mother sat herself at future meals. On the fourth day, when I came to visit, Mother greeted me with a smile as she proudly showed me around "her" house, and she paused at the large mahogany buffet in the dining room on which were placed sets of china cups and saucers of various patterns, many of which she had owned herself among the seventeen sets of dishes at Willow Lake. She pointed to some of them and said, "Muriel, these will belong to you some day, so why don't you take them now and enjoy them."

The nursing care at Hudson House was exemplary, but in the next year and a half, Mother fell twice and had to be hospitalized for several days until she was well enough to return to the home. After her second hospitalization, I was advised by the home physician that Mother needed more specialized nursing care than they could give her at Hudson House, and we should start our search for a permanent nursing home. *Here we go again,* I thought.

We tried a nursing home in Hyde Park, about twenty miles away, but ultimately, we realized this place was undesirable: Mother fell out of bed there twice and was taken by ambulance to the hospital, where she was X-rayed for fractures (of which there, thankfully, were none), and I found her lying on urine-soaked sheets a few times. My own mother, living in Connecticut, was a frequent visitor to a nursing home in her town, as several of her widowed peers were patients there, and she raved about the warm and wonderful care they received. So Mel and I traveled to Meriden and found the staff to be as interested and caring as my mother had pre-dicted. Yes, the patients were tied into wheelchairs, but it was for their own safety, and there was no odor of urine. The place was a bright and cheer-ful one-story building, with doors and windows that opened onto pretty, flowered walkways and gardens. There was a well-staffed complement of nurses and aides in every wing, and we felt positive that Mother would get the nursing care she needed.

As added incentive, my mother and sister both assured me that they would visit Mel's mother weekly and report to us if any problems arose. Fortunately, this never happened, as her care turned out to be superlative, and I never had any complaints on that score when making the one-and-a-half-hour drive to Meriden to visit with her. At one point, Suzy made the trip to Meriden from California, where she was working on her doctorate in clinical psychology, so that she could visit with Mother. She had written to the director of the home, asking if she would be allowed to stay in an empty room in order to spend as much time as possible with her grand-mother. The amazed director reported to me that in all the years he had been in this business, no child or grandchild of a patient had ever made this unselfish request, and he was happy to grant her wish. She repeated this act of love when my own mother was a patient in the same home a few years later.

Mother soon joined the ranks of those tied in wheelchairs, and after the second year at the home, she stopped talking completely. Mel had made tapes of her favorite music, which he played for her, but she showed no sign of recognition, and she refused to eat the food goodies we brought that she had always enjoyed. She sat in her chair, head back, eyes closed, totally mute, apparently oblivious to our presence, though we never knew for sure if she was aware that we were there. She died of pneumonia at the end of her fifth year in the nursing home. ❧

CHAPTER THIRTY-THREE

WHO IS ARTHUR DIEHL?

I WAS BOMBARDED BY QUESTIONS from the five different auction-eers I was interviewing—"Who is this artist, Arthur Diehl? Is he American or foreign born? Are his paintings on exhibit in any major art museums? Where did your mother-in-law acquire so many of his paintings?"—but I had few answers for them.

Each auctioneer impressed upon me the fact that the more informa-tion he had about the artist and his background, the better price he could command when the contents of Mother's nineteen-room mansion were auctioned off. The financial aspect was paramount in importance when disposing of all furnishings, so I realized that it would behoove me to track down whatever information I could gather about Arthur Diehl.

I couldn't question Mother about the artist for whom she seemed to have an affinity—her disease had claimed her by this point, and she was oblivious to the sale of her home. There were at least fifty of Die-hl's oil paintings, and they were hung in every one of Willow Lake's rooms, including the master bath and maid's room. They were in elab-orate gilt frames and were of every shape and size, ranging from twelve-by-sixteen-inch portrait-size paintings to huge paintings, four to five feet in diameter.

About forty of the paintings were scenes of Venice: the Grand Canal with gondoliers, the Piazza San Marco, orange-tile-roofed buildings, Moor-ish-looking arches, flower markets, and young peasant girls carrying water jugs or flower baskets. There was one partially draped female nude that had been in the master bath (for modesty's sake)—it found a home with our daughter—and several scenes of beaches peppered with well-dressed bathers, apparently from an earlier era. There was only one of the large paintings that I liked well enough to not relinquish to the auctioneers; it now adorns one of our living room walls.

This was a peaceful Turneresque seaside scene featuring fishing boats, with distant windmills barely visible through the early-morning mist.

My antipathy to most of the paintings lay in the fact that every household in Mel's family, on both his father's and mother's sides, displayed the identical scenes on their walls—the tile roofs, Grand Canal, Moorish archways, etc. The only difference was that the paintings in the homes on his mother's side of the family were signed by Arthur V. Diehl, and those on his father's side were signed by Bert, Mel's aunt, who was a student at Yale School of Art. Family lore tells that Aunt Bert honed her art skills by copying directly from Diehl, who had set up a stand for selling his paintings on or near the grounds of the art school. Apparently, his prices were very moderate, as Mel's mother and her sister, who both appreciated bargains, bought up his stock by the dozens. Aunt Bert painted prodigiously and gave gifts of her paintings to her four siblings and parents; hence, every household had the same scenes on their walls. On visiting their homes, I would have a sense of déjà vu, and viewing the constant repetition of art in each home was monotonous and distasteful for me.

To the unschooled eye, the paintings were "pretty," evocative of past eras, peaceful in content, and colorful, but were they good art? Beauty is supposedly in the eye of the beholder, but I didn't know how to respond to the auctioneer who complained, "His brush strokes are too short, which means he was in a hurry, so he can't be an artist of any repute."

Not being an art connoisseur, I only knew that I wanted none of these paintings (other than the single Turneresque seascape) adorning our walls. We had enough paintings of our own without joining the family circus.

To satisfy the auctioneers' queries about the artist, I began contacting art associations, libraries, and museums throughout the United States, but my search was fruitless—I either received a negative response or no response at all. Then I moved on to contacting our embassies in the European capitals, again with no results. I came to the conclusion that this was a lost cause; no one in the art world seemed to know of an Arthur V. Diehl.

Before the auction took place, I removed eight of the paintings to Mother's new downsized apartment. In a rush to get her settled in, I was grateful when friends volunteered to help with moving Mother's things while I was busy elsewhere. I later called to thank them for their efforts, and that was when one of the volunteers, Doris, asked, "Where in the world did Mel's mother get so many Arthur Diehl paintings?"

"In New Haven, I guess," I replied, "where her sister lives. Why do you ask?"

"Oh, my sister was engaged to his son at one time," she answered, "when he was going to Yale."

I couldn't have been more shocked if I'd been hit by a lightning bolt. For months I had been searching halfway around the world for someone who knew something, no matter how little, about this artist, and the answer was found in my own backyard. Pumping Doris for more information, I learned that the artist had been born in London but had lived in the United States for years and had died on Cape Cod many years ago. She and her sister had been invited to tea by Arthur Diehl's widow, who was then living in New York City.

To complete the picture of Arthur Diehl for my own curiosity—the auction was over before I learned this information—I wrote to the Yale Alumni Association, asking for the address of the son, and my request was forwarded directly to him. Soon after, I received a very pleasant and detailed letter from Arthur's son about his father's final years, spent painting daily on the beach at Sandwich, Massachusetts. He had become such a well-known figure to the townspeople who clustered around his easel that when he died, a wing of the Sandwich Museum was dedicated to Arthur Diehl and housed dozens of his paintings.

Some thirty years later, with the advent of the Internet and search engines, I eventually learned that Arthur Diehl, who was born in 1870, was a multitalented person; he also was a poet, singer, actor, and music director at various times in his life. He arrived in Provincetown, Massachusetts, in 1912, with his third wife, and he summered on the Cape until his death in 1929. According to Artist Archives of the Provincetown Art Association and Museum, "he painted swiftly under the gaze of many onlookers, keeping up a stream of comment, able to produce up to twenty-five paintings in a day, selling them directly and never to dealers, and always indifferent to price and artistic reputation."

Belatedly, all the auctioneers' questions were answered. &

CHAPTER THIRTY-FOUR

THE ENIGMA NAMED EVELYN

I WAS ON THE PHONE with the New York State Employment Agency and not getting too much help.

"I'm really sorry, Mrs. E., that I can't help you out. I only have one person available for three days a week."

"I'll take that one person," I begged. "I'm desperate. I have to fill in for my husband's office manager who is in surgery right now, and it will be weeks before she returns to work. I need someone to do the housekeeping and also be here when the kids get off the school bus. So what's wrong with that one person you have?"

I could almost see the agency secretary squirming uneasily in her seat as she searched for words. "Well, there's really nothing wrong with her. She's honest and her cleaning is impeccable from all reports."

"So?" I demanded.

"I've sent her out on three jobs this past month," sighed the secretary, "and she left each job after one week saying she didn't like the people or the job. I'd hate to stick you with her and then have her leave after one week when you won't be free to break in someone new."

"I'm willing to take the chance," I said, "as I told you, I'm desperate!"

We must have passed muster, because Evelyn came to work and stayed for twenty-eight years. If it hadn't been for heart problems when she was sixty-eight years old, she would have stayed longer.

There was nothing particularly spectacular or revelatory about my first meeting with Evelyn. She appeared at our front door at the designated time, bundled up against the frigid winter weather in a worn but clean quilted beige parka. A green knitted hat covered her head and ears, leaving her white-skinned, expressionless, Miss Piggy-like face exposed. She didn't exactly erupt with information about herself—that took the first ten years—but on this visit she did say that yes, she was a widow with ten kids, ranging in age from six to twenty years old; and no, she didn't like the three previous jobs she was sent on; and yes, she did like doing housework, period.

Evelyn was all business, here to work and not talk. And clean—she did that with a vengeance! The house was spotless when she left each day, and she turned out to be the best housekeeper I ever would have. In time, our home became "her home," and I tracked garden mud on "her floors," and the three tiers of plants in front of the dining room window became "her plants" (she talked to them as she watered them). I often gave her cuttings from the plants, which she treasured, and once, about twenty years later, when my purple passion plant died, probably from old age, Evelyn brought me a replacement cutting from the original one I had given her.

I learned a few more facts about Evelyn over the years as we lunched together at the kitchen counter, once she knew me well enough to confide that her deceased husband had been a handsome alcoholic with a vicious temper and could never hold a job. During the drunken binges he would beat her and the kids, and these beatings caused her to have several miscarriages, which she admitted "was just as well because I didn't know how to turn off the pregnancies, and it was a real relief when he died."

Ten years after his death, though, when she and the kids had saved up enough money to purchase a fitting memorial, he became almost sanctified in her mind. I was shown a photo of the gravestone, with Evelyn squatting next to it, with a most sorrowful expression on her face, and one arm cradling the stone protectively. The inscription read: "Here lies Dennis G., beloved husband of Evelyn," and under that were three sloping lines of names reading:

"Loving father to James, Charles, Bridget, Mary, William, Ellen, Dorothy, Al—."

"It's a beautiful stone, Evelyn," I marveled, "but why didn't they finish writing Albert's name, and what about the other two kids whose names are missing?"

"They ran outta space," was her reply, "and they woulda charged me more to put them on the back, so this is good enough."

Evelyn's passion for cleaning was surpassed only by her honesty, in word and deed. Every dollar bill or coin found in the washing machine or under the living room seat cushions was duly deposited on the kitchen counter, down to the lowliest penny. "I ain't so poor that I take what don't belong to me," she would declare righteously. Many of her truthful utterances have lived on in our family over the decades, particularly one she made as I was packing our suitcase. "Where yez all goin'?" she inquired.

"To Boston," I replied, "for my nursing-class reunion. Look, Evelyn, here's a photo of me as a student nurse in my apron and bib—that was thirty-six years ago."

Evelyn studied the photo for a while, and as she handed it back to me, she sighed and uttered what became a classic, unforgettable phrase: "Ain't it awful what time does to a person?" This unvarnished comment was passed around through the family so often that, even now, instead of greeting each other after long absences with the trite (and untruthful) "You haven't changed a bit," we just grin and say, "Ain't it awful?"

I learned, in time, to understand Evelyn's unique vocabulary. I kept hearing about the "flint" on the clean clothes before I realized she was talking about lint. Her favorite department store was Kreejis—Kreejis carried the best line of everything. When I tried to pinpoint the location of Kreejis and heard that it was across from Woolworth, then—ah, yes! How could I have been so stupid? Of course, it was Kresge.

Evelyn's unemotional facade applied only to the humans in our family; she truly adored our black Labrador retriever, named Goniff (meaning *thief*). Goniff retrieved all the neighborhood garbage, which he buried in my flower gardens, and each spring my trowel would unearth empty cans, ham and beef bones, foil packages of cigarette butts, etc. Whenever we were away from home for vacations or business meetings, Evelyn would move in to keep Goniff company, but we always felt *he* kept *her* company, because she would croon lovingly to him as she watched TV and always dropped him tidbits of whatever she was eating. She warned me frequently that Goniff was her real reason for continuing to work, now that her kids had jobs. "And when he dies," she said, "I ain't comin' to work no more." She actually did quit work when Goniff died at the age of seventeen, but she called three weeks later to ask if she could come back, as she missed the house. And the house missed her!

The day after one of her dog-sitting sessions, I answered the front doorbell to find a uniformed state trooper. I was surprised when he asked about the condition of the house and grounds upon our return home. "Everything was fine, as always," I replied. "Why?"

"Well," he replied, almost ready to burst into laughter, "it seems that your housekeeper had a family party while you were gone, and one of the grandchildren pushed the panic button on the security system. When the two fire engines and two police cars answered the call, there were about forty people all over the place—playing baseball on the back lawn; a bunch of them raising hell in the pool; some of them cooking on the grills—they sure were having a ball. I just thought I'd let you know so you can tape up the panic button if she has any more parties the next time you go away."

On Evelyn's next work day, I casually mentioned the visit from the state trooper, ending with, "I hope all your family had a good time."

"Oh, yeah," she enthused. "We had a family party, just like the one you have every year, and all the kids and their friends and the grandchildren was here, and they had such a good time. I kinda forgot to tell you about it, but I knew you'd be glad Goniff had kids to play with, and he got real good exercise, chasing the baseball." Anything for Goniff. And except for scuffed up areas on the grass from the baseball game and the trash can overflowing with beer and Coca-Cola cans, there was no evidence of the mob scene a couple of days previously.

Over the years, Evelyn's appearance remained constant. She wore the same style of clothing she had always worn: simple cotton housedresses in the summer and polyester slacks in the winter. Her pale face never wore makeup, and she kept the same short-cut, straw-colored hair, parted on the side, with the longer strands held in place by a black metal bobby pin. It came as a shock to me when I realized, in about Evelyn's twenty-sixth year with us, that she was actually wearing lipstick and rouge, and her work clothes were much dressier and more stylish. These changes occurred about the time I had arranged for her to clean house for an eighty-five-year-old widower, whose wife had died the previous year; their fourteen-room Victorian house was begging for Evelyn's loving care.

She kept me appraised as to the neglect the house had suffered. And she also mentioned, "Between you and me, he's still a good lookin' man for his age. I seen the pitcher of his wife in her bedroom, and she sure wasn't no beauty." Once she started working for Mr. M. (she couldn't pronounce his "long Eye-talian name"), Evelyn talked more in a few months than she had in all the previous years she had worked for us. Not surprisingly, Mr. M. soon became Mr. Joe, and she would relate in great detail just how Mr. Joe had held the ladder for her when she took down the kitchen curtains for an overdue laundering. And when Mr. Joe drove her to the bus stop on a stormy day, she was all smiles as she related how he held the door for her; smiles were very rare for Evelyn.

Then the questions started coming. Did I think Mr. Joe was dating any women? Did I think Mr. Joe would get married again? Did he like blondes, brunettes or redheads? I pleaded ignorance to all her questions, but I did give her my color preference when she brought three wigs to show me. They were all the same style, a tight-fitting cap of Shirley Temple-type ringlets and in colors of brassy red, peroxide blonde, and jet black. Frankly, I preferred her natural straw-colored short hairdo but didn't dare shatter her illusions about her self-perceived glamour. She changed her wigs with the days of the week: red for Monday, blonde for Wednesday, and black for Friday. I don't remember her ever telling me which color Mr. Joe preferred.

Mr. Joe made trips twice monthly to Charlotte, North Carolina, to visit with an old army buddy, and he gave Evelyn the keys to his home so that she could come in and clean in his absence. To her, this action was tantamount to a declaration of romantic intentions, and he was promoted from Mr. Joe to just Joe. Then, when Evelyn informed me that she had told her kids that she would probably be living in Joe's home very soon, I felt I had better alert Joe to Evelyn's intentions.

The poor guy was horrified—he had been completely oblivious to her misinterpretation of any of his actions and had always been the epitome of chivalry. A relationship with Evelyn was the farthest thing from his mind—at the time, Joe was actively involved in rekindling a World War II romance with an army nurse, which had started in New Guinea about fifty-five years ago. Who suspected that the "old army buddy" he went to visit in North Carolina was a female?

Whether Evelyn's fixation on Joe was the catalyst, I'll never know, but two weeks later, Joe appeared at our poolside, proudly escorting his eighty-year-old, petite, white-haired, wrinkled bride, Nadine. Nadine had it all. She was charming, poised, outgoing, and warm, with a marvelous sense of humor. She played several different musical instruments and had a lovely singing voice. She also held two PhDs—one in nursing and one in music—and had many books published in her tenure as nursing administrator. She wasn't too proud, either, to wear a twenty-year-old bathing suit held together by safety pins that had belonged to Joe's former wife, who'd been built like an Amazon.

We were delighted in the happiness radiating from the faces of the newlyweds, but I was concerned for Evelyn and how she could save face with her family, to whom she had already announced her marriage plans. I mentioned my concern to Joe, who had already considered the least painful way out for her. His plan was to tell her that he was putting the house on the market and moving to North Carolina to take care of his army buddy. All true.

Evelyn's disappointment was obvious when she informed me, a few days later, that she wouldn't be working for Joe anymore, as he was moving to take care of his old army friend. "I would expect him to do something nice like that—he's just that kinda guy," she observed, and I agreed with her.

Despite the termination of the Joe affair, Evelyn continued to wear her wigs: red for Monday, blonde for Wednesday, and black for Friday. And when a heart attack ended her life two years later, the blonde wig was the headpiece of choice for her burial. With her head cushioned on a pillow of pale blue satin and wearing a party dress of white lace (probably purchased for a wedding that never was to be), Evelyn looked, in death, the way she had aspired to look for Joe: glamorous. ❧

CHAPTER THIRTY-FIVE

RETRIBUTION

THE INVITATION WAS BEAUTIFUL, with the outline of the city of Jerusalem imprinted in gold and soft pastel colors. It was thrilling for Mel and me to receive this invitation to the long-anticipated bar mitzvah of our oldest grandson, Morgan Engelman O'Reilly, but it was also very disquieting for me. For forty years, the mere mention of the words "bar mitzvah" set off a chain reaction of painful memories I'd wanted to forget—but never will.

It started off so perfectly, a gorgeous day in May, with 135 friends and family members in attendance, to help celebrate the bar mitzvah of our son, Corky. We beamed with pride as Corky went through all the ritual of this occasion with an ease, knowledge, and aplomb derived from four years of study that truly imbued him with the spirit of his heritage and faith.

Following the ceremony, the cocktail hour, with its sinful hors d'oeuvres, and then a seven-course dinner were pronounced by all to be a gastronomic success. As Mel and I went from table to table to greet each guest personally, we basked in the praise heaped upon our son for his inspiring performance, and we felt that the long hours of planning for this milestone had paid off.

Out-of-town guests, who were staying at hotels for the weekend, had been invited back to our home at night for an informal catered meal of cold cuts and salads, so we could have a chance to relax and really visit with each person. Those who were returning to their respective cities at the conclusion of the bar mitzvah dinner were asked to stop by the house for a cold drink and fruit en route home, and many were happy to do so. It had been such a satisfying, uplifting day, that people were loathe to leave the party atmosphere.

At this point, the nightmare event occurred.

People were milling around our house and grounds, checking out the gardens and flowering shrubs, which were all in bloom at this particular season, and enjoying the cold drinks and fruit the caterer had prepared earlier. I was joyously rehashing the day with a cousin when Mel approached me with a sense of urgency. "You'd better come in the house and see what's going on—you're not going to have any food left for the company who are coming tonight."

I rushed indoors and saw, to my consternation, that the caterer had left trays of cold cuts, breads, salads, and deserts on the dining room table and buffet. This wouldn't have been so terrible, but many of the guests, who had just consumed pounds of hors d'oeuvres and a seven-course dinner not more than an hour ago, were now making corned beef and pastrami sandwiches to fortify themselves for their trips home.

Mel was right; there wouldn't be enough food for the guests that night. My six foot four Uncle Dolph (who gave the most generous of checks) was about to spear some corned beef for "a bite for the road" when Mel snatched the huge tray of meats and made his way down to the cellar with it. I still can see Uncle Dolph, standing at the dining room table, looking bewildered, one hand holding a plate with one slice of rye bread, and the other hand holding an empty serving fork. "W-w-what happened?" stammered Uncle Dolph. Out of the corner of my eye, I could see Mel deftly removing the rest of the food platters, and I just wanted to sink through the floor in embarrassment. I tried to explain to my uncle that the food was for company coming that evening, but he wasn't listening. He put down his plate and called to his wife, "Come on, Roselle, we're going."

I fled to our bedroom, locked the door, and paced the floor in agitation. I was filled with a sense of humiliation that I hope to never experience again. I reviewed the events of the day and thought that this was retribution for being so proud, so secure in the knowledge that we did everything right. It took me a good half hour to settle down enough to come out and face the rest of the guests, who, fortunately for me, were leaving. I smiled and accepted their words of praise for Corky's wonderful performance, the marvelous meal, and the day in general, but their words were just a meaningless mumble to me, for my head was in a whirl and nothing penetrated.

Mel was able to replenish some of the missing cold cuts from a local food store—not as good as the caterer's, but they filled up the blank spaces on the trays. The evening guests, unaware of the calamitous happenings a few hours earlier, mingled, visited, and ate, but I was still in a daze, talking and smiling but my mind was a blank.

Uncle Dolph is long gone, but whenever I hear the words "bar mitzvah," he becomes very much alive for me, still trying to spear some corned beef that wasn't there. ❧

CHAPTER THIRTY-SIX

STOP THE CLOCK

AT THE AGE OF EIGHT OR NINE, I was a dedicated reader of the obituary page. It was fascinating to learn the ages of the deceased and categorize them mentally:

Newborn to age twenty—too young to die.

Ages twenty to forty—they've lived half of their lives.

Ages forty to sixty—old enough to die.

Over sixty—should have died already.

Thoughts of dying and being buried deep in the ground terrorized me as a child, and for years my nightly prayers beseeched God to let me live forever. As I matured, I gradually adjusted the categories to keep in step with my advancing years. For me, at this point in time, there is only one category: too young to die.

On my mother's fiftieth birthday, I posed this question to her: "Mom, now that your life is more than half over, if it was in your power, would you like to go back in time and not get any older?"

Her reply resounding. "No, not at all! I've enjoyed every year and look forward to what next year will bring."

On every five-year milestone birthday, I repeated this question to her and always received the same response. On her eightieth birthday, the reply to my question was different. "No, I would not go back one single year," she said, "but I'd just like to stop the clock; it's going too fast."

This was the philosophy of a woman, widowed at thirty-eight, with three young kids to bring up and no money in the till. She turned her sewing accomplishments into an alteration business that eventually became a specialty dress business. By the time she retired at eighty-five, her clients came from all over Connecticut. They came, not only for the quality and style of the garments she carried but also for her salesmanship—or lack of it—because she was truthful.

She would tell a customer, "You can't wear that dress; it accentuates your hips," or "That color is not good on you; your skin is too sallow," or "You are too short-waisted to wear this style of dress." She was blunt, all right, but her customers knew she spoke the truth, though it hurt. I grew up with the pronouncement, as she fitted a dress to me, "Muriel, you have a figure like an old gnarled apple tree." And she was right—I was short-waisted with a big belly, big busted with small shoulders, and no hips or behind. Every dress I wore required extensive alterations.

The clock finally stopped at age ninety-six, when she had been bedridden for a year in a nursing home and needed to be fed and diapered. When I would come to visit, she'd say, "Muriel, what am I hanging around for? I've had a good life and done everything I wanted to do, and I'm ready to go. Can't you give me a pill so I can get it done and over with?"

She was aware also that her mind was wandering, for she would have occasional lapses of living in the past and then would apologize for it. When she finally did die from the usual age-related pneumonia, I didn't grieve because I was glad for her—glad that this undignified existence, with no quality to it whatsoever, was finished.

My mother's voice echoes in my mind as I celebrate each birthday. I wouldn't want to go back and redo any years, and it will be interesting to see what next year brings, but I, too, would like to stop the clock. It *is* going too fast. ❧

CHAPTER THIRTY-SEVEN

ROSES AND ASHES

THE CLIMBING ROSE BUSH my grandmother planted seventy-five years ago produced the most delicately scented blossoms of the palest pink velvet-like texture. In no time at all, the porch trellis that supported and guided the groping branches was completely filled with dark green, shiny leaves and clusters of full-blown roses and buds just starting to unfold.

Every June, when the roses were their most prolific, my sister, Ruth, and I would present a large bouquet of these roses to our teachers on the last day of school. This was an annual ritual that I anticipated as much as it's being the last day of the school year, and I would blush happily as the teacher exclaimed over the beauty and fragrance of the roses.

When we moved into our new home, my grandmother presented my mother with a cutting from her rose bush. "Marion," she said, "I want you to plant this cutting of my rose bush so you can enjoy your own as much as we have all enjoyed mine, and you will think of me."

This little twig rooted quickly and in a few short years became as prolific as its forebear, and like my grandmother's, our porch trellis was completely covered, and the vines entwined themselves still farther along the porch railings. When we sat on the porch in the summer, our view of the street was almost obliterated by the prickly overgrowth of the ever-seeking and ever-expanding branches.

Years later, when Mel and I built our home, my mother came to visit, bearing her gift of Grandma's climbing rose cuttings. Of course, these cuttings flourished like their predecessors, and each spring as I pruned and fertilized, I looked forward to the coming weeks when my labors would be blessed with a profusion of those gorgeous pink blooms.

After the first buds appeared, then it was a running battle between me and the Japanese beetles, and it was imperative that I be victorious in time for the Family Party.

Mel and I hosted the Family Party every summer, and it was a matter of my reputation as a gardener that was at stake. My aunts, uncles, and mother always gravitated toward the rose garden to discuss the merits of my roses, as compared to Grandma's, and they would reminisce about childhood events and Grandma herself, long deceased.

A good twenty years before Mother died, she informed me of her burial wishes. "I want my ashes to be buried under Grandma's roses. Each year, when the family is here, I would like you all to share a drink with me, so I can be with you in spirit. I just want my usual one shot of Canadian Club on two rocks. Remember, Muriel, no more than two rocks."

It is now eight years since Mom's ashes were strewn under the roses, and as I work in that area, I'll praise her. "Hey, Mom, we're loaded with flowers this year. You're doing great!" Or sometimes, it's "Mom, you're slacking off! The beetles are getting ahead of us."

On the day of the Family Party, weather permitting, during the late-afternoon poolside activities, one of the cousins will invariably ask, "When are we going to give Aunt Marion her drink?" That let's me know it's time, so I pour one shot of Canadian Club over two rocks, and we all make our way to the rose garden, carrying our own drinks. With family members fanned out around the rose-covered trellis, I pour Mom's drink around its base. "Here you are, Mom. I know you're thirsty."

We drain our glasses and then read in unison a lovely poem entitled "We Remember You," recalling not only my mother but the memories of all the other departed family members. It is a joyous occasion, and we linger around the roses, dredging up oft-repeated family stories. I know each year that Mom enjoys our visit and her drink, and perhaps the Canadian Club will encourage the Japanese beetles to alight elsewhere.

Mom's presence isn't felt in our yard alone, because when she died, my sister Ruth said, "I'd like some of Mother's ashes to put under Grandma's roses in my garden." Then, my brother, Art, requested his share of the ashes to be buried in the cemetery plot next to our father, who had been waiting for her all those years. It is good that Mom had no more than three kids, or we might have run out of ashes. ❧

CHAPTER THIRTY-EIGHT

THE SKIER

I SHOULD HAVE HAD A PRENUPTIAL AGREEMENT to the effect that it is not the duty of a wife to learn to ski, but I was naïve and unschooled in the ways of husbands—especially the part where they pounce upon wives, shortly after the wedding, with the unexpected pronouncement: "You really have to learn to ski." Who could foretell that two pieces of wood called skis could indirectly impact the rest of my life?

Mel came into our union with the fully developed skills of an expert tennis player, swimmer, and skier, which I accepted, even though I didn't expect these attributes to affect me in any way. Little did I know! I had always been a klutz when it came to sports; in school, I was the last to be chosen for the dodge ball or basketball teams. It was enough that I could ride a two-wheel bike, even no hands sometimes; execute a wobbly fifteen-foot-long span on ice skates; perform a glorified dog paddle at the beach; and roller skate. But now, he wanted me to ski.

In short order I was being measured for skis and pole, boots, mittens, and ski outfit. I was part of that elite group that traveled hours over snow and ice-packed roads to ski resorts, where I would have preferred drinking hot chocolate before an open fire in a ski lodge to traveling down the slopes. Instead, I was subjected to spending frigid hours outdoors in a beginners ski class that mostly comprised five-year-olds.

As I feared, skiing did not come easily to me, and when the five-year-olds went on to a more advanced class, I remained where I was. I couldn't learn to snowplow, the basic rudiment in skiing. To snowplow, one's ski tips had to be angled inward to control the speed generated by skis being parallel, a feat I could never master. When I gained too much momentum, I would panic, plop myself down, and slide to the bottom of the slope on my rear end.

This charade of beginner's classes went on for eight years, in ski areas in New York, Massachusetts, and Vermont, where I was the longest reigning beginning skier on record. Mel would purchase the embroidered emblems from each ski resort we frequented, which I dutifully sewed on to the sleeves of my ski jacket. This created the erroneous impression that I was a real pro, having skied the well-known slopes, but that was only until they saw me maneuvering on skis.

One winter's expedition was to Big Bromley in Vermont, where the sixteen-below-zero temperature saw me bundled up in so many clothes that when I fell down—which was often—it took a half half-hour before I could get back up on my skis. While floundering in the snow, cold, exhausted, and disgusted, the tempting thought crossed my mind that if I broke a leg, that would solve my problems, and Mel would leave me alone with this skiing business. I really hit my low point that weekend. Not to say that I didn't enjoy the camaraderie of our friends on these excursions and the après-ski cocktail parties—that was fun—but skiing, I could live without it.

Shortly after my low-point weekend, while on a one-day ski trip two hours from home, the unexpected, yet long-delayed miracle occurred. Atop the beginners ski slope with the five-year-olds, my skis pointing down-ward, the instructor gave me a shove, and I went sailing down the slope to the accompaniment of his yelling, "Snowplow! Snowplow!" And suddenly, my feet did what they hadn't been able to do for eight years—and I was controlling my speed. I reached the bottom of the slope on my feet for the very first time, thrilled and exhilarated, eager to do a repeat performance, which I did, again and again. From that point on, I was emancipated; I was the one to initiate every ski trip, and now that I could control my speed, I was eager to accompany Mel down the expert trails.

The honeymoon didn't last long, though, for while following Mel one sunny, cold day on top of Killington Mountain in Vermont, I became over-confident and inadvertently made the mistake of crossing my skis in deep snow. I recall a wrenching of my right knee and then lying flat on my back, unable to move and minus my skis, which were sliding down the mountain without me. Mel appeared shortly after that, and then, other skiers, who volunteered to ski down to notify the ski patrol to send help. Lying there in the snow, I was in no pain, just conscious that my shirt and underwear were pulled out of my pants and that the snow was wet and cold on my back, which was overstimulating my bladder. That full bladder was the worst discomfort I suffered during the toboggan trip down the mountain and on the ambulance ride to the hospital. Arriving at the emergency room (where I was given a bedpan), I noticed at least a dozen pairs of ski boots lined up at the doorway, so apparently I was in good company.

X-rays revealed no fractures, though my knee ligaments were torn, necessitating an ankle-to-buttock plaster walking cast, to be worn for six weeks. Mel and our two kids, who were with us, took this dictate with the thinking that this finished my skiing for this winter. It not only finished my skiing for the remainder of that winter but all future winters, though we didn't realize it at the time.

Two months later, after my cast was removed and my dried with-ered-looking leg was starting to rejuvenate, my knee was checked by a widely known orthopedist in New York, a doctor for whom I had worked when I was single. His practice included many luminaries from stage, screen, and TV, and I knew from my working days in that office that this physician was infallible. His final prognosis for me was that I would not be skiing again; my knee joint would become arthritic; the patella would eventually need to be removed; and I would end up walking with a limp. To my way of thinking, there were lots worse things than having a gimpy leg, but it bothered Mel. To compensate for the anticipated disability, and while I could still walk normally, he told me to make plans for a six-week trip to Europe to visit family, friends, and old haunts from my wartime years, going and returning on the S.S. *France.*

It was a dream come true; every minute of every day was thrilling and exciting and only the precursor of many more trips to follow: to Europe, Asia, Central and South America, and the Middle East, as well as many places in the United States. I'd had a taste of travel and was now insatia-ble. My life was a constant study of travel books, maps, and brochures. I could just taste the places I read about. Already fluent in French, I learned to speak Italian and Spanish and took History of Art courses so we could understand the works of art and architecture we encountered in our travels.

I even conducted art classes with our kids and Mel every Sunday night for six months prior to our taking the kids to Europe. They griped the whole six months but once confronted with the works of art we had studied, they were belatedly grateful. There are still so many places on my "Must See" list that we have not yet visited; so we just have to live long enough to do so.

I *had* to learn to ski, but from the resultant promised disability was sown the seeds of our interest and love for travel, which dominated the rest of our lives. Fifty years after the fact, I am still waiting for my knee to become arthritic, have my patella removed, and walk with a limp. Here's to more infallible doctors! 🐚

Après-ski cocktail party, with daughter Suzy autographing Muriel's cast.

CHAPTER THIRTY-NINE

THE USER

HERB'S PHONE CALL opened a can of worms that I was unprepared to deal with, unleashing a chain of memories never before fathomed. Sarah's husband had invited us to a surprise sixtieth birthday party for her, and as part of the evening's entertainment, Herb asked me to relate some of the experiences Sarah and I shared during our three years in the Army Nurse Corps in World War II.

She was a good fifteen years older than I, a new young graduate nurse. I stood in awe of her skills as a top-notch psychiatric nurse and as a worldly, well-read individual who could discourse on any subject. We all appreciated her sense of humor, as she was a great raconteur of Morris and Becky jokes, told with a Yiddish accent that was even funnier than the joke itself. Her wit could be caustic, too, leaving one with the sensation of having been stung by an unseen assailant.

Physically, Sarah did not have a Miss America build—she was short and squat, with a big bosom and thick torso set on two widely spaced legs. When she walked, she lumbered along, resembling a small tank in slow motion. Though her body was not physically attractive, she was lucky to have a full head of wavy, short blonde hair and pretty green eyes, which helped compensate for her thin-lipped mouth and overly plump cheeks.

Sarah was like my second skin. Her last name was only two initials away from mine, alphabetically, and in the army, every phase of your life—eating, sleeping, drilling, traveling—was related to where your last name was located in the alphabet. The only instance where this rule did not apply was in the practical application of our nursing skills, when we were assigned to areas of the hospital commensurate with our ability or experience in that field.

Researching my memory bank for episodes to relate, I was shocked to discover that now, in my maturity, the pictures that I mentally recalled were of a person far different from the Sarah I had genuinely liked and admired then. I recalled the fifteen-mile hikes we took at Fort Devens while preparing for overseas duty. Of the one hundred females participating, the only one to return in the ambulance stationed at the halfway mark was Sarah. She always had a blister.

I recalled crossing the Atlantic in December of '43, when eight of us were assigned to an eight-by-ten-foot stateroom, lined on two and three walls with three tiers of cots. Alphabetically, Sarah should have had one of the uppermost cots, but she edged me out of my lower cot with her rationalization: "You're younger than I am and heights make me dizzy."

I recalled landing at the staging area in England, where we were housed in those frigid, dark Quonset huts—the ones heated by the coke-burning stoves that threw very little heat. Still, they had to be fed during the night at specified hours, and Sarah always slept through her shift. It was because of her that we'd awaken to ice-covered wash water in our steel helmets. Her alarm clock never worked.

I recalled the dressing table and stool I constructed from three orange crates for our cement-block hut at our hospital site in North Wales. And guess who usurped my dressing table most of the time? When I'd remonstrate with her that I wanted to use *my* dressing table to comb *my* hair, she would glare at me and sputter, "For God's sake, one would think you had the crown jewels stashed away in your precious table. Have patience; I'm almost finished."

I recalled crossing the English Channel after D-Day, the trip that took four days due to the sunken ships blocking the Channel. This was the trip where the staterooms were infested with bedbugs, so we slept up on deck for three nights. But where was Sarah? Sleeping in sick bay, of course, on a cot bed. She'd developed a sudden cold.

I recalled the seven weeks we lived in tents in the Normandy cow pasture, where we had a rigid regime of baseball and softball games as well as daily calisthenics and drilling twice a day to keep us occupied. And where was Sarah while we drilled and did calisthenics in the hot sun? Playing poker with the medical officers in their adjacent cow pasture. I should have been so smart.

I must acknowledge, though, that we were all glad of Sarah's company in our long tents of thirty women at night. Once darkness fell, a complete blackout had to be observed, as Kraut planes, called "Bedcheck Charlie," flew over each night, and there was nothing else to do but take to our cots. On the one night each week designated as "Dirty Night," Sarah would again regale us with her delightful Morris and Becky Yiddish jokes as would others who had jokes to contribute at this time. It helped break the monotony of our long evenings.

I recalled the three days and nights on the crowded troop train, going from Paris to Liège, Belgium. We sat two abreast in a seat, with our gear piled around us, getting up only when nature called or to stretch our legs every few hours. At night, while trying to sleep in our sitting positions, some of us were exhausted enough to try stretching out in the aisle but gave it up almost immediately when we realized we were obstructing traffic. Sarah had a bad back, though, so there she was, stretched out full-body length, unconcerned that she was blocking the aisle for anyone who had to use the facilities.

I recalled how stressed out we all were during the Battle of the Bulge, from weeks of working around the clock in our tent hospital, being hit by buzz bombs, and fearing imminent capture. Several of the medical contingent of enlisted men and two medical officers cracked up under the constant strain and had to be evacuated to hospitals back in France. It was understandable, and we felt the utmost compassion for those who had to leave the outfit under those conditions. But when Sarah feigned symptoms of battle fatigue, no one was surprised—she was the only nurse to desert. Three months later, she surfaced back in Reims, France, running the R&R center for nurses in a lovely chateau in the heart of the city, with a cadre of French men and women to maintain the premises and cook. Our hospital unit had moved back to France when the war in Europe was over, so I had many encounters with Sarah on our overnight passes to Reims. Sarah enjoyed displaying her own suite of rooms and invited us to share one of the gourmet meals she consumed three times a day. Now, she resembled a full-size tank, still in slow motion. I'm not an authority on brothels, but her life there reminded me of a madam enjoying her harem of women.

These are my memories of Sarah, resurrected at her husband's request for her surprise birthday party. I can only conclude that she was devious and a user. Applying one of her tricks, I suddenly developed a severe back condition that precluded us from attending her party. ❧

CHAPTER FORTY

YA WIN SOME, YA LOSE SOME

We did not *need* a second dog in our household. I did not *want* a second dog. But we got a second dog—a three-month-old black-and-tan Doberman Pinscher with cropped tail and ears, which were still taped in a stand-up position.

If we hadn't attended the annual Westminster Dog Show and if we hadn't descended to the lower level to "just look" at the different breeds of dogs, the next five years of my life would have been a lot more peaceful. But who could foretell then? All I know is that it was unanimous for the four of us when this frisky pup wagged the stump of his tail and jumped up in happy recognition of his future family as we approached him and his drowsy siblings.

Once the business transactions were completed and instructions given for picking him up at his Long Island kennel the following week, we headed for home. Our heads were abuzz with strange dog terminology, and we were given a sheaf of papers to study and forms to fill out and send to the American Kennel Club, known as the AKC. This was nothing like purchasing Suzy's dog, Cindy, a black-and-white Springer Spaniel from the SPCA, where we made a contribution, got a list of her shots, and that was it.

It seems that we inadvertently purchased into Doberman royalty, as this newest pup of ours had a grandfather who was the greatest living Doberman ever, Champion Rancho Dobe's Storm, and his father, another great among dog annals, Champion Top Skipper. These names meant nothing to us; we just wanted a household pet, but now we had to submit our own genealogy to the AKC to demonstrate our fitness as his owners. As befitting such an illustrious family, we had to come up with a suitable name for this newcomer, and he was duly registered with the AKC as

Skipper's Caesar of Dutchess—Skipper after his father, Caesar to designate power, and Dutchess for our home county.

Despite Caesar's elegant lineage and the Doberman reputation for intelligence, it hurts me to admit that Caesar was dumb. We could never break him of the habit of chewing drapes, dust ruffles, and bedspreads; the brass bureau drawer handles turned green, bearing permanent evidence of Caesar lifting his leg on the furniture; the paint on front and back doors was gouged and peeling because he scratched instead of barking when he wanted to go out; and I didn't have an uninterrupted night's sleep from the day we brought him into our home.

We had constructed a lovely bedroom under the cellar stairs for him, complete with a wire-mesh window, rubber tile floor, electric light, and a thick Land's End cushion bed filled with redwood shavings, conducive to good sleep. Each night, however, between 1:00 and 2:00 a.m., Caesar would awaken and give a few gentle yips, which then graduated to a series of sharp staccato barks that brought me stumbling, half asleep, down the stairs to let him out. There was no alternative, unless I enjoyed cleaning up a mess the next morning, which I did not. So I would let him out the back door and sit at the kitchen counter, my head resting on my arms, craving sleep, waiting for this stupid dog to get tired of his backyard meanderings and come in, usually an hour or more later.

Oh, Caesar was loveable all right. He thought he was a lap dog and would snuggle up to us in a chair and poke our elbows with his nose to be continually petted. The watchdog tendencies Dobermans are noted for were completely lacking in Caesar, and he was so sociable that when guests would depart from our house, he was ready to walk out the door with them. We always knew if burglars ever came to our home, Caesar would lead them to the loot, and then go off with them. So much for his sense of loyalty.

We tried dog obedience training, and he failed to graduate with his class, so I enrolled him in a second obedience training class. Three months later, although I was well trained in the commands of sit, stay, and heel, Caesar wasn't, and he would still run off when his leash was removed. The instructor took pity on me and awarded Caesar a diploma. He did feel though, that even with Caesar's shortcomings in the obedience department, he had the makings of a champion and should be appraised by an expert Doberman handler. This dog didn't know enough to come out of the rain, and yet he had the makings of a champion.

Those few sentences from the instructor sealed my fate for years to come. I spent them chauffeuring Caesar to dog handlers in New York, New Jersey, Connecticut, and Massachusetts, and then after a weekend of his participating in dog shows, I had to travel to pick up His Highness and bring him home until it was time for the next show. Sometimes, if the show wasn't too far away, we would pack the kids in the car and take off for the shows to watch him strutting around the ring with his handler, and it was always exciting when he took a first or second prize.

When we eventually moved out of our home, among the attic junk I had to dispose of were three cartons of Caesar's ribbons from dog shows and a lot of poor-quality silver-plate punch bowls, sugar and creamer sets, fruit dishes, and serving dishes, all blackened with tarnish.

We realized, later rather than sooner, that Caesar was probably hyperactive. When he was outdoors, he wanted to come in, and when he was in, he wanted out, so I was jumping up every few minutes to take care of his desires. And if I didn't move quickly enough, the latest paint job on the doors was ruined. Besides his hyperactivity, he was a poor eater, which was catastrophic for a show dog. Every day, I made up a big bowl of dog food mix, rolled the contents into golf ball-size balls, and shoved them, one at a time, down Caesar's gullet, holding his jaw shut until each ball was ingested. The beef and vegetable stews I made for him were unappreciated by him, though tempting for the kids, coming home hungry from school. They were quick to lift the cover off the pot to sample the contents, to the accompaniment of my screams, "Don't touch that! It's for Caesar!"

Besides catering to his poor appetite, I was told to strengthen his rear leg muscles. This was accomplished by tying him to the rear bumper of the car, with plenty of slack, and trotting him down the road at ten miles per hour for one half-hour daily. The animal activists weren't around then, or I would have been tarred and feathered.

Eventually, Caesar garnered enough points to win his championship, and the day he won Best in Class at Westminster was a never-to-be-forgotten thrill. Mel had closed his office for that day, and we took the kids out of school for this great occasion. The adrenaline was flowing in all of us as we applauded and yelled, and I was hyperventilating from the excitement and tension. I forgot the hours spent cooking, driving, training, and going without sleep, and the horrendous expenses involved in ascending these heights. We were now part and parcel of the show people who spoke a language of their own, which had been so foreign to us a few years earlier. Caesar was appearing in most of the dog magazines as "Ch. Skipper's Caesar of Dutchess," and was appropriately compared to his famous forebears,

After his Westminster win, we received a phone call from a Washington state breeder, who wanted Caesar shipped out to him, as he was interested in using him at stud, if his head was the correct shape. I cried for two days after we put him on the plane because I missed him so, but by the third day, I suddenly smartened up. I began to realize how wonderful it was to sit for an evening without getting up to let him out, and to sleep through a night, and to not have to force-feed him or trot him behind the car down the road. I actually had time on my hands, and I loved it. Upon his return from Washington, Caesar's handler wanted to take him out on the show circuit for the next six months, and I didn't fight it—it was a relief.

We kept in touch weekly with Caesar's handler, Bill, who loved Caesar as we did, and we knew Caesar was in the best of hands. Unexpectedly, we had to summon Bill to bring Caesar home one weekend, as the bible of dog journals wanted some new photographs of this champ. Caesar proved he hadn't forgotten us as he smothered us with sloppy kisses and raced around the yard excitedly, checking out familiar trees and shrubs. Then he spotted Cindy, his old Springer Spaniel playmate and, in a flash, was mounting her. He had been at stud in the months he was away, so his relationship with her had changed— little girl dogs, even though spayed, were now meant for purposes other than chasing balls. Bill yanked him off her back, and we moved indoors to prepare for our dinner party that night for fourteen guests. Our many friends, who had been witness to his shenanigans as a pup, were anxious to see the end product, the local champion Doberman.

As usual, the cocktail party preceding dinner was in high gear, as Mel believed in pouring double-strength drinks so he wouldn't have to refill them as often. After their initial appraisal of Caesar, the guests forgot about him as he wandered in and out of the living room and the noise level and laughter rose higher and higher. No one was feeling any pain at that point. I saw Cindy, out of the corner of my eye, move hesitantly into the room, looking for an empty space. Suddenly, I heard Bill's voice yell, "Caesar, *no!*" He yanked Caesar off Cindy's back and as he did so, Caesar's paw flew up, raking the skin on Bill's face. As we stared, horror stricken, at the blood pouring down Bill's face, again the paw shot up, raking the face again.

Mel grabbed Caesar and brought him down to his cellar bedroom, while I brought wet cloths to staunch the bleeding, which had just about ceased. The party atmosphere of a few minutes ago had dissipated like a pricked balloon, and now it was more like being at a wake. Bill apologized profusely, taking the blame on himself for not being more under control in handling Caesar, who was still in a state of excitement over being home. Mel took Bill to the hospital, where a surgeon friend of ours did a spectacular job of suturing the wounds (six months later, there were no visible scars).

I ushered the remaining twelve guests into the dining room to serve a belated dinner, while a muted conversation among the guests resumed. If the meal was any good that night, I'll never know, as I couldn't taste a thing. My mind was in a whirl, and I could only see Bill looking up at us as though in a stupor, with the blood running down his face. It was a relief when the guests took an early departure, and Mel arrived home shortly after, leaving Bill in the hospital for overnight observation.

In our five years' ownership of Caesar, this was the first time he had shown any aggressive tendency, but anything was possible after this. Bill had four young daughters at home, so we couldn't possibly let him take Caesar back with him, though he pleaded to do so. I was burned out from the all-consuming job of maintaining this show dog and was enjoying my freedom too much now to have Caesar back home. We deliberated his fate for several weeks, while boarding him out, and then gave him to a family we knew would love and nurture him, rejecting a few offers to purchase Caesar, as we felt he would be exploited for commercial reasons alone. Did we have any compunctions about giving away this dog we had professed to love? Yes, of course we did, but we feared a resurgence of the aggressiveness he demonstrated that one fateful night; more important, we missed the pattern of life we'd had before the advent of Caesar.

He had been away from us so much of the time with a series of different handlers caring for him that we felt it would not be traumatic for Caesar to adapt to a new family. They had been advised of the one episode and still wanted him, so we were comfortable with our decision.

We did not follow any show career he might have had with his new family; we had lost interest. The show dog circuit was a closed chapter in our lives. ᷓ

CHAPTER FORTY-ONE

THE INVITATION

ALL VESTIGES OF CIVILIZATION seemed to disappear once we left the Bar Harbor Motel, where we had spent the night en route to our final destination, Corea, Maine, just forty-five miles away. Whoever heard of Corea, Maine, and spelled with a C, no less? We certainly hadn't, until that letter from Marie arrived, inviting us to visit in their newly built home. Mel and I had tentatively discussed exploring Maine on our summer vacation but once we heard from Marie, it became a fait accompli.

I mulled over my excitement generated by the receipt of the invitation to visit, as I had heard nothing from Marie in the ten years since we last saw each other in June 1945, when our army hospital unit left Liège, Belgium, shortly after the war in Europe was officially over. My immediate mental vision of Marie was not of her blonde hair, green eyes, and generous mouth but of her bare, purplish-red legs, stockingless in the frigid winter of 1944–45, due to the shortages (or lack) of everyday necessities.

Marie was one of the young Belgian women hired by the army to do odd jobs at the sixteenth-century chateau that housed the nurses, and we became fast friends. We nurses, sympathetic to the Belgian workers' deprivations, were happy to ply them with articles of clothing and food from the PX and our own supplies, which earned us their eternal gratitude. Marie enjoyed practicing her fractured English with me so she could better communicate with her American fiancé, Albert, and I became more fluent, employing my three years of high-school French in our frequent conversations. Fraternizing with the Germans had been frowned upon, and as the Belgian men had been conscripted by the Germans, when the young American liberators came on the scene, it didn't take long before most of the single women had an American fiancé in a matter of weeks. It was mutual, though, for the men had been away from home and family for over a year and hungered for female companionship.

When I said good-bye to Marie in '45, I pressed upon her my home-town address, "just in case" she should ever come to the United States, a much-sought-after destination at the time, never dreaming it would actually happen. According to her letter, she'd married Albert, a lobster fisherman in civilian life, and had been living in his parents' home in Corea for several years, long enough for her to bear three children. Her father-in-law helped Albert construct a house next door to theirs, and Marie was euphoric, having a home of her own now and able to make her own decisions at long last.

So, here we were, driving on an almost-deserted highway with few homes or gas stations, the landscape becoming more remote with each passing mile.

The barren, windswept cliffs plunged down to meet the sun-dappled waves that crashed noisily against them, and except for the few circling seagulls, we were alone in this vast expanse of sea and sky. I had the eerie sensation of being at the end of the world and was relieved when we reached the roadside marker indicating the turnoff to Corea, two miles away. As we approached the harbor, the stench of dead fish, seaweed, and salt water assailed our nostrils and permeated our clothes, remaining with us long after we had departed from this area. We learned later that this unpleasant smell was due to the harbor being dredged; the hot August sun baking the dead fish and seaweed created this stench.

We slowly drove up what appeared to be the main street, perhaps the only street in this little fishing hamlet, searching for the "new, white house" on the right side. We drove the length of the street without spotting it, turned around, and went back to our starting point to look again for that new, white house. Almost missing it, we finally saw Marie—a much larger version of her former self—standing in the doorway of what seemed to be more a cabin than a house, for it was one-quarter the size of the neighboring homes. Marie rushed to our car to greet us, with hugs and tears for me, reminiscent of the day we parted ten years ago.

A tall, lanky, and laconic Albert strolled over to our car and waited patiently for introductions. A cigarette dangled from his lips and appeared to be permanently affixed there for the duration of our visit. Introductions completed, we were ushered indoors to explore this new home of which they were so proud.

We oohed and aahed in all the right places but secretly, we were appalled at the lack of amenities and by the minuscule rooms. The three bedrooms each contained a bed, wooden clothing pegs on the wall, and a shelf that held piles of folded clothes. There was no closet, no bureau, and no door for privacy, just a velvet-like curtain on a pole that stretched across the doorway. I was grateful at this time that Marie had informed us in advance that we would be sleeping in her in-laws' home next door, which was so much bigger. With the three children Marie and Albert had produced, there certainly was no room in this tiny house for guests. Whatever her home living conditions in Belgium were, Marie seemed oblivious to the lack of comforts that Mel and I were immediately aware of, and she only exuded an aura of contentment.

We moved on to the kitchen, which was also the dining room and living room. It housed a large, black, coal-fed stove, no doubt very efficient, and a cast-iron sink, apparently used as a holding area for soiled dishes until water from the outdoor pump could be brought in for washing. This rang an alarm bell in my brain, and when I asked to be shown the lavatory, I was directed to the outhouse, a couple of hundred feet to the rear of the building. Back in the kitchen again, I noticed the shiny, new white refrigerator in the corner, so, yes, there was electricity, and a bare electric light bulb in the center of the ceiling proved the point.

From the light bulb's pull chain dangled sticky flypaper twirling in a breeze that drifted in from the open screened window. This flypaper was covered with the bodies of dead and living black flies, some still struggling to escape their entrapment. The open, unscreened back door was the scene of a steady stream of whole generations of black flies zooming in and out. This prompted Mel to go out to our car and retrieve that morning's edition of the *New York Times*, purchased at our Bar Harbor Motel. He returned with the *Times* rolled up and proceeded to swat the flies as they landed on the walls and furniture. I always said Mel would get out of his coffin to swat flies—he couldn't stand them.

"These flies are a nuisance," remarked the unperturbed Marie. "They won't be so bad when the harbor dredging is finished, and we have learned to just live with them."

My unspoken thoughts were that if they closed the back door that had no screen, it might lessen the fly traffic.

The table was set for dinner, which would be mashed potatoes and fresh lobster from Albert's lobster traps. Mel doesn't eat lobster, so Albert went to the harbor and came back with a fish he had already beheaded, scaled, and gutted. While the lobster and fish were cooking, Marie took a quart bottle of mayonnaise out of the new white refrigerator, and with a rubber spatula removed the entire contents of the jar into a deep soup dish, which she placed on the table. The remaining population of flies that Mel hadn't killed off immediately swarmed to the mound of mayonnaise and in a minute's time, the entire contents of that soup dish was covered with still struggling little black creatures.

Mel and I exchanged wary glances with each other as the shy children were called in from their outdoor play to sit at the table with the guests. Although the lobster was fresh and succulent, I didn't have much appetite for it, nor did Mel with his fried fish. Marie and her family calmly picked the black specks off the mayonnaise, which they placed in small mounds on their dinner plates. (Mel and I, however, ate no mayonnaise with our meal.) The bowl of mashed potatoes fared better; although it still attracted a few of the flying creatures, they were able to alight on the potato mound and then fly off at will.

We raved over the freshness of the lobster and fish, which we were "much too full" to finish, though in reality, we were famished. Boxed cookies and tea comprised our desert, which fortunately, didn't entice our flying friends. We sat at the kitchen table for a couple of hours, as Marie and I reminisced about our days together in Belgium, and then the photos of our two kids were exhibited and clucked over by Marie and Albert. Mel plied Albert with questions about his military service and the lobster business, as there didn't seem to be anything else to discuss with the reticent Albert.

We were relieved when a sudden thunder clap announced an impending rain storm, and Marie rushed to get us next door to her in-laws' home before the rains fell. As this house was so much larger than Marie and Albert's, I expected to find a bathroom here, but when I inquired as to its location, my hostess stepped to the window and pointed into the night-time blackness.

"The outhouse is at the end of the grape arbor, so I'll leave this flash-light here with you. We don't have any indoor plumbing, so you'll have to use this pitcher and basin for washing. Because it's raining so hard now, I would suggest you use the chamber pot under the bed. Just be sure to empty it in the morning."

So much for all the creature comforts I had learned to enjoy since my army days.

The big double bed was comfortable, and Mel fell asleep immediately, though my stomach, growling with hunger pangs, kept me awake for hours. By morning, the rains had ceased, and after taking care of the chamber pot and thanking our hosts, we went next door to take our leave of Marie and Albert. We declined breakfast with the excuse that we had a dinner engagement for that night and had several hundred miles to cover.

We never saw Marie and Albert again, though Marie and I corresponded frequently for many years. I did order from her the exquisitely patterned hand-knit baby sweaters she made to earn extra money, and they made wonderful baby gifts. Each time, though, that a package arrived from Corea with my latest order, I had to keep the opened package on the back porch for several days to air out—these items reeked of Albert's tobacco, dead fish, salt air, and seaweed. ❧

CHAPTER FORTY-TWO

PRISCILLA

IT WAS TRULY LOVE at first sight. In her naked beauty, innocence, and grace, she stood out among the scores of sculpted stone contenders for my attention. Her head was tilted back slightly, as if listening to the song of a bird, and a mysterious half-smile lingered on her serene face. One arm was outstretched entreatingly, and the other was placed just beneath her budding breasts, as if trying to conceal her nudity. There she stood, one leg slightly in advance of the other, almost on tiptoe, probably to better hear the bird's song.

"I've just got to have her for a Father's Day gift for Mel," I said, "and I have just the place for her—in the middle of my perennial flower garden. I guess I'll need the pedestal too, won't I?"

My question was directed to Elliot, the horticulturist and landscape gardener who was known throughout the county, not only for the quality of the plants, flowers, and shrubs that he sold but also for the unique, one-of-a-kind outdoor statuary that filled a huge area beyond the greenhouses.

"Oh, definitely," Elliot's replied. "She needs the height of the pedestal, and with its Grecian scroll motif, it blends in nicely with the grace of the figure. I hate to see her go because she is the prettiest piece in my collection, and I had to talk long and hard for the sculptor to part with her. But I know she'll look beautiful in your perennial garden under the silver maple tree, which will be a perfect backdrop for her. Make sure you take good care of her," he teased, "or I'll come and pick her up."

On Father's Day morning, bubbling with repressed anticipation, our two kids, Suzy and Corky, and I led Mel outdoors over the dew-covered lawn to view his gift. We anxiously awaited his reaction.

"Well, now, this is really a nicer gift than shirts or ties," Mel remarked, "and she is such a beautiful work of art, she deserves her own name for posterity. She's definitely flat-chested and sort of prissy looking, so I think we'll call her Priscilla."

And that is how Priscilla became a much-loved member of our family, standing sweetly on her pedestal, in all kinds of weather, under the protecting branches of the silver maple tree. The birds sang above her and left their droppings on her, which fazed her not. In the spring, summer, and fall, she was flanked by the ever-changing masses of color from the perennials, and in the winter, she proudly wore the clumps of snow that adhered to protected areas of her body. At night, a spotlight outlined her silhouette in the blackness, and we never tired of enjoying her from the dining room picture window.

In the third autumn of Priscilla's residence within our family, while weeding around the base of the pedestal, I happened to note a four-inch-long crack in Priscilla's outstretched arm that seemed to have arrived overnight. Surely, it hadn't been there when I weeded yesterday, but it alarmed me enough to call Elliot immediately, who sounded as concerned as I was. Within a few hours, Elliot drove up in his truck, anxious to make a diagnosis. He frowned as he studied the affected part.

"So, what do you think?" I anxiously asked.

"I think I have to bring Priscilla back with me and have the sculptor take a look. I don't really know why the crack occurred or how to prevent it from widening. I'll keep her in the greenhouse, out of the elements, until I can get her creator to come and see what's what. He usually comes to this part of the country every fall, which should be any time within the next month."

"All right, Elliot, you're the doctor," I replied reluctantly. "Just make sure she's home for Thanksgiving. I'm having the whole family here, and the house and grounds will look bare without her."

Assuring me that Priscilla would surely be on the mend by Thanksgiving, Elliot tenderly lifted her off the pedestal and strapped her securely in the body of the truck, cushioned by heavy quilts and bales of straw. Somehow, with her departure, weeding wasn't fun or inspiring.

September and October passed with no Priscilla to grace the bare, lonesome pedestal. I left word in Elliot's office that Thanksgiving was approaching, and we needed Priscilla home for the holiday. By mail, two days later, I received a handwritten letter from Elliot, informing me that Priscilla's creator hadn't arrived yet, and besides, Priscilla was happy in her new surroundings and didn't seem to miss us at all.

I fired off an indignant reply to Elliot, accusing him of alienation of Priscilla's affections. Her first allegiance was to us, her family. The missive ended with a fervent plea, "Suzy and Corky miss their sister terribly, and our Thanksgiving dinner will be a sad one if we have to look out that picture window at an empty pedestal."

Priscilla never made it home for Thanksgiving, and becoming concerned about Christmas approaching, I sent Elliot a letter, demanding Priscilla's presence for the upcoming holiday and visit from Santa. Elliot's reply was disheartening: "Dear Muriel," it read, "I hate to tell you this, but Priscilla has become very much enamored of a Jewish boy named David who lives in the greenhouse, and I don't think you should interfere with this romance." Ha, I remembered that David with the slingshot, who didn't compare in artistry to Priscilla. As an aside, Elliot wrote that the sculptor still hadn't made an appearance.

Two weeks later, Elliot sent a brief note: "This is just to prepare you that you are going to become grandparents, as Priscilla is pregnant. She certainly will be spending Christmas in the greenhouse, as she doesn't want to leave David."

This shocking news demanded an immediate reply to Elliot, castigating him for not taking better care of our daughter, leaving her without proper supervision in the presence of a young man, and we felt he should bring her home so we could at least be sure she had the proper prenatal care. Our entreaties fell on deaf ears, for Priscilla did not make it home for Christmas, and that empty space under the silver maple tree was more bleak than ever.

January came and went, and the notes from Elliot continued to arrive, detailing Priscilla's morning sickness, and that he refused to bring her home to us in this delicate state and with her fracture still unattended. We despaired of ever getting her back.

The first week in February, there was a longer letter than usual from Elliot, and this one contained the good news that Priscilla's fracture had been repaired, and she had been newly outfitted in a fresh protective coat that would prevent future fractures. There was also the sad news that we would not be grandparents after all, as Priscilla'd had a miscarriage. Allowing for recuperation time, she was due to return to us the following day.

The next morning I shoveled a path through a foot of snow out to the garden and the awaiting pedestal, where Priscilla was gently placed a few hours later. Alighting from the school bus at the foot of our U-shaped driveway, Corky and Suzy noticed a much-loved figure back where she belonged and ran into the house, calling out, "Priscilla's home!"

It was a happy day for us to welcome her back, and that night, under the spotlight's beam, the empty space was filled with the white, nymph-like beauty of our newly refurbished and returned Priscilla.

Over the next forty years, Priscilla maintained her half-smile as she listened to the song of the birds or sheltered pockets of snow in the crook of her arm, and she remained in good health with no further fractures. When the time arrived that we sold our home to make the permanent move to Florida, the buyers were anxious to keep Priscilla. We debated whether to take her and just keep her in a storage room (as our new homeowners association did not allow outdoor statuary), but our buyers made the offer to share her with us. We immediately refused the offer of sharing, as we still wanted to maintain ownership of her, but we did stipulate that Priscilla could remain in the garden on her pedestal until such time that we might possibly move and have her as part of our household again.

So far, it hasn't happened, but while there's life, there's hope. ❧

Corky and Suzy coming home from school,
the day Priscilla returned.

Priscilla

CHAPTER FORTY-THREE

I HEAR YOU, PART I

"COME ON IN, and see for yourself how large and luxurious this RV is—two bedrooms, each with its own bathroom and shower; good-size living room with TV; comfortable dining area that seats six; and fully equipped kitchen with our own washer and dryer. No need to use the community laundry."

It took all of ten seconds to say, "Yes, we'll go with you."

Our friends Jan and Nel, from the Netherlands, were visiting us during one of Jan's frequent IBM business trips and were urging us to tour Greece and Yugoslavia with them that upcoming summer. They had their own camper back in Holland in which they frequently traveled to other European countries, but it was small, and for this occasion, Jan planned to buy the RV (recreational vehicle) we had checked out and have it shipped over to him. He would then have it available for taking family members on future vacation trips.

For the duration of their visit with us, we planned dates and itinerary of our four-week tour, with Jan doing the driving. He was not only an expert driver and auto mechanic but was familiar with both countries, having toured them before, and he looked forward to showing us the historical and geographical points of interest.

Two months before our departure for Europe, Jan called to say his order for the RV could not be filled, so he was about to substitute it with the largest camper available and wanted our OK. A camper would be a lot easier on fuel consumption, he said, and we would make better time on the mountainous roads between Yugoslavia and Greece.

What did we know about campers? Nothing. So it was "Sure, go ahead, Jan. Do what you think best." Eight weeks and one sleepless airborne night later, we were greeted at the Frankfort airport by Jan and Nel, and after collecting our luggage, we headed for the parking garage, where we would view our home for the next month. Only then did we learn there was a big difference between a camper and an RV. This little shed on wheels was one-quarter the size of the RV that we had seen. My mindset was still with two separate bedrooms and bath plus spacious living and dining areas, so it was a shock to view our cramped quarters.

Jan proudly escorted us through our "home," from front bumper to rear bumper, all twenty-eight feet in length. It had one bedroom—theirs—with a doorway but no door to close it off from the rest of the camper. Through clenched teeth I asked, "And where do Mel and I sleep, Jan?" After all, though we were sharing expenses of the trip, he had purchased the camper so we were, in reality, his guests.

"Oh, you'll sleep on the kitchen table, Muriel," he informed me, "and Mel will sleep in that space up over the driver's seat."

I've slept on beds, hammocks, bunks, and on the ground, but I've never slept on a kitchen table. As I looked askance at the wooden tabletop, Jan reassured me, "The cushions on the benches here open up and will serve as your mattress. Don't worry, Muriel, it will be very comfortable." Jan wasn't aware that if a trophy was awarded to the world's worst sleeper, I would win it, hands down.

The shelf over the driver's seat where Mel would sleep was long enough for a body to ooze itself in sideways, provided he kept his head folded down to his chest; otherwise, the roof of the camper was dangerously close. Fortunately, Mel is a good sleeper, as well as being thin and agile enough to clamber up to his perch, so sleeping arrangements didn't seem to faze him at all.

While I was digesting these sleeping arrangements, Jan discussed the matter of the bathroom, which apparently was there mostly for cosmetic purposes, as we wouldn't be able to use it. It seems that the holding tank on this camper had to be emptied manually, rather than by a vacuum hose found on most models of campers, and this one was difficult to extricate from the camper, besides being an unpleasant task at best. "Only for dire emergency purposes" could we use the commode, and the sink water was to be used sparingly.

I thought of the weeks ahead with a rapidly sinking heart. "So, Jan, what do we do for washing and otherwise?" I inquired, again through clenched teeth. (At this rate, my teeth would be ground down to the gum line.)

"Absolutely no problem" he promptly replied. "I have made reservations at various campgrounds throughout Yugoslavia and Greece where we will be each night, and they have wonderful facilities there for servicing the people in campers. They will have bathrooms, showers, and laundry facilities, and you will never have to stand in line. When we get to our Austrian campgrounds tonight, I'll show you how they function. But for now, I think we should get going, as I'd like to be there between 9 and 10 p.m."

Jan climbed into the driver's seat, and Mel joined him in the passenger seat as we took off through the Frankfort traffic, heading for the Austrian border. Nel and I took the two easy chairs flanking the picture window and were soon caught up in exchanging news about our respective families and mutual friends. I tried valiantly to appreciate the changing scenery and to be enthusiastic about the trip ahead of us, but my stomach churned each time I thought about the bathroom situation and sleeping on that kitchen table. We stopped for a late lunch at a small restaurant along the highway. When we finished eating, Jan advised us to be sure to use the restrooms, as we would not be near any rest areas until we arrived at our campgrounds for the night. Another churn of the stomach.

Several hours later, and still a few hours from our campgrounds, I tapped Jan's shoulder. "Jan, I have to 'go' and can't wait a few hours."

"OK, Muriel," said Jan patiently, "Just wait until we get to a wooded area; you can find a spot behind some shrubs."

With my luck, I thought, the way this trip is going, *I'll probably land in some poison ivy.*

A few miles down the road, Jan found a suitable area and parked the camper, and both Nel and I climbed out and found bushes that concealed us from passing cars. Mission accomplished, and we got back into the vehicle and were on our way again.

By this time, I was beginning to seriously feel the effects of jet lag, not having slept at all on the plane. I also was agonizing inwardly as I allowed myself to dwell on the coming night and the sleeping arrangements. Mel was oblivious to my concerns—he can sleep anywhere and is also built like a camel.

Dinner, which Nel had purchased in advance, in our lovely little home on wheels consisted of cold cuts, tomatoes, savory Dutch cheeses for which Holland is famous, and crusty hard rolls. Jan ate his meal in sandwich form while driving. I might have enjoyed the meal if my stomach hadn't been in knots as we ate (where I would soon sleep), and if I hadn't been so terribly tired.

And so we drove on into the night, finally arriving at the Austrian campground at 10 p.m., everyone exhausted and ready for sleep. Jan parked the camper in its reserved slot and then escorted us to the ablutions building. We walked the equivalent of two city blocks on gravel paths, past one darkened camper after another, all from different European countries. The building was brightly lighted, with rows of spotlessly clean sinks for washing and showers; the opposite side of the building was lined with toilet stalls. On each stall door was a large sign in many languages advising occupants that all toilet tissue must be placed in pails, and not flushed down the toilet. At age 65, could I learn a new way?

Once back in our camper, Jan readied my bed on the kitchen table, unfolding the bench cushions and handing me the sheets and a blanket to finish making my bed. No hospital corners on this bed. Jan and Nel said their good nights and disappeared through the doorway into their bedroom, while Mel scrambled up to his perch, throwing me a kiss from on high from his supine position, as I hurriedly donned my pajamas. He didn't dare lift his head, as his nose was about four inches from the ceiling. My robe, flashlight, and slippers were at my feet, as I knew I'd be taking that two-block walk at some point during the night. Before I could even get my sleep mask on and ear plugs in place, a horrible rumbling noise emanated from the bedroom—and it gained in intensity until it reached an explosive crescendo. I was about to call out to Jan to ask what this noise was, but when it continued with a certain rhythm and regularity, I resigned myself to being up all night with his snoring. How could Nel—or anyone else sleep—with that racket?

I was so exhausted that I hoped I would fall asleep anyhow, but sleep evaded me, and my body was trembling with fatigue. After an hour of timing the snoring cycle, sleep was farther away than ever, so I reached down for my flashlight and found my little bottle of sleeping pills, used for emergency situations. Two hours later, the pill hadn't worked and the snoring pattern was right on schedule. By now, besides being tired, I was boiling mad—mad at myself for being in this predicament and mad at Jan and Nel for initiating it.

Well, I thought, *I might as well go to the john and get that over with for the night.* So I slipped on my robe and slippers, grabbed the flashlight, and made my way out of the camper. I fumed and agitated all the way over, praying, "Please, God, get me out of this," and "God, I can't stand another night on that kitchen table," and just plain "Please, God, help me!" I really didn't expect much help, as we were committed to this trip for a month and God has more important jobs.

Back once again on my Beautyrest mattress, I turned and tossed for another hour or two and then, finally, fell asleep, despite the snoring, as dawn was breaking. One hour later, Jan announced wake-up time, as he wanted to be on the road by 9 a.m., and we had to wash and have our breakfast at the campground restaurant before heading to Yugoslavia. Like a zombie, I removed my bedding, dressed, washed, and ate, not feeling very sociable and afraid to open my mouth for fear of ruining this beautiful friendship of ours.

Back in the camper and on the road, leaving Austria, my muddled brain was trying to work out a solution to get us out of this mess, and the only thing I could come up with was to have an appendicitis attack. I couldn't have pneumonia because I wasn't coughing, and another option, breaking an arm or leg, was something I didn't care to do.

We were two hours driving time into Yugoslavia when suddenly there was a loud explosion from under the hood of the camper. The motor sputtered a few times and then ceased running completely. Attempts to restart were futile, so we piled out of the camper to push while Jan steered the vehicle to the side of the road, out of traffic. We looked around and observed that we were in the middle of nowhere—no apparent signs of life or civilization as far as the eye could see. On both sides of the highway were low, flat meadows, peppered with an occasional clump of trees or shrubs, and no animals grazing these fields.

Jan lifted the hood to evaluate the situation and busied himself probing and pulling and testing. Ten minutes later, he gravely informed us there was a serious problem that necessitated a new part, which might take several days to acquire. It was now 3 p.m. on a Friday afternoon, the beginning of a weekend, and we were a good hour's drive away from Llubljana the nearest large city. And would any of the garages there have our needed part?

Our foursome stood by the side of the road, three of them pondering the next step, the fourth—me—reveling in the unexpected dissipation of all my anxieties, tension, fatigue, and anger. It all rolled off me, one wave after another, as the skies above seemed to open up and a heavenly voice boomed down, "Muriel, I hear you!" ❧

CHAPTER FORTY-FOUR

I HEAR YOU, PART II

HE REALLY HEARD ME! I exulted inwardly, recalling my fervent pleas for help, not more than twelve hours ago. For tonight, at least, there would be no kitchen table, and hopefully, no snoring Jan six feet from my ears. If we should have to sleep on the ground in the field adjacent to the highway, there was enough space to distance myself from the unwanted sound effects. I felt giddy with relief, and I'm sure the others must have wondered about my smiles and enthusiasm, both of which I had not generated since we started this trip (which now, with Divine Intervention, was becoming a great lark for me).

There was very little traffic on the highway, and the few cars that sped by paid no heed to our little group by the side of the road; no one stopped to offer aid.

We scanned the horizon again, hoping to see some form of life and luckily, barely visible in the far distance, we saw the outlines of a building. If it was a barn, then somewhere in the vicinity there must be a house—with a telephone.

Jan locked the camper, and we scrambled over the highway guard rails, on to the almost level expanse of meadow that stretched on and on into the distance. We were fortunate that the ground was dry, and though in some areas the weeds were waist high, the going was smooth, and we didn't encounter any deep ruts or gullies. We walked single file, conserving our breath, each wrapped in his or her own thoughts. We were about halfway to our destination when we realized that the building was indeed a house, and there was a female figure there, who appeared to be working in a garden, alternately stooping and standing. We quickened our pace, and about fifteen minutes later arrived at the perimeter of this property.

I was at the head of the line and called out "Hello!" in the friendliest voice I could muster, so this woman would realize this band of strangers was not to be feared. She stood up quickly, wearing a questioning but pleasant expression, as I held out my hand and asked, "Do you speak English?" She understood that much but shook her head, uttering one word that sounded like "Nein." Between the four of us, we tried out the different languages we were familiar with. "Parlez-vous francais?" "Nein." "Habla espagnole?" "Nein." "Sprechen sie deutsch?" "Nein." "Parla italiano?" "Hollandaise?" "Nein."

By now, we were all smiling, although it seemed that we had exhausted our repertoire.

Even though we got nowhere language-wise, when I gestured toward the distant highway and said "Auto kaput," she understood immediately, clucked some sympathetic sound, and motioned for us to follow her into the house so she could telephone "polizia." After her call was completed, through hand motions and apparently some Slavic words, we understood that the highway police would locate the camper and summon a tow truck. It would take about two hours before the tow truck could arrive at the dead camper position, and then we would be towed into Llubljana. Our hostess, named Marta, shook hands with all of us as we gave her our names and respective countries. She nodded pleasantly when Jan and Nel indicated they were Dutch, and when Mel and I said we were from America, she smiled broadly and purred, "Ah, Amerika" a couple of times. When we went on to say we were from New York, she shrieked excitedly, "Nuevo Djork! Nuevo Djork!" If we had come from Mars, she couldn't have been happier, and when her husband walked into the room and she introduced us, she kept repeating to him, "Nuevo Djork! Nuevo Djork!" (At that point in time, Americans were loved in Europe.)

Marta and her husband excused themselves so she could prepare coffee, and we had a chance to examine this low-ceiling farmhouse of fairly modern construction. The living room was furnished with substantially built, highly polished, dark wood chairs and a couch with upholstered cushions, and the walls were hung with inexpensive replicas of famous paintings and crucifixes. A bible and religious statue was placed on the coffee table, conveying the impression that this was a family that took their religious faith seriously. The room was immaculate and apparently not often used.

Marta served coffee and cookies to us as we waited for the police and tow truck. Though we did not speak her Slavic language, by dint of hand and eye motions, voice inflections, and a word here and there in French, German, Italian, Dutch, and Yiddish, we carried on a lively conversation. We learned about their two children, ages ten and twelve, and their grades in school; we heard about the expensive price of coffee and how they went to the Austrian border to purchase it; we discussed politics in Yugoslavia and America; and we talked about their favorite American movie stars, and the crops her farmer husband grew and the difficulties of marketing them. Language was no barrier, and by the time we had to start our trek across the fields to meet the tow truck, we were fast friends, exchanging addresses and hugs. Mel took photos of everyone, which we later sent to our benefactress.

We made the return walk through the fields faster than the earlier trek, buoyed by the fact that help was on its way and because the last couple of hours had been so pleasant. Shortly after we arrived back at the camper, a tow truck arrived, and we exchanged introductions with the nice-looking young driver. Again, the information that we were from America, from New York, elicited high interest from the driver, Michael. He indicated we would be in Llubljana in one hour, and all four of us would have to sit in the front seat in the cab, as there was no back seat and no area in the rear of the truck where we could sit. Once the camper was securely fastened to the tow truck, Mel and Jan took their seats next to Michael, and then Nel and I seated ourselves on our spouses' laps. Our conversation with Michael was in the same vein as with Marta and her husband. Michael did not speak any of the languages we were familiar with, but we understood each other very well, with our pronouncements accompanied by much giggling.

My first question to Michael concerned the availability of hotels in Llubljana, and I was happily reassured to learn there were many, even a Holiday Inn. Oh, joy! A real bed in the solitude of our own room, minus Jan's explosive snoring—the camper repairs could take a month, as far as I was concerned.

The drive passed quickly enough, though it seemed longer to Mel and Jan with the loads on their laps—Nel and I were frequently asked to shift our positions on their thighs. As we approached Llubljana, traffic picked up tremendously, and at a very busy highway intersection, Michael located the garage that the highway "polizia" had described to him. We drove through the entrance of a huge outdoor parking lot, filled with all manner of disabled vehicles, and pulled up at a dilapidated one-story building that was both office and repair garage for the trucks, cars, busses, and campers awaiting attention. A security worker informed Michael that the office was closed for the weekend, but the disabled camper could be parked there until the office reopened Monday morning.

Jan and Nel elected to stay with the camper in the parking lot and planned to meet us at the Holiday Inn lobby the next morning. Their bicycles were strapped to the rear of the camper, so transportation for them was assured, and even if Holiday Inn had no room for us, we would still use the hotel lobby as a central meeting place. We quickly packed a suitcase with enough clothes for an extended hotel stay, if necessary, and after hugging Nel and Jan; we joined Michael in the front seat of the tow truck and took our leave.

Civilization never looked as good as it did when we drove into the heart of the city. Even though only thirty-six hours had elapsed since we had first stepped into the ill-fated camper, it seemed more like weeks, and I was euphoric out from under its confines. Michael drove us directly to the hotel and waited in the truck until we were assured there was a room available. We exchanged addresses amid our fervent thanks, and Michael promised to contact us if he ever came to America.

Back in the busy hotel lobby thronged with people speaking a dozen different foreign languages, we followed the bellhop to our large high-ceilinged bedroom. Not only did we have our own bathroom with flush toilet, but we also had two queen-size beds, a far cry from my kitchen-table bed and Mel's shelf up over the driver's seat. "This is more like it!" I exclaimed to Mel. "Let's go out and celebrate our liberation."

"That's fine for now," replied Mel, "but eventually, the camper will be repaired, and you'll still have to sleep on the kitchen table and put up with Jan's snoring."

"Well, in the meantime, I'll catch up on my sleep, so I'll be in a better frame of mind," I insisted. "And now that I know what to expect of camper life, I'll be prepared mentally for the next chapter."

I had eight nights to catch up on my sleep; the camper could not be repaired and once this was determined, we had to wait for a new one to be driven from Munich to Llubljana. The wait wasn't wasted, though, as we had the opportunity to become acquainted with our host city and its environs, which we would have not been able to do before the breakdown. Every morning, Nel and Jan rode their bikes to our hotel after breakfast, and we explored the city to our heart's content. We visited the colorful open-air flower and food markets and attended evening concerts—one night we had box seats at the opera and experienced a lovely production of *La Bohème* for the munificent fee of the equivalent of $2.38.

One particularly beautiful sunny day, we followed the sound of music and came across an orchestra playing on the broad expanse of steps before a public building. The music was lively and of our vintage, so of course we had to stop, listen, and enjoy. Before we realized what was happening, we were all dancing in the street along with the locals and the tourists. The dancers sidelined themselves when the orchestra burst into a number with an extremely fast tempo, and we were stunned to see our quiet, laid-back Nel, whirling and twirling to the beat of the music, the lone dancer, wreathed in smiles. One male dancer joined her and soon another claimed the privilege of being her partner, and then, Jan decided it was time for us to move on. To this day, I still have the vision of Nel, whirling with outstretched arms and smiling face, to the accompanying applause of her audience.

We sampled different restaurants and took bus and train tours to points of historical significance, such as the mountain caves where the Partisans hid out in their war against the Germans. A day's outing by bus took us to the scenic mountain resort of Lake Bled, where we mingled with the natives and tourists who came to enjoy this pristine lake, which reflected myriad evergreen trees that grew around it.

All too soon, the eight days passed and our new camper arrived from Munich, as scheduled. It was time to continue on our trip along the Adriatic to Dubrovnik and then over the mountains to Greece. Although I was well rested and thought I was better prepared for bedding on the kitchen table, each time I turned and could feel the seams of the seat cushions that served as my mattress, I was reminded of the story of *The Princess and the Pea.*

The new camper was an improvement over the old one, as it did have a holding tank that could be emptied automatically at each campground, so we were able to use the bathroom and not have to resort to bushes along the highway. What did not change was Jan's snoring, which I attempted to interrupt by pointing my flashlight beam in his face and imploring, "Jan, wake up! You're snoring." It was a futile gesture, though, because although he did wake briefly, the snoring would resume before I was back on my table. I had no alternative but to resort to sleeping pills for the duration of the trip, except for the few nights we spent in hotels.

The remainder of the trip was uneventful and yet exciting, as we explored all the sites in Greece that we had studied in our history books in school and were now seeing for ourselves. I didn't have to plead for Divine Intervention for the duration of our trip. ❧

Jan supervising the disabled camper being unloaded in Llubljana.

CHAPTER FORTY-FIVE

THE HIGH THAT WAS LOW

THE MEMORY IS OF A TIME IN THE '60S when our college-student daughter, Suzy, was home for Christmas vacation. She had learned to bake marijuana brownies, using my famous family brownie recipe—which did *not* include marijuana among the ingredients. Though she had perfected the recipe, no academic credits for this endeavor were received.

Anxious to initiate my husband and me into the pleasures of this unknown substance, she baked a batch of brownies one day, and the tantalizing, mouth-watering smell was as enticing as ever. Two squares of brownies were left on a plate for me to sample, but I was still wary about the effects of this infamous marijuana, so I settled for one square; it was as delicious as it smelled.

"Now what's supposed to happen?" I asked Suzy.

"Oh, in twenty minutes or so, you'll start to feel wonderful, happy, and completely relaxed."

Twenty minutes passed and nothing happened, but then, while in the midst of a phone conversation, strange physical sensations began overtaking me. My entire body was wracked with cold, which seemed to emanate from my bones outward, through layers of muscle to the skin. The light in the room dimmed, and everything looked and felt gray. As I endeavored to keep my balance on the stool at the kitchen counter, I looked at the wall clock, and time was standing still. I stared at the second hand and after what seemed like an hour, the hand moved ponderously to the next indicator.

"Suzy, come and get me," I called, "and help me move to the lounge chair in the den. My legs are too unsteady for me to walk. And get me a blanket, too, 'cause I'm freezing."

Suzy very solicitously helped settle me into the den chair, as I complained that I felt "just awful" and must have had an overdose of marijuana from *that* brownie. She burst into tears and sobbed, "You were supposed to feel good, but maybe you shouldn't have eaten both brownies."

"But I only ate one brownie," I countered.

"Well, I put out two," she insisted.

A small sigh from across the room solved the mystery of the second brownie. There was Goniff, our black lab, completely zonked out on the floor. He was unable to move a muscle, and the tail that usually thumped at the mention of his name was motionless. His eyes were the only movable part of him, and when I called his name, he just rolled his eyes piteously at me.

What a pair we were, both zonked out on a heavenly marijuana brownie! ❧

CHAPTER FORTY-SIX

GAMES PEOPLE PLAY

SHE MAY HAVE BEEN TINY in stature, but she could move mountains—and she was my best friend.

Sarah wasn't at all pretty, though she might have been considered cute, not just because of her petite build but also because of her long-lashed, wide, searching green eyes and untamably curly, carrot-red hair. She had an unremarkable nose and doll-like lips that she would purse over her slightly protruding front teeth when lost in thought.

I didn't meet Sarah until a few years after Mel and I got married, though Mel had often spoken of his dental-school classmate Morty and his wife, Sarah, who had left nursing school in her second year to marry Morty upon his graduation. He'd started a dental practice in New Hampshire, and by the time our paths crossed, they were the parents of two girls: Julie, age five, and Sharon, age two, who were being cared for at home by Sarah's mother so the young couple could celebrate their sixth anniversary in New York.

En route home, they stopped off for a visit with us in Wappingers Falls, and this meeting heralded a rekindling of Mel's friendship with Morty, the first time they had seen each other since graduation. For Sarah and me, there was an instant bonding that I had never felt with previous women friends, and she admitted to the same feelings, as if we had always been friends. I enjoyed her sense of humor, in contrast to her more serious husband, and we shared so many similar philosophies and interests that in that one short meeting, we knew we would be dear friends, if not best friends, forever.

That encounter soon led to our reciprocal visit to their New Hampshire home over a long weekend. We were shocked beyond all comprehension to meet five-year-old, Julie, and learn that she was a crippled post-polio victim, a fact that Sarah had never mentioned when discussing her children. To me, it was heartbreaking to see this happy and complacent child with one eye focused in the wrong direction, a mouth turned up at one end, and an inverted hand, walking with a staggering gait as she shifted her hip with each step. Sharon, on the other hand, seemed to be a perfectly formed, pretty little brunette, normal in all respects but with a petulant mouth and whiny voice (which never changed over the years).

Sarah set the tone upon our meeting Julie. The introduction was so matter-of-fact that she made the residual polio defects sound as normal as the common cold. "I want you to meet Julie," she said, "who had poliomyelitis and has a few problems right now, but as she grows older, with treatment and exercises, she will be able to do everything she wants to do."

I admired Sarah tremendously for her positive offhand attitude and wondered if I could be so nonchalant if either of my two children had been stricken like this child. Later in this same visit, I was awestruck when, in discussing long-term plans for herself and Morty, Sarah talked about the time "when Julie and Sharon are both married."

I thought to myself, *You poor, dear, blind mother! What normal man is going to marry your crippled daughter, even with her rose-petal complexion and sweet inquisitive disposition?*

I ate my unspoken words over the years to come, for Sarah pushed her daughter to do everything her peers could do. Julie had a portable typewriter in first grade that she could manipulate with her inverted hand; she had dancing lessons to help in maintaining her balance and physiotherapy for the twisted gait; and she was active in her Girl Scout troop, which included all the swimming, camping, and boating activities in which the average child indulges. By the time she was sixteen, though Morty rebelled, Sarah insisted on driving lessons, and Julie earned her driver's license on the first road test. Morty was an interested and good father to his daughters, but his professional life was all-consuming and the brunt of raising the girls fell on Sarah, who seemed to thrive on adversity.

The day came when we danced at Julie's wedding, shortly after she received her PhD in English and her college-classmate husband earned his law degree. Julie's eye problem had been corrected surgically; the slightly turned-up mouth was barely noticeable, and onlookers saw only the sparkling eyes in Julie's glowing face. She really was a pretty bride.

My relationship with Sarah deepened yearly, fueled by our frequent letters, weekly phone calls, and long weekend visits to each other's homes, three to four times a year. The host couple always planned special activities for the visiting couple. Sarah exposed us to local museums and theater; we climbed Mt. Monadnock, and visited Dartmouth College and local ski areas. When it was our turn to host, we took the visitors to the Roosevelt Museum and Homestead at Hyde Park, the Vanderbilt mansion, and West Point across the Hudson River. Our freezers were stocked with cooked dinners in advance of the arrivals, so we didn't have to spend precious time in the kitchen when we could be catching up on each other's activities and exchanging confidences. Sarah really enjoyed cooking, while I didn't, so her meals were always extra-special for us, and my high opinion of her capabilities increased upon each meeting.

Not only was she an excellent homemaker and mother, but she excelled as a volunteer worker for civic organizations, starting first with the local polio-myelitis association, for which she raised funds, tirelessly and successfully, over the years, always exceeding her quota. She eventually became president, a title she retained for many years, and traveled frequently for meetings with state and national officers of the organization. Sarah was seen often on local TV and in the newspapers, lauding the businesses and philanthropists who abetted her cause. She exuded a self-confidence and savoir faire that certainly was not present when we first met. I was bursting with pride over my dearest friend's accomplishments and reputation.

With all her public exposure, Sarah had to dress the part, and the family coffers didn't allow for her excellent but expensive taste in clothes—but she planned well. As she once explained to me, she would frequent the most exclusive shops in town and make her choice from the size 2 dresses that she wore. Then she'd give the store manager her name and phone number and ask her to call if the dress she'd chosen was not sold at the shop's half-price sale. She invariably got the dress long before the sale, especially if it was a slow-moving stock season. I had such faith in Sarah's good taste that I frequently had her pick out dress accessories, scarves, or handbags for me when I had something special in mind. Despite her poverty-stricken youth when hand-me-downs were her lot, she quickly developed a sense of style and appreciation for quality, which applied not only to clothes but also to her general pattern of living.

Mingling now in different social and civic circles, Sarah undertook to improve her culinary skills by enrolling in cooking and wine-tasting courses, and before long, she was invited to discuss her favorite recipes with accompanying wines on the radio, on TV, in local newspapers, and at various women's organizations. And as with everything else that caught her interest, there was no room for improvement.

Moving upward culturally, Sarah became interested in art, and on one of our New Hampshire visits, she introduced us to two artists, George and Armando, both sculptors who worked in marble. Their creations were highly sought, not only locally but countrywide, and Armando even had European commissions. Any hostess who nabbed them as dinner guests could be assured of a highly successful social event, not only because of their renown as artists, but because they were music and theatre savants, charming, funny, and crazy, and they enjoyed people. Of course, it was love at first sight for all of us at one of Sarah's Sunday brunches, and from that day forward we became "The Group." This was typical of Sarah's talent in bringing people of like interests together, and we had many fun-filled visits as "The Group," which extended to sightseeing in various parts of the country and in the Caribbean in winter months.

Shortly after Julie's wedding, with Sharon's college graduation coming up and another wedding lurking in the not too distant future, Sarah joined the ranks of the employed, where she would now be paid for her abilities and execution of them. I was never sure of her exact title but knew that she was hired by the local university to work assisting Harvey, the chief of the psychology department, and Jim, the assistant psychologist. Morty seemed pleased that she was earning a salary for her efforts.

From that time on, subtle changes in Sarah were noted on our visits to their home, obvious to Armando and George also, although Morty was oblivious. Sarah talked incessantly about her job, the goings-on in the psychology department, and her two bosses, and no matter what subject we were discussing, she would manage to interject the names of the psychologists. Of course, she was enamored of her job, but over the next two years, instead of toning down the glamour and importance of her job, the constant name-dropping and recital of the daily office anecdotes increased. We had built up a healthy disregard for this Harvey and Jim team long before we met them, but then Sarah started including them and their wives in all of her dinner parties.

On meeting the two bigwigs for the first time, we were surprised to note that they were mere mortals like the rest of us, not at all exceptional in physical appearance—they certainly wouldn't stand out in any crowd. We waited for pearls of wisdom to issue forth from their lips, but their conversation remained within normal bounds, though Harvey was much more impressed with his self-importance than Jim. The wives were attractive and pleasant women, seemingly glad to be invited out.

Now on our visits, instead of Sarah and I sitting down for our girlie chats and catching up, I would accompany her to the gourmet food and wine stores for her last-minute dinner party purchases. Instead of meals precooked and in the freezer so we could have more time for enjoying each other's company, I sat in the kitchen, attempting to talk to Sarah, while she was trying to concentrate on intricate recipes or running down to the freezer in the basement for a needed ingredient. No longer did she ask about mutual friends at home, our activities, or the doings of our kids, and my questions to her were answered in monosyllables. Mel and Morty talked shop in the den, while I simmered in frustration on my kitchen stool. I mourned the lost intimacy that Sarah and I once shared and was unhappy with Sarah's continual preoccupation with fancy dinner parties each time we came.

These evenings were a striking display of Sarah's culinary abilities and social skills, with the meal preceded by an array of mouthwatering hors d'oeuvres and enough rounds of drinks to guarantee a loosening of the tightest of tongues. By the time dinner was served, everyone was in fine spirits, and the conversation was sparkling, witty, and congenial. Sarah scintillated, sitting at the foot of the beautifully appointed dinner table, flanked on either side by Harvey and Jim, while their wives were to the right and left of Morty at the head of the table. Sarah hung on to every word of her dinner partners, especially Harvey, who delighted in monopolizing the conversation. At one such event, Armando, my dinner partner, whispered to me, "What does she see in those two stuffed shirts?"

I nodded my head in complete agreement. I finally summoned up enough courage to mention to Sarah that I missed the old days when we were just "The Group" and had time to visit with each other and discuss topics of the day and what was going on in our lives.

Sarah stared at me in hurt, wide-eyed amazement and vehemently protested, "I'm shocked that you feel this way, because these dinner parties are actually held for the purpose of entertaining you and Mel, and we want to show you off to our friends." So, the guilt trip was mine, but how many times did she have to show us off to the two psychologists and their wives?

Three months later, we again headed to New Hampshire for Sharon's wedding. Mel and I were relieved to be seated with Armando and George and not the two bosses and their wives, who, for once, were not seated with the host and hostess. As usual, Sarah's talents as a hostess were remarkable, as was her ability to stage a successful wedding weekend for two hundred people. The wedding was lovely, though Sarah seemed to be somewhat distracted throughout the weekend, which we attributed to the routine anxieties one encounters at an event of this magnitude. At the conclusion of the festivities, while Sarah and Morty were still involved with out-of-town family guests, Mel and I headed home. We discussed highlights of the weekend, and I knew that Sarah would be interested to hear about another of her successful productions from the onlooker's viewpoint.

A few days later, I called Sarah to thank her again for the weekend and to rehash the event, as we always had in the past, when we were good for an hour's long-distance call. Sarah accepted my words of gratitude and praise graciously, but gone from her conversation was the feeling of closeness and warmth that existed between us in former days, and she seemed to be five thousand miles away in thought. Seeking to make conversation, to prolong this phone call, I mentioned that our daughter, Suzy, had applied to graduate school to earn her PhD in clinical psychology. I was shocked by Sarah's cold response: "I hope she doesn't expect me to use my influence to get her into a school."

My hurt but quick retort was "Suzy doesn't need or want any help from you. She has had nothing but A's on report cards all her life and will get accepted on her own merit."

I could have said, "Since when does one and a half years of nurse's training qualify you for a psychology degree?" But of course, I was too stunned to think logically and could only wonder what in the world had happened to Sarah for our relationship to sink to this low. Was it something I had said or done? Was it my complaint about the continual dinner parties for the two psychologists on our visits that prompted this explosion? But no, there had been changes in her attitude before that time, which we couldn't account for. At any rate, the phone call was terminated then, mutually. (And of course, Suzy was accepted into the school of her choice without Sarah's intervention. The head of the department, to this day, proclaims that Suzy was the best student he ever had.)

I was depressed and saddened that the woman I had considered my best friend for more than twenty-two years had become a complete stranger. And now, where did we go from here? Who should make the next move? It would be our turn to host "The Group" in three months, but after this episode with Sarah, I didn't know what to expect.

The answer came a week later, when Mel and I received an anguished phone call from Morty, who was almost incoherent as he sobbed over the phone that Sarah had requested a divorce and had moved out of the house to live with Harvey. Harvey had left his wife and four children, setting in motion plans for his divorce. Further talk between gulping sobs elicited the information that Sarah admitted to her growing infatuation and affair with Harvey, which had commenced shortly after she was hired. Twenty-eight years of what Morty had assumed was a happy marriage was down the drain. Trying to console him was futile; the shock was still too new and too great for him to assimilate, and we could only offer our condolences and the offer of a sympathetic ear when he needed to unburden himself.

Reeling in astonishment and sorrow at this news, Mel and I stared at each other, trying to understand and make sense of Morty's heartbroken message, and the more we talked about it, the more I understood the games

Sarah had been playing the past two years. Once Harvey entered her life, our visits to their home provided additional bait for capturing him completely. The dinner parties, supposedly for the purpose of entertaining Mel and me, were actually for Sarah to show off her remarkable talents as the perfect hostess, chef, and socialite. Harvey was aware of her capabilities in the office, but it was important for him to know how well she could function as a homemaker also. By including Jim and his wife in each invitation, Sarah showed no partiality toward either boss; everything was open and above board.

At this turn of events, I felt violated, as Sarah had used our friendship to further her own ends in a manner that could only be described as deceitful.

Several weeks later, I received a phone call from a penitent Sarah, who apologized for not confiding in me, her "dearest friend," and hoped our relationship would continue, even though she had left Morty. I wished her well but said that there was no more relationship to continue.

I never saw her again.

Eighteen months later, Sarah's place in "The Group" was filled by Morty's second wife, to whom he has now been happily married for many years. Time and distances have limited the frequency of our reunions, but when we do get together, we pick up where we left off, as if it was yesterday. ❧

CHAPTER FORTY-SEVEN

THE GIVE AWAY

STACIA WAS AN UNFORGETTABLE CREATURE who happened to be the only applicant responding to my ad for a cleaning woman, so I had no recourse but to hire her. She was delivered to our home two days a week by her boyfriend, who came roaring up the driveway on his motorcycle with Stacia clinging to him from her back seat. They were identically clad in helmets and black leather pants and jackets, which Stacia removed on arrival, changing into cotton slacks, more suitable for house cleaning. She donned her leather uniform again at the end of the workday, ready for her motorcycle ride home.

Her appearance was unremarkable—medium height and build; short, dark blond, straight hair with bangs reaching down to her eyebrows; and a bland, expressionless, plump face—but she had one outstanding feature, and that was her voice. It was a high-pitched, nasal, sing-song sound, glass-shattering shrill, and I was tempted to cover my ears each time she addressed a question to me in her heavy Polish-accented voice. I flinched each time I heard, "Meesa Hengamen, what I clean now?" Or, "Meesa Hengamen, where I find cleanser?" Stacia went through three cans of cleanser in the five weeks she worked for me, her theory being that the more Dutch Cleanser she applied to the countertops, sinks, bathtubs, showers, and toilet seats, the cleaner they were. Ours was just an ordinary two-bathroom home that she was cleaning, not a hotel, and her theory might have been plausible if she at least made an effort to rinse the cleanser off. Instead, a thick, gritty layer remained on every surface she had attacked so viciously with the cleanser. A bathtub filled with hot water does not dissolve the grit on the bottom, and that is not conducive to bathing, nor is grit on a toilet seat conducive to sitting there.

I just couldn't get across to Stacia the message of removing cleanser, so I wasn't too disappointed the day she called to say her boyfriend had a new job out of town, and she was going with him.

I'd answered the phone to hear her high-pitched, nasal, whiny voice query, "Meesa Hengamen?"

"Hello, Stacia," I replied.

Complete surprise was obvious in Stacia's question: "How you know dis Stacia?" ❧

CHAPTER FORTY-EIGHT

BOUND UP

"ARE YOU SUFFERING FROM IRREGULARITY? Has impotence ended your sex life? Are you suffering from an enlarged prostate or menopause?" My ears are assaulted daily by radio and TV ads that would have shocked me years ago. Today, all bodily functions are discussed openly in the media, presumably in the interest of educating the public. So in that context, perhaps it is permissible to discuss my problem: I was born constipated.

Early in life, I learned to accommodate this particular affliction by acquiring my own arsenal of over-the-counter medicaments, and I became quite an authority on the effects of Alophen, cascara, Ex-Lax, mineral oil, Milk of Magnesia, Epsom salts, senna leaf tea, glycerin suppositories, and all the others.

As a student nurse, I was always happy to dispense my wares to needy classmates from my storehouse of laxatives. When I discovered a product called Dr. Hinkle's Compound, my classmates dubbed them "little Brown Bombers," for they were potent, and they worked! One of the ingredients was strychnine—bound to either cure you or kill you. I did have to stop dispensing this particular pill, though, after one of my disciples became incapacitated with cramps and diarrhea after only one Brown Bomber, and was off duty for three days.

Years later, as Mel and I were rounding up a six-week European trip in Paris, I had exhausted all my supplies and could have used a few "Brown Bombers" at that point. After a miserable night, I asked Mel to go to the American pharmacy and purchase an enema bag, guaranteed to stimulate peristalsis.

Two hours later, Mel returned to the hotel, carrying the means for my survival but weary from his trials of having to communicate my needs in his almost non-existent French vocabulary. The American pharmacy had been closed, so he'd had to go to a French pharmacy and try to convey to them what he wanted to purchase. He rubbed his belly and groaned, but got only blank stares. He pointed to his buttocks. No response.

Finally, he came up with what I thought was a brilliant command of his limited French vocabulary when he asked, "Avez-vous douche pour la derriere?" Translated, it meant "Have you a shower for the behind?" This bit of brilliance got him nowhere, so he had to return to our hotel, where the concierge wrote out the proper French terminology on a piece of paper. Back at the pharmacy, the pharmacist read the precious words of liberation for me, smiled broadly, and then broke out in a torrent of French that sounded as if he were saying, "Oh this! Why didn't you say so?"

Eight years later in Llubljana, Yugoslavia, while on the camper trip with Jan and Nel, we encountered a similar situation; namely, I had exhausted my supplies. The hotel receptionist spoke English but was unfamiliar with the word "laxative". The hotel general manager, who spoke English with a typical British accent, walked over to us and asked if he could be of assistance, but again, "laxative" wasn't in his English vocabulary.

Finally, in exasperation, Mel saved the day by asking the manager, "Do you know the meaning of the word "s-h-i-t?"

The manager drew himself up haughtily and replied, with great disdain, "Of course I do."

Mel pointed at me with his index finger. "Well, she can't!"

At this, the eyes of the manager met those of the receptionist, who was trying to stifle a laugh, and they both howled with laughter while the tears ran down their faces. Success was ours! ❧

CHAPTER FORTY-NINE

THE OPIATE

IN ALL MY LIFE, I could never purchase ready-made garments. (My mother, you might remember, always compared my body to an "old, gnarled apple tree.") So it was a major catastrophe for me when the seamstress I'd had for many years moved away. Most of my friends could wear dresses right off the rack, so they had no recommendations for a replacement seamstress.

My salvation lay in a tiny ad in the local newspaper that offered alterations for men and women. I immediately called the number listed, and my call was answered by a sweet, lilting, slightly foreign-sounding female voice. Her name, I soon learned, was Masako, and she was Japanese. We set up a time for the following morning, when I would bring my latest purchases to her home, which was also her workplace.

Masako's four-bedroom home was in a new, medium-priced residential district near the local schools. She had four children—Dick Jr.,15; Martha,14; Bill, 12; and Charlie,10. Masako's husband, Dick Sr., was a captain in the army and had been in Vietnam for the past six months. She shyly confided how she had met her tall, handsome husband when he was serving in the Army of Occupation at the conclusion of World War II; it had been a case of love at first sight for both of them.

It was certainly easy to see how he would have been smitten with her, for she was beautiful-petite, with a creamy complexion, her coal-black hair fell in soft waves around her face, framing her clear, almond-shaped dark eyes. Masako's rosebud mouth smiled frequently, showing a perfect set of white teeth, and the voice that issued forth flowed as smoothly as quicksilver.

She and Dick had settled in our town shortly before he was recalled to active duty, and she had taken on alterations as a way to supplement his captain's salary, which didn't go too far with four growing children to feed and clothe. Masako missed her husband very much, referring frequently to their past life together and anticipating the day he would return home. Belying her appearance of fragility, she was firm and decisive in handling her children, demanding the highest standards in obedience, manners, and their school work.

As expected, Masako's workmanship was perfect, but she dismissed my praise by crediting her school curriculum, where sewing and embroidery were required for women, and the study of the English language was required for all students. This accounted for her mastery of our language, which she spoke with few grammatical errors. When she was at loss for a word, she would blush deeply, then flutter her long eyelashes and turn her head aside, as she asked me to supply the word she was seeking. We soon became fast friends. Masako hungered for adult companionship, and I often invited her to our home for dinner, sometimes with her children but often without them.

Besides having a happy disposition and laughing easily, Masako was extremely intelligent and eager to improve her knowledge of her adopted country and our way of life. Mel was readily sympathetic to her plight of being a single parent. He enjoyed her company on these visits and was happy to answer questions she had about finances, dental care, the political situation, or any number of other topics. She reciprocated these dinners by inviting us to her home for marvelous Japanese meals of sukiyaki and tempura, which were not part of our usual home or restaurant cuisine. On one occasion at our house, Masako brought up the subject of Dick's parents, who weren't supportive of her situation. They weren't happy that their one and only child, the all-American boy, had married a "Jap." Even the births of the four grandchildren hadn't healed the breach between them. By default, we became the family Masako didn't have while Dick was away.

Several months after our meeting, it was Mel and me who Masako called to sob out the terrible news that Dick Sr. had been killed in action. Mel and I rushed over to comfort her and the bewildered children as best we could. Soon after, Masako took the kids to Texas to meet their paternal grandparents for the first time, hoping to share in their mutual grief and perhaps effect some feeling of family closeness. A slight thaw in relations was achieved—Dick's folks did learn the names, ages, and physical characteristics of each child—but their emotions were too tightly bottled for them to express any warmth toward the children. They seemed to favor the two children who didn't have almond-shaped eyes, as they looked for any resemblances they could find to their dead son. On return, Masako felt that the trip hadn't been a total loss, but the warmth and closeness she had hoped to find still eluded her. After sending a profuse thank-you letter to her in-laws for their almost indifferent hospitality, Masako declared that she could not force the relationship, and any further moves were up to them.

The pall of Dick's death still hung over the entire family for weeks after their return from Texas—and then a happy event occurred that brightened all their lives. This was the arrival of Masako's parents from Japan, whom she hadn't seen since she departed from Japan as a young bride so many years ago. She had always been close to her parents and communicated by mail and phone. They were distraught to learn the news about Dick, as they had learned to love their American son-in-law during his years in their country. Their impending visit was a godsend to this grief-stricken family; now, they had something good to look forward to.

Masako was delighted when I suggested she bring her parents over for afternoon tea, though I had some trepidation about entertaining two people who neither spoke nor understood a word of English. Mel had picked up a few Japanese phrases when he had served in Japan at the conclusion of World War II, but I wondered how much he could milk those phrases over a few hours' visit. "How are you?"; "Good morning"; "Thank you"; "You're welcome"—that wouldn't take us too far.

It turned out to be a wonderful afternoon for all of us, with Masako, beaming for the first time in months, translating when necessary. By dint of gestures, facial expressions, and sounding out words in Japanese and English, we made ourselves understood and shared a lot of laughter. The laughter increased when we opened the package containing the bottle of sake and the lovely porcelain sake cups her parents brought to us as a house gift. It was then that Mel and I learned from her parents that the word "yoparai" meant "drunk," and we were all a little "yoparai" by the time they left.

I was astonished to see the mother of dainty, petite Masako was built like a female Buddha—she was extremely short and fat, and when seated in an upholstered living room chair, her feet didn't reach the floor. When she smiled or laughed, which was often, she displayed several shiny gold teeth, a sign of affluence at the time, but they certainly didn't add to the American ideal of beauty. Her husband—a good-looking man of slight height and build—doted on her. I decided it must have been his genes that Masako inherited. Masako later confided that her mother had a cardiac condition, which so worried her father that he made sure she didn't lift a finger to do anything for herself, She remained sedentary while he plied her with sweets and delicacies to demonstrate the depths of his affection.

The month-long visit by her parents did wonders for elevating Masako's spirits, and she and the children resumed the pattern of life they'd had before they received the news of Dick's death. Masako's life was a busy one—between caring for her children and running her alteration business, which had increased to the point where she had to refuse new clients, she had no time to wallow in grief.

This phase was too good to last, though, for a phone call from her father several months after her parents returned to Japan brought the sad news of her mother's sudden death from a heart attack. After making quick arrangements with a neighbor to care for the children, Masako flew to Japan to be with her shocked and grieving father, who seemed to have aged twenty years since his visit to this country. He was so bereft without his wife that he found it difficult to make the slightest decision—whether to dress, to eat, to walk—and Masako feared greatly for his mental state.

She appealed to her one sister to keep a close eye on her father until the grief had lessened. Not too surprisingly, six months after the death of her mother, Masako received a phone call from her sister. Their father had committed hara kiri on his wife's grave, as he could no longer live without her. He had plunged a sword into his chest up to its hilt, and that's how he was found by Masako's sister, the sword still in position. A note to Masako and her sister was found on the ground, detailing his wish to die to be with his beloved wife in another world.

The year following the death of her parents was almost as traumatic as the one after Dick's death. Masako struggled to keep her grief encapsulated and not inflict her sorrow upon the children. Through the intervention of our local congressman, Dick Jr. was accepted as a cadet at West Point Military Academy, which was financially advantageous for Masako, as his college expenses would not be a strain.

Martha, however, a tall, pretty girl with Japanese features, became her mother's worst nightmare almost overnight. She refused to participate in family life and hibernated in her room when not in school. She often was absent at mealtimes, though Masako could hear her puttering in the kitchen long after they had all gone to bed. Then, ramshackle cars started appearing in their driveway at night, driven by slovenly, long-haired young men. Their cars were painted with strange symbols and anti-war sentiments, and the radios were always blaring for the world to hear the music of their generation. They never came to the door to ask for Martha; instead, they sat in their cars, tooting their horns in an almost constant blast, until Martha ran out to join them, even as she attempted to work her arms into her coat or jacket.

When Masako intercepted Martha on her return home, usually in the very early morning hours, she reeked of alcohol and—as Masako later learned—marijuana. All efforts to reason with Martha failed. Her nightly excursions continued, her school marks plunged, and then, there were nights when she didn't come home, showing up twenty-four hours later. On one occasion, the police brought her home after finding her lying in a gutter, completely stoned on drugs. Masako was at her lowest ebb by now, much worse than when Dick died. She felt she was at fault somehow, that she had failed as a mother. We tried to convince her that she was wrong in her self-denunciation, and that it was the time we were living through that was responsible—the sentiments for and against the Vietnam war that were dividing the country; protesters defected to Canada to avoid being drafted; and "guru" Timothy Leary, a leading proponent of taking LSD, was indirectly responsible for the mental and physical deaths of the thousands of young people he encouraged to "turn on, tune in, drop out."

The final blow came when Martha disappeared completely. A month later, Masako received a brief phone call from Martha from somewhere in Wyoming; she only said that she was now eighteen and free to run her own life. She told Masako not to try to find her. And as she hung up, she blurted out, "I'm pregnant, too; stay away."

For the sake of her sons Bill and Charlie, still at home, Masako tried to maintain their daily routine. We tried to help with daily phone calls, and invitations to join us when dining out with other friends. I even tried a little match-making with our divorced male friends, but was unsuccessful in my attempts. Masako was amenable to the idea of dating, but the first man on my match-making list was an enthusiastic athlete, who lost interest when he discovered Masako couldn't participate in the hobbies he loved—skiing, tennis, and sail boating—and which took up 95 percent of his spare time. The second man, a music professor at a local university, was only interested in getting Masako into bed for his own pleasure, but they both realized she wouldn't fit into his academic milieu.

Our pushing Masako out in the world to meet other men proved to be a stimulus for her, which she took one step further by joining an Arthur Murray dance class. It was there, on her very first night, that she met Ray, a divorced IBM engineer. Ray was a pleasant-looking, laid-back, affable individual, always anxious to please, who had been awarded custody of his eight-year-old son when his wife left him. I thought perhaps his wife had left because he was so agreeable to everything that he seemed boring, but he was nice—and very interested in Masako.

In the few months before this relationship culminated in marriage, Masako, still digging deeper to "atone for her shortcomings as a mother," found religion—and in a big way. In no time, she had Ray going to prayer meetings with her several nights a week, and these meetings probably were responsible for her emergence from the black cloud of depression that had engulfed her since the death of her parents and Martha's defection from the family. She was a different Masako now, though, for she had become hardened by these tragedies and Dick's death. Apparently, she needed the crutch that this new religion provided, and Ray's willing participation in it helped his cause in wooing Masako.

They were married in a brief ceremony by a justice of the peace, attended only by Bill and Charlie (Dick Jr. was away at West Point) and Ray's son, Peter. We visited them occasionally in their new home, and Ray was always the pleasant host, quick to offer drinks under Masako's directions. Her Japanese dishes were still a treat, and we enjoyed our meals there, though the conversation usually centered on the children or the stimulating speakers they'd had in their religion classes.

By the time Dick Jr. was a senior at West Point, Bill was a midshipman at Annapolis, which left only Masako's Charlie and Ray's son Peter at home. There was no news from Martha; her name was never mentioned.

As time went on, Masako became even more deeply involved in her religious scene; in fact, she was fanatical on the subject. A year after their wedding, she persuaded Ray to quit his safe, secure job (with benefits) at IBM so that they could become missionaries as soon as Charlie went off to college. Peter had gone to live with his mother, who was happy to have her son again as long as she didn't have to put up with his father.

We had frequent letters and occasional phone calls from Masako from Florida, where she and Ray were sent for their missionary training, and she sounded happy and fulfilled. During one of these calls, she joyfully announced that she had heard from Martha, who was now married to a "very nice man with a good job" and loved her fatherless son as his own. From Florida, Masako and Ray were sent to a mission in the Philippines, where they ministered to native Indian tribes, providing articles of clothing and school supplies. They also taught the basics of reading and writing in the Tagalog language, and, most important of all, the story of the Bible, their main mission being to convert the native people to Christianity.

The phone calls to us eventually ceased, though we did receive very religious Christmas and Easter cards from them. About two years after their move to the Philippines, they returned to the States to see their children before embarking on their newest mission assignment to Japan. We visited one evening, happy to see each other again, and learned the news of Martha—they'd been to see her and had met their son-in-law, who really was a very fine young man and now the father of Martha's second child.

When discussing their missionary work, Masako was so imbued with the subject that her chin quivered with emotion in her religious fervor. She strove to convince us to follow in her footsteps to attain true happiness, not only in this life but also in our afterlife. We gently declined her invitation, saying we were very content with our Judaic beliefs, but we were happy for her and that she had found peace at last.

Fifteen years have passed since we last heard from Masako, but if there are any Shintoists, Confucianists, or Buddhists left in Japan, I'm sure it isn't for lack of effort on her part. &

CHAPTER FIFTY

UNFINISHED BUSINESS

ANGELO WAS THE ANSWER to a committee chairman's prayer, for he was available to work and didn't hesitate to volunteer for jobs that no one else would consider taking. I first met him at an organizational neighborhood meeting, and as my chief volunteer, it was natural that I learned about Angelo and his personal life. He talked frequently about his IBM job and how he met his wife, Santina, there. He bemoaned the fact they were never able to have children, which he attributed to his teenage encounter with polio, which also left him with a gimpy leg.

According to Angelo, Santina's housekeeping and cooking skills could not be equaled, and she was the most efficient secretary ever hired by *the* IBM. (I could never understand why higher-salaried employees seemed to work at IBM, and the lower echelons referred to working *for the* IBM) I assumed that Santina's job there must have drained her physically, for she never attended any of our neighborhood meetings. I finally asked Angelo if Santina was too tired to attend our monthly meetings, as we could have used her secretarial abilities. "Oh," he replied, looking a little shame-faced, "Santina died three years ago, but she did everything so perfectly that I sometimes forget she is not here. I keep the house just as neat and shining as she did, and I learned to cook her recipes; I don't mind saying that I'm almost as good as she is."

"*Was,*" I wanted to correct him, but I kept my mouth shut. Was this man out of touch with reality? Apparently, he hadn't come to terms with his wife's death.

"You'll have to come to the house and see for yourself how well I take care of it and how I do everything just the way Santina wanted," pronounced Angelo, and I didn't have the heart to refuse him. At the conclusion of the meeting, I followed Angelo's car to his home. It was at the top of a steep hill, which could be treacherous during the snow and ice seasons, but his panoramic view of the majestic Hudson River down below was breathtaking and must have compensated for the winter inconveniences.

The house was a ranch-style frame dwelling, perhaps fifteen years old and beautifully maintained, as it appeared to have received a recent paint job. The shrubs growing against the house were evenly trimmed, not a twig sprouting out of its smooth alignment, and the flower borders of marigolds, petunias, and impatiens had been freshly manicured, with not a weed growing in between. The large expanse of lawn around the house looked as if it had just been mowed—the overall picture was one of neatness, neatness, neatness. I don't know whether Santina's jurisdiction applied to the exterior of the house as well as inside, but Angelo was either well trained by her or was a perfectionist himself.

Once inside, I felt the spirit of Santina hovering, as Angelo proudly led me from room to room, indicating the different photos of Santina and explaining when and where the photos had been taken. The hardwood floors gleamed, the couch cushions and pillows were plumped up as if they had never been sat on, and there wasn't a speck of dust on the highly polished mahogany furniture. Two floor-to-ceiling bookcases flanked the stone fireplace and were filled with books by authors of substance and stacks of long-playing operatic and classical records. We stopped briefly in my tour to discuss some of the books and records I was familiar with. The kitchen was as pristine as the living room and dining room—not even a spoon in the empty dish drainer. It was hard to believe, from what I had seen so far, that anyone actually lived in this house.

I was regaled constantly with pertinent bits of information: "This is the chair that Santina always sat in"; "Santina picked out this flower pattern and made the drapes herself. She could sew anything"; "This is where we watched Santina's favorite programs at night." Throwing open the doors of a huge china cabinet, he said, "These dishes belonged to Santina's mother, and she loved them. I don't use them because I don't want to break any."

The three bedrooms also were occupied by the ghost of Santina, and by the time Angelo opened his bureau drawers to show me how his underwear and socks were folded in neat piles—the way Santina had always done—I was feeling very intimidated thinking of my casual housekeeping. He even ironed his wash-and-wear shirts! My home never would have passed her inspection—or Angelo's—and I vowed to myself that I would never let Angelo bring Mel through this home, in case this neatness obsession was contagious.

I praised Angelo for his meticulous housekeeping and took my leave.

En route home, I pondered Angelo's refusal to let go of Santina and thought that perhaps, in time, he would tire of living alone and might seek out feminine companionship. He was only in his late fifties and was intelligent, nice-looking, well dressed, and apparently quite comfortable financially. He enjoyed being with people and was very informative on topics of the day, as well as on music and literature—when he could forget Santina for a while. That rarely happened.

I eventually broached the subject of his dating and was shocked but pleased when Angelo admitted that it was lonesome living in his home on the hill, and he would be interested in meeting the right type of woman.

"But Angelo," I warned him, "when the right woman presents herself, you will scare her off if you keep repeating how wonderful Santina was, because no woman wants to be compared to her predecessor. You know, Santina has been gone now for almost five years, so its time to get on with your life with someone new, if you really don't enjoy being alone.

"You're right, Muriel," agreed Angelo. "And I'll try not to talk about Santina if you'll try to help me find the right type of woman."

Wow! This was just up my alley, as I enjoyed being able to introduce available women to available men. I had been responsible for fourteen marriages so far, with only one divorce, and that was after a ten-years-and-two-kids marriage, so my record was pretty good.

About two months after this conversation with Angelo, I received a phone call from a twice-widowed friend living in California, who had come to town to visit her daughter. Janet was a pretty, short, blonde, plumpish barrel-of-fun. She was a live wire, never refusing an invitation for dinner, dancing, or even a movie, and she was excellent company. Her sense of humor was infectious, and she would laugh hilariously at items that struck her funny bone. When the spirit moved her, she would spontaneously burst into song or execute a few dance steps, using a couch pillow as her partner.

I was well aware that Janet was the exact opposite to steady, meticulous, sincere Angelo, but as a starter for the dating game, I felt Angelo would be comfortable with her. There were no other unattached women on the horizon at this point, and who knew? Perhaps opposites might attract.

Once Angelo had Janet's name and phone number, he lost no time in setting up a date with her. He asked me about the really good restaurants in the area and whether he should wear a tie for the occasion. My most important advice, however—and my final word—was "Do *not* mention Santina's name if you want this evening to be a success."

I eagerly awaited calls from both parties the next day to learn of the success or failure of their meeting. When the phone rang at 8:30 a.m., I knew it would be one of them.

"Muriel?" It was Janet, who could say no more before bursting into paroxysms of laughter, unable to proceed. Her laughter gradually subsided, and she attempted to speak, but she again was overcome with gales of laughter.

"What's so funny?" I yelled into the phone, trying to make myself heard over the sound of her laughter.

Getting control of her voice, Janet bubbled, "Do you know where Angelo took me last night?"

"No," I replied. "We discussed several restaurants, but I don't know where you ended up."

"We ended up," replied Janet, "in the cemetery, visiting Santina. Friday is Angelo's regular night for putting flowers on Santina's grave, and by the time he clipped the grass around the stone and read the inscription to me, it was too late to keep our dinner reservation."

"So he didn't even take you out for dinner?" I asked in horror.

"Oh, he took me out for dinner, all right," laughed Janet. "We went to the McDonald's across from the cemetery for a hamburger and fries."

I didn't attempt to alleviate Angelo's lonesome state after that. He had too much unfinished business. ❧

CHAPTER FIFTY-ONE

THE CHEAP SEATS

"WHY IN THE WORLD do you want to go to Sicily? You'll probably get knocked off by the Mafia."

This was typical of the remarks leveled at us, once we announced we were going on an eight-day tour of Sicily. But my response was ready, for I had done my research and could enumerate, without pause, all the reasons we had to go: "It is a beautiful island, populated by warm, emotional people and blessed with a temperate climate. There are Greek ruins in better shape than the ones in Greece. Sicily has Mt. Etna, a live volcano. There are catacombs in Palermo, where dead people were mummified hundreds of years ago and are supposedly hanging on the walls. And lastly, the price of the tour, which includes airfare, is so cheap, we can't afford not to go."

When I made our reservations at the tour office, I was asked if we wanted to upgrade our seats to business class. The cost was $900, each, so I immediately refused, insisting on getting the cheap seats in tourist class. I was warned that the plane would be full, and we would be sitting in the seven-abreast seats, but I felt we could manage that. I would rather have the extra dollars to spend in Sicily.

Angelo, our widower neighbor, was joining us on the tour. At this point in time, he was beginning to emerge from his chrysalis of grief and was eager to rejoin the world of the living. The idea of going to Sicily rejuvenated him, for his grandparents had been born on the island, and he hoped to find cousins there—and perhaps a prospective bride.

So there we were on the plane, jam-packed into our seven-abreast seats, when a female of huge proportions—the likes of which we had never seen—settled herself into the aisle seat next to Mel. It was hard to guess her age—she had a pretty face, but her small head was attached to her body by three chins, creating an impression of a peanut sitting atop a grapefruit. She had to raise the armrest to fit into her seat, and her enormous thighs were squashed up against Mel's. After a period of time, Mel wedged some of the journals he'd been reading down between their thighs, and he whispered to me that they helped deflect some of the heat she was radiating. Whenever she or he shifted position the journals had to be reinserted, a fact they were both aware of, although Mel's movements were limited as much as possible to just breathing.

Once, when she got up to visit the lavatory, Mel made a beeline for the tour director, who was sitting a few rows in front of us, to ask if his seat could be changed. He received an emphatic no in response and was reminded that there were no empty seats on the plane, and that he'd had the opportunity to upgrade his seat but had opted for the cheap one. Furthermore, we would be occupying the same seats for the return flight.

Mel grumbled to me that just thinking about the return trip was going to dampen his enjoyment of the tour and I, like the good wife I am, volunteered to change seats with him at that time. Fate intervened, though—thanks to Angelo, we had different seats for the trip home.

We arrived at our hotel, a large, rambling, stone structure about fifteen miles from Palermo, and were assigned to our rooms. We parted from Angelo then, making our way across the marble floor to the elevator, marveling at the high ceilings and Old World splendor of the lobby. Once in our room, I was intent on unpacking our luggage, when the phone rang, and I recognized the panic-stricken voice of the hotel manager, imploring me in Italian to come. From my rusty knowledge of the language, I understood that "amico," "accidentato" and "gamba," meant "friend," "broken," and "leg."

Mel and I rushed down to the lobby, where we were guided to the barroom by the agitated manager and found Angelo stretched out on a leather couch, calmly drinking a double-shot of scotch. "What happened?" we inquired in unison.

"Well, I was headed for my room, and the marble floor had just been washed, and I slipped on it. I could hear something snap, so I know it's broken. The manager called for an ambulance, which will be coming from Palermo, so I'm afraid I'll miss out on the whole tour of Sicily. I just hope

I'll be able to go back with you when you go."

The scotch that Angelo was consuming seemed to alleviate his pain, and he was well through his second double-scotch, talkative, and happy to be conversing in Italian with the staff, when the ambulance arrived with four men, who we assumed would carry the stretcher. But they had no stretcher, just two wooden straight-backed chairs, upon which they placed Angelo; he sat in one chair and his legs were outstretched in the other. Two men each held the legs of the chairs, as they thrust Angelo aloft and carried him out to the ambulance, where they then headed for the hospital in Palermo. The next day, we asked the hotel manager to call the hospital to find out Angelo's condition, which was reported as good. Surgery had been performed to position his fractured leg, which was now encased in plaster. The second post-operative day, as the tour bus headed for Palermo to visit the cathedral, Mel and I were dropped off at the sprawling hospital compound, bearing a camouflaged bottle of scotch for the patient. We must have looked like foreigners, for everyone we encountered smiled and uttered the word "Americani," as they motioned us in the direction of Angelo's floor.

He was in a semi-private room, though until we reached it, we were astounded to see a huge open ward with patients being attended to by their families. A dozen women dressed in black with shawls were bathing, shaving, or feeding their family member, and young children clustered around or on the beds. Angelo's room was pleasant. It had two beds and one large window, through which the sunshine was pouring, magnifying the grime on the glass.

We were introduced to his roommate, who had suffered a fractured arm. He had become Angelo's best buddy by this time, and they carried on rapid-fire conversations in Italian. We learned that his roommate's wife had supplied Angelo with bedding and eating utensils, as it was hospital policy to bring your own when hospitalized. Angelo was clearly having a wonderful time, was not in pain, and was enjoying the notoriety of being an "Americani" here. Our bringing the scotch was an added dividend, which he later declared had saved his life and afforded him star treatment from his physician.

Knowing that Angelo was enjoying his hospital stay, we had no guilt feelings about not visiting him daily, so we were able to make the most of our tour of the island, which was everything we had hoped for and more. The weather, the people, the Greek ruins, and the smoking Mt. Etna were thrilling, and the visit to the catacombs were unbelievable. The Cappuccini friars were proficient in the art of mummification, beginning in the sixteenth century, and had the bodies of eight thousand children and adults, fully dressed, either encased in glass or propped up, suspended from the walls as though they were hanging on meat hooks. It was macabre but fascinating to see. Seared into my memory was one blonde, blue-eyed little girl, perhaps three years old, in her glass coffin for two hundred years, who seemed to be looking right at us.

The week passed all too soon for us. Angelo was delivered back to the hotel on the day before our departure, his leg cast covered with names of the hospital staff and his roommate, along with messages written in Italian. At the hotel he reigned as King for a Day on the couch in the bar, and the widows and divorcees in our tour group made sure to inscribe messages with their phone numbers in any empty areas they found on the cast. Angelo didn't seem to regret not being able to find any relatives while in Sicily, and he certainly had enough phone numbers to keep him occupied for a while when he returned home.

We didn't know what arrangements were made for special seating for Angelo on the return trip, as his leg had to be elevated, so the three of us were delighted and relieved when we were assigned to front bulkhead seats, where we could sit with Angelo. His leg was propped up on our carry-on luggage, piled on the floor in front of him. and we had abundant foot and leg space. We came home in much better style than the trip over and did not miss the companionship of our too-well-endowed seat mate, who, thanks to our reassignment, enjoyed two cheap seats of her own. ❧

CHAPTER FIFTY-TWO

MY FOUR BEST MARRIAGES

AS OF THIS WRITING, my one-and-only Mel and I have been married for fifty-seven years. I was responsible, however, for bringing about fourteen marriages, over a period of fifty years or more, due to my matchmaking prowess. What follows are the four marriages I consider to be the best.

I think some people are endowed with a certain gene that functions like an antenna, picking up signals when a guy or gal is available and looking for a mate, and if my supposition is true, then I surely possess that gene. This avocation of mine started long before my peers were even old enough to think of marriage, as far back as seventh or eighth grade, when I was the go-between for passing notes from "him" to "her" or vice versa. I was a true romantic at heart and delighted in promoting these classroom crushes.

Over the years, my playing the role of Cupid continued—and became serious business. Actually, throughout my matchmaking "career," when I found a good, available man for one of my friends, I would experience a sensation similar to an adrenaline rush. Bingo! Hit the jackpot on this one! Very rarely, someone might comment that I was trying to control lives of others by playing God. My response always was that I was "just introducing two adults to each other and the rest is up to them."

Perhaps this same matchmaking gene is responsible for my proclivity for "picking up people" as Mel calls it. "Why do you have to talk to everyone in line," he often asks, "whether at the grocery checkout or at the line in the ladies room?"

I don't know why, really; I guess I just like people, and if helping them find a spouse makes them happy, then I'm happy.

MATCH NO. 1

MY FIRST MATCH was that of my nursing-school classmate, Doris, and Paul, whom I had known most of my life. Paul and I were playmates at age four and went through public school together. When we both ended up in the Boston area after high school; I was in nurses training in Cambridge, and he was majoring in business at Boston University. It was natural that he would call me. We met a few times, but once we discussed hometown news, we discovered that we actually had very little to talk about—we each had our own interests.

Paul's chatter about the outside world and the ills of society reminded me of Doris, who spoke in similar fashion. She had known nothing but extreme poverty all her life—brought up in the Great Depression as we all were, she knew first hand how it felt to go to bed on an empty stomach. Her parents had emigrated from "the Old Country" and were struggling to feed their five kids on the meager income her father earned as a junk man—and Doris later admitted that the only reason she went into nurses training was because as a student nurse, she would get her room and board and an education for a small financial outlay. She was familiar with the politics of our time (the only one in our class to read the newspapers from beginning to end) and her vocabulary was sprinkled with words such as welfare, socialism, Marxism, capitalism, and communism, terms I had heard but couldn't accurately define. She and Paul were both so concerned with the world situation, not part of my world of medicine; it just seemed so right to bring the two of them together. Surely, Paul would understand all these-isms that had such prominence in Doris's vocabulary.

Apparently, he did, for he married her three years later on her return to the United States after she served as an army nurse in the Pacific Theater of Operations. Her years in the military hadn't dampened Doris's ardor for the underdog (the oppressed, the blacks), and for the rest of her life, she was in the forefront of the marches and the protests, ready to crusade for her strong beliefs.

Paul, now a well-to-do businessman, was much more moderate; he dealt with the public on a daily basis and never was the firebrand that his wife was. He saw black where she saw white, and their heated discussions and arguments were no secret to their friends or to their three children, who grew up to be free thinkers and successful in their own fields of endeavor.

Every year on their anniversary—even on their fiftieth—Doris has uttered the same well-known phrase to family and friends, as she rolls her eyes and crosses her fingers: "Well, we made it through another year."

Now married sixty years, Doris confided to me recently, "You know, we're actually going to make it."

MATCH NO. 2

THIS MATCH WAS A PUSHOVER FOR ME, for aside from introducing the two characters involved, that was it—no frequent phone calls, cajoling, and expounding on each other's virtues for me. These were two mature adults, who knew what they wanted and recognized it when the opportunity presented itself.

Bill was Mel's second cousin, a good fifteen years older than we were, who had lost his blind wife, due to her severe diabetic condition. His wife, Martha, had been bedridden for the last three years of her life, and Bill lovingly cared for her without complaint, bathing, dressing, and feeding her, in addition to doing all the household shopping and maintaining their apartment.

Over the years we had always enjoyed their company at family celebrations and the times they traveled from Boston to visit with Mel's parents who lived nearby. We knew Bill to be jovial, always with a funny story to tell, and he was a marvelous chef, especially Chinese dishes. Aware of his being alone now, I called Bill one night, about three months after Martha's death, and asked solicitously, "Bill, how are you doing?"

"Muriel," he replied, "I am so lonesome. I can't stand walking into this apartment with no one to talk to. I miss Martha terribly. and the emptiness of this place is getting to me."

"Well. then," I began, "why don't you do something about it?" "What do you mean?"

"I mean, find yourself some female companionship, a woman to take out for dinner or go to a movie with. Just so you can look forward to being with someone at the end of the day, rather than going home to an empty apartment."

After silence for a few seconds, Bill sighed. "I wouldn't know where to begin. I don't know any single women."

"Come to Wappingers Falls" was my quick response. "There are dozens of single or widowed women around, just dying to meet a nice guy like you, and I'll make sure you get to meet them."

"Sounds good to me," he agreed. Then, as an afterthought, he added, "But Muriel, it's only three months since Martha died. Would people think I was being disrespectful to her memory?"

"Bill, Martha's dead and you're alive," I reasoned. "You were a wonderful husband to her for the thirty years you were married, especially the three years she was bedridden, so now you deserve some fun and enjoyment out of life. Go for it!"

That clinched it. A date was set for the following weekend, and by the next day I had lined up two women for Bill to meet. Bill's Friday night date was with Helen, a fifty-five-year-old spinster and businesswoman, who had dated every bachelor and widower in the county for years but always ended up just a friend and never a wife.

But as Bill explained the morning after his date, "She's a nice girl, but she's looking for a doctor, and I'm just a lowly liquor-store owner."

We struck oil with his Saturday night date! Liz was a short and somewhat stocky red-haired widow, attractive, intelligent, outgoing, and easy to be with. She was secretary to a high school principal, and thanks to frequent school vacations, had traveled extensively since the death of her husband fifteen years earlier. She had interesting stories to recount. Bill's breakfast report on Liz was: "Her conversation is stimulating, she's a lot of fun, and there are a lot of similarities in our backgrounds. Her hair is red, and my mother's and Martha's hair were red. And both of our mothers were named Jenny. I'm coming back to see her next weekend." Wow, I liked hearing that!

He came the next weekend, and we saw him for all of five minutes. The rest of the weekend was spent with Liz. The following weekend, Liz drove to Boston to visit with Bill, prior to leaving on a two-week cruise she had planned before meeting Bill. While she was gone, Bill worried to me on the phone, "I hope she doesn't meet any other men on this cruise."

But, I soothed him. "Bill, she hasn't met one good man in fifteen years, so why should it happen now?"

He worried needlessly, for only Bill was on her mind, and they had a lover's reunion on her return, at which time they became engaged. One year to the week that Martha died, Bill and Liz became man and wife at a beautiful wedding ceremony in one of Boston's fine restaurants. They had twenty-two happy years together before they were separated by death.

MATCH NO. 3

MATCH NO. 3 occurred as the result of the period in our lives when Mel and I were deeply embroiled in an environmental battle with the town. We had galvanized the 250 families living within a rural three-square-mile radius, whose wells had dried due to overconstruction of apartment complexes in the area. Into our hectic existence of meetings, protests, planning, publicizing, and dealing with the politicians came Leland and Sharon, two individuals we never would have met under ordinary circumstances.

Leland was a newspaper reporter on environmental issues, specifically water, for the largest county newspaper. He became aware of our organization after reading of my presentation to the County Board of Supervisors on the grave water situation in our part of the town, as well as my numerous letters to the editor of our newspaper. After the first phone call, which was all business, Leland took to calling me two nights a week to learn of any progress we might be making in our fight, and the more we talked, the more personal these phone calls became. I was glad to get his calls, because each one resulted in more newspaper publicity for our organization the next day. But once the business was taken care of, we discussed other important issues; namely, his love life—or lack of it.

Long after Mel had gone to bed, I would be on the phone with Leland, listening to the story of his life and his unsuccessful attempts in attracting women. He was rather unsophisticated—certainly not the man-about-town type—but he wasn't physically unattractive. He was of medium height and solidly built, with a pleasant but serious face. He always had a pencil behind his ear and notebook in hand, which, he thought, gave him an air of authority.

One night, after hearing his latest litany of complaints against the Jewish girls, who apparently would accompany him to a fine restaurant for an expensive meal but then wouldn't even kiss him goodnight, I made a suggestion. "Leland, if the Jewish girls don't appreciate you, try dating a gentile girl. She might be more interested in you as a fine person than in the importance of being seen in a fancy restaurant."

"My family would kill me if I brought home someone who wasn't Jewish," he replied, "but I'm willing to give it a try—if I could even find one." "I'll help you look," I promised.

With Leland's utter lack of sophistication and inability to play games, the only type of woman who would be interested in him would be someone who would be grateful for any attention from a man. I found her just a few nights later at one of our environmental meetings, when Matt, an IBM executive, introduced me to his secretary, who lived in our area with her parents and grandparents. Matt told me in an aside that Sharon was the best secretary he'd ever had, and he wasn't worried about losing her through marriage—she was grossly overweight, even though she was a pretty blue-eyed brunette with a kewpie-doll mouth and creamy complexion. "Poor girl," Matt confided, "she's never had a date in her life."

The light bulb in my head turned on immediately.

I engaged Sharon in conversation and found her to be charming, sweet, and knowledgeable about important issues. I was impressed with her integrity and lack of self-consciousness about her size. I couldn't wait for Leland's post-meeting phone call, so I could tell him about Sharon. When I described her to Leland, I was honest about her size, but I also mentioned her charming personality, ending with the age-old axiom, "Remember, Leland, beauty is only skin deep."

The rest is history. Sharon and Leland had a marvelous two-year friendship and courtship, and the more they saw of each other, the thinner Sharon became. She accompanied Leland on his rounds to the county rivers and streams, measuring flood levels and learning other technologies in dealing with them, and in time Sharon could discuss the subject almost as expertly as Leland. Their wedding was a lovely affair—the ceremony was performed by a rabbi, which pleased Leland's family, even though Sharon wasn't Jewish, and Sharon's family was thrilled that she'd found a man who could love, support, and care for her. Mel was asked to be an usher and as a special honor, hold one of the four poles of the canopy sheltering the bride and groom during the ceremony.

As I was standing at the bar after the ceremony, I gushed to the two men standing next to me, "Didn't the bride look beautiful?" And indeed she did, for Sharon was aglow with happiness that radiated from her smiling face.

The man to my right happened to be Leland's father. "You think she's beautiful?" he snorted.

"Yes," I quickly responded, "and I introduced them."

The man to my left agreed, "She's my niece, and he's darned lucky to get a nice girl like her."

Later that night, Leland's mother called me at home to thank me effusively for making her son "the happiest man alive," for which she would be eternally grateful. She'd been aware of her youngest son's search for a woman to share his life, and she was happy to welcome Sharon into the family. Leland's father eventually softened and learned to focus on Sharon's fine qualities, not her size.

Sharon and Leland were idyllically happy and became even more so when their daughter was born a couple of years later. They never failed to invite us to their home for various celebrations and always acknowledged their gratitude to us for their happiness. During her pregnancy, Sharon regained the weight she had lost before marriage and was twice the size she was when I first met her. Still, that didn't seem to diminish Leland's love for his wife.

She, in turn, adored him, and when he eventually lost his legs due to diabetes, she lovingly cared for him and was often seen wheeling him around town in the wheelchair, into restaurants, stores, or movie houses. When he died in the twenty-first year of their marriage, Sharon called me almost immediately. And, in a conversation similar to the one I'd had with her mother-in-law twenty-one years earlier, she thanked me for being responsible for her and Leland's wonderfully happy life together.

MATCH NO. 4

FRANKLY, I WAS MORE THAN A LITTLE MIFFED when my long-time friend Helen wasn't interested in Mel's second cousin Bill, because, as Bill had put it, "She wants a doctor." But when a doctor literally fell into my lap, it was too good an opportunity to turn down. It was three years later, Bill was happily married to Liz, and Helen, at fifty-eight, was still looking—and still hopeful.

And she was still attractive, trim-figured and petite, always wearing the high heels that called attention to her shapely legs. She had honed her dealing-with-the-public skills over the years while working in her mother's dry goods store before becoming an electrolysis technician. She now maintained her own office, the only one in town and for miles around, that catered to hirsute women. Apparently, there was a big demand for her services, judging from her lifestyle, because she lacked for nothing in her business and personal life.

Helen's large, lavishly decorated apartment in a new building complex was a far cry from the dark tenement apartment she had been sharing with her mother and three brothers when I first met her, twenty-five years earlier. Now, she luxuriated in the opulence of her own apartment, with its velvet-upholstered chairs, marble end tables, and gold-flecked draperies. It reflected the very feminine tastes of a twentieth-century modern American woman in control of her life.

Surprisingly though, her speech was peppered with Yiddish words and phrases one didn't expect to hear, and she still referred to her brothers, as did her mother, as Moishela, Fishela and Yossel.

Helen drove an expensive, late-model car and had season tickets for many cultural events, where she could be seen by the "right" people. She was outgoing and witty, and she was a fantastic cook—she'd not only perfected her mother's recipes from the Old Country, delicious as well as artery clogging, but also mastered Italian and French cooking, turning out entrees and desserts equal to those in the finest restaurants. So, with all this going for her, why was she "still looking" at fifty-eight, having dated every eligible male for miles around over the years? Well, as she admitted, she wanted a doctor, and there weren't many of them around who weren't married.

Then, there was Milton, a much-loved family physician in a nearby town, short in stature but big of heart—he had delivered most of the present generation of the kids in town. His wife, Charlotte, who had been his office nurse for twenty-five of the thirty years of their marriage, succumbed to cancer after a three-year battle with the disease. She was the direct antithesis of Helen,. a dyed-in-the-wool Southern belle from Charleston, who never lost her southern drawl or adapted to "the northerners" way of life. Though she was born into a Jewish family, she never joined any of the local Jewish women's organizations, nor did she accompany Milton to their synagogue on the high holy days.

After her death, Milton was engulfed by sympathy, love, and dinner invitations from the whole town, and he was eating better and enjoying it more than all the years of eating Charlotte's southern recipes. About a year after Charlotte's death, Milton disclosed that the news of his being a widower and "available" had spread throughout our county, as well as into the two adjacent counties, and he was being inundated with dinner invitations from unknown widows and friends of widows. He had been dating one particular widow—Jean—for a couple of months when he asked if he could bring her over, ostensibly for a swim in my pool, but also to solicit my opinion of Jean.

Well, Jean came, but she didn't conquer. Milton and I came to the same conclusion that day: she wasn't for him. While wearing her brief two-piece swimsuit, Jean was so loaded down with gold jewelry that I was sure she'd sink to the bottom of the pool if she tried to swim, which she didn't, for fear of messing her coiffeur. She was a very sophisticated New Yorker, anxious to snare a rich doctor, and would certainly never make this "country-style" family doctor happy. I was glad that Milton came to this realization before I verbalized my feelings. By this time, he admitted, he was tired of meeting different women, yet he didn't enjoy living alone.

A week after the episode with Jean, I received a phone call from Helen. She was aware of Milton's widower status and also that we were friends of his. "You have fixed me up with a dozen men over the years. How come you haven't introduced me to your friend Milton?"

I didn't want to admit to her that she was the exact opposite of Milton's tall, cool, Southern belle, late wife. But I also still remembered her rejection of Cousin Bill. *Well*, I argued with myself, *Milton is lonesome, and who knows? Maybe he'll like her.* "Oh, sure, Helen, I'll be glad to arrange a meeting," I answered glibly. "Milton has been kept so busy by all the widows for miles around that I didn't think he needed any help from me."

Unabashed, Helen informed me, "Yes, but *I* need your help. And he knows my brothers, so it's not as if my family would be totally strange to him."

"You're absolutely right," I agreed. "I'll get to work on it immediately. Just let me know which nights are good for you, and I'll invite you both over for drinks, and then we'll go out for dinner."

"Better still, why don't you bring him to my place for drinks? I'd like him to see my apartment."

Wow, I thought, *she's pulling out all stops.* I knew Helen was very proud of her apartment, and it certainly wouldn't hurt for Milton to see how she lived.

Milton was still living in the home he had built for Charlotte over thirty years ago. The neighborhood wasn't particularly fashionable now, and his home furnishings looked seedy, having been neglected since Charlotte became ill.

The date was set up with a willing Milton, who was happy to have us as a buffer with a new female to escort. Going to Helen's apartment was an excellent idea, for Milton was impressed with the newness of her home and the way she had furnished it. He was also delighted with the delectable appetizers Helen served with our drinks, so many different ones that we had no appetite for our dinner at the French restaurant.

Looking particularly attractive that night, Helen was warm, interesting, and charming. She displayed her marvelous sense of humor as she related amusing incidents of her practice and details of her early days, lifting heavy bolts of material in her mother's dry goods store, and I am sure Milton must have been comparing her mentally to Jean, the jewelry bedecked sophisticated New Yorker. The evening flew by quickly and was enjoyed by all. Back at Helen's apartment, Mel and I waited in the car as Milton escorted her to the door.

"Nice girl," Milton said on entering the car, "and her appetizers were great! Let's do this again."

We had a repeat performance a week later, only this time, Helen insisted on cooking the dinner—and with that, Milton was hooked, proving the truth of that old adage about the way to a man's heart. He found his way to Helen's apartment frequently in the next several months for sumptuous meals, yet never gained an ounce. We often ran into them at various restaurants, sometimes alone but often dining with her family. Milton seemed totally comfortable in the presence of her brothers and their wives, and Helen was familiar enough with Milton by now to address him as "Moische," or "Moishela," the same endearing Yiddish appellations she used for her brother Morris. Her speech was sprinkled with Yiddish phrases and terms that I'm sure were strange to Milton, but he just wore his gentle smile.

We weren't too surprised when Helen called, weeks later, to announce that she and Milton had been married a few days earlier. We were happy for both of them. It took years, but Helen finally got her doctor.

Seventeen years later, after Milton's death, I received a short but heartfelt note from Helen that read: "Thank you for the happiest seventeen years of my life."

CONCLUSION

I REGRET TO SAY it is now almost twenty years since I made my last match, but not because of lack of effort or interest on my part. It's because of lack of available, walking, breathing manpower, a scarce commodity in this era of women outliving men.

Did I have any failures in my fourteen marriages? Well, yes, and I do have to qualify this, because one couple divorced after two kids and ten years later, so it wasn't a total loss. She happened to be Mel's first cousin too, and I wasn't in the best of family graces for a while. How could I know that he had wed and shed four other wives, long before I met him? She learned the true facts, that she was wife #5, on their honeymoon, but cared enough about him at the time to stay and give birth to, and raise the two boys who have been her pride and joy.

I haven't given up on my avocation, for my eyes are *always peeled*, but it's almost a losing battle these days. That adrenaline rush when I struck oil was always wonderful, and I admit I enjoyed that warm, glowing feeling when I was thanked for making a difference in a few lives.

No way am I totally altruistic, cause I got my kicks too! ❧

CHAPTER FIFTY-THREE

LOVE IN BLOOM

I WAS ON MY WAY out the back door, eager to get rid of those fast-growing weeds that were sullying my pristine tulip garden, when the sound of the musical front door chime stopped me abruptly. I deposited my gardening toolbox on the countertop and glanced at the kitchen clock, as if that could tell me the identity of whoever was ringing my bell. It didn't, of course, and—so I headed down the front hall. I could see the outline of a woman outside the screen door—she seemed to be of medium height and build, possibly fiftyish, and a total stranger to me.

"Can I help you?" I inquired.

She seemed a little uncomfortable. "Are you the lady of the house?"
"Yes, I'm Mrs. Engelman."

"Well," she tentatively began, "I hope you won't think me rude, but we have a question." She nodded her head toward the male driver of the strange car parked in the driveway. "We love to drive out in the country at this time of year to see the various trees in blossom, and for the past few years, we have been just entranced by that grove of pink trees growing at the base of your driveway, as well as that one tree with white blossoms growing near them. We haven't seen them elsewhere on our rambles on these back roads and wondered what the names of the trees are."

If one truly has cockles in the heart, I could feel mine warming and swelling, for this stranger touched on my pride and joy. Of all the beautiful flowering trees and shrubs in our yard, the Red Bud Trees and the Lady Apple Tree, which I called my Bride Tree were the loves of my life. I identified the trees for her and stepped out on the porch to enjoy her company momentarily, as we stood for several minutes, our gazes transfixed at the vista of clouds of tiny hot-pink flowers that clung closely to the branches of the redbud trees, which looked oriental in their growing pattern. They provided the perfect backdrop for the one Lady apple tree in full bloom, the snow-white blossoms so thick and profuse, no branches or twigs were visible. What else could this tree resemble but a bride?

She then asked, "Would you mind very much if we parked the car at the bottom of your driveway so we could sit and enjoy this magnificent sight? I see other cars slow up as they pass by your house, and apparently a lot of people feel the same way we do, but we have the time to really stop and look."

I smiled broadly. "Lady, you made my day! It's so gratifying to realize that others enjoy the fruits of our labors, so stay for as long as you care to. I have to get back to weeding my tulips." I took myself off to the backyard, where I spent the next couple of hours on my knees, doing what I enjoy most: weeding. Time flew and when the job was finished to my satisfaction, I decided to get into the house and start preparing dinner for that night, as Mel would be home in an hour or so. I had no sooner gotten into the kitchen when the front door bell chimed. Again, I could see the figure of the same woman through the screen, but this time her husband was standing there beside her.

"Don't tell me you've been here all this time looking at the trees!" I exclaimed.

"Yes, we enjoyed every minute of it," she replied enthusiastically. "We just wanted to thank you so much for allowing us this afternoon of pleasure."

Her husband nodded in agreement. "I hope in the future you will allow us to come again to enjoy the beauty you have here."

I was so pleased by their words that I was ready to hug them both, but instead, I said, "I have a great idea. If you want to give me your names and phone number, when the trees are just starting to bloom next year, I'll call you, so you won't have to worry about missing out on them." My suggestion didn't get the response I expected, so I quickly added, "If you're not home, I'll leave a message on your answering machine."

It was then that the woman looked at her "husband" and said haltingly, "I don't know if that's a good idea, because my husband might just get the message."

And he looked at her as he replied, "Yeah, I don't think you'd better do that because my wife might wonder what it's all about."

If they came the following year, they didn't bother to announce themselves, but I hope they did. ❧

CHAPTER FIFTY-FOUR

SURPRISE!

CHRISTOPHER COLUMBUS did not discover Copper Canyon in northern Mexico. The travel agents discovered it in the late 1980s, and once they unleashed the publicity of their great find, our mail was bombarded by them daily. Their travel brochures, in bold headlines, blared: "Come visit the "Grand Canyon" of Mexico, deeper and more scenic than the United States' Grand Canyon! Come visit with the Tarahumara Indians, still living in caves. Come visit in a community of blonde, blue-eyed Mexicans!" On and on it went.

How could I resist? I couldn't. We planned a trip for the first week in October, when the temperature was bound to be perfect for traveling.

The first two days were spent in a colonial town where many American retirees had settled, often living in rambling haciendas and on grounds that took up a whole city block. Living was cheap then for the retirees, who paid no taxes, and they were able to hire a dozen or more workers to maintain their houses and grounds for a mere pittance of salary.

On the third day, we boarded the Chihuahua el Pacifico Railroad for our 8000-foot climb to Copper Canyon, through eighty-three tunnels and over thirty-five trestles. The scenery was exciting and dramatic, but after a few hours with our noses glued to the train windows, we welcomed the "sumptuous box lunch" described in the travel brochure. The train attendant came through the cars distributing cans of soda and Styrofoam boxes, which we hurriedly opened—and closed almost immediately. Our lunch consisted of one dried roll, with a dead-looking gray slice of something housed between the halves of the roll, accompanied by a small foil packet of mustard. A few die-hards bit into their rolls but then, with resigned expressions, quickly closed the lid of their boxes. As we all rummaged in our carry-on luggage for any food items, the train attendant collected the untouched meals in their boxes and stacked them in large garbage bags.

About twenty minutes later, the train came to a stop at a clearing bordered by a fringe of trees, beyond which we could see, several hundred yards away, a small settlement of homes—more like shacks, really, constructed of wood and corrugated metal. We idly watched the train attendant as he made several trips from the train to a platform, where he deposited the seven or eight garbage bags containing the uneaten "sumptuous box lunches." After his last bag was deposited on the platform, he boarded the train, which began moving slowly.

We watched in horrified amazement as five young boys materialized from the fringe of trees and raced toward the garbage bags, where they tried to drag away more than one of the bags, which were almost as tall as they were. They headed for the shacks beyond the trees as we occupants of the train exchanged shocked glances with each other. Apparently our lunches would yet be appreciated. This was our first confrontation with real poverty in Mexico.

The second confrontation occurred while visiting a boarding school run by the Church for the teenage boys of the Tarahumara Indians, who still lived in caves. They were a shy, gentle people who fashioned their handicrafts in the ways of their ancestors and were known for their amazing endurance in long-distance running. As there were no local schools in the vicinity of their cave homes, the boys were sent miles away, to be taught by the dedicated priests in a stark, rambling wooden building that housed about seventy boys at that time.

We toured the premises and marveled at the accomplishments of the priests in educating these cave-dweller boys and at the crude but utilitarian classrooms and sleeping quarters. As we were shown through the large dining hall, our young priest-guide indicated the many wooden picnic-style tables and benches, which the boys would not have experienced in their caves. A large stone fireplace in the middle of one wall of the room provided heat in the winter. On the wall directly over the fireplace mantel, a narrow rack held about fifteen small black brushes, each about six inches in length.

"What are those brushes used for?" I asked our guide.

"Oh, those are the toothbrushes we have taught the boys to use," he answered. "They take turns using them, as we don't have enough to go around."

Again, we who replace our toothbrushes every couple of months, exchanged shocked, sympathetic glances with each other. (Several weeks later, the school was the recipient of several cartons of toothbrushes donated by Lactona, a dental toothbrush manufacturer, at the urging of Mel, the dentist.)

Our next destination was to the community of blonde, blue-eyed Mexicans described in the travel brochures. My curiosity was piqued, as Mexicans are always depicted as being dark-complexioned, with dark hair and eyes, but in this instance, the brochures didn't lie. What we learned at this settlement was that over fifty years earlier, a band of Mennonites from Germany emigrated to Mexico and started their own commune, becoming Mexican citizens.

We were guided through the various buildings of this settlement, including a couple of private homes, and then we were let loose to purchase their handcrafted goods, including knit and crocheted articles, wooden ornaments, aprons, dolls, and pot holders. I purchased two sets of pot holders I didn't need, but I was grateful later on for having made the purchase. While concluding my purchase, I became unpleasantly aware of feeling squeamish, and when our guide began ushering the tour bus occupants into the huge dining hall for a Mennonite lunch, eating was the farthest thing from my mind. I told Mel to enjoy his lunch and took myself and my bag of potholders to the empty bus, where I stretched out on a rear seat. Lying flat seemed to accentuate the feelings of nausea, so I tried sitting up, wondering all the while what I could have eaten that was different from the rest of the tour group. The sitting position didn't help the situation, either; I became more miserable—I felt as if I was going to die, and yet I was afraid that I wouldn't die!

One interminable half-hour later, the bus occupants began straggling back to the bus, and Mel rejoined me on the back bench seat, concerned about my worsened condition. When every seat was filled, the bus started up with a lurch, and that had me looking around wildly for a bathroom that wasn't there. And there was no nearby open window out of which I could hang my head.

"I have to throw up!" I frantically announced to Mel.

With a quick movement, Mel removed the potholders from the plastic bag and handed it to me to use, and oh, what blessed relief as my stomach disgorged its contents!

"Now what?" I asked, wiping my mouth with a tissue, holding the half-full bag out in front of me.

"This," replied Mel, as he grabbed the bag and knotted it securely. He then stepped to the seat in front of us, opened the window, and reaching over the heads of the two occupants, threw out the bag with a mighty pitch. As he took his seat again next to me, we both turned to look out the back window of the bus. I experienced a horrible sense of déjà vu as three little boys rushed to the site of the pitched bag by the side of the road. The tallest one of the three reached it first, grabbed it, and ran off, with the other two following him in hot pursuit.

Our eyes met again, in shocked disbelief. ❧

CHAPTER FIFTY-FIVE

MISSION ACCOMPLISHED

IT WAS A SIMPLE REQUEST that I couldn't refuse, though it was unexpected and most unusual. It was the first and only time I had been asked to write information for an obituary notice by someone who was still very much alive—my old army buddy Uppie. We had been in close contact with each other for the past forty-eight years, since the end of World War II. Uppie was third in command of the nurses, a captain, head of the psychiatric nursing section, and the oldest nurse in our hospital outfit, while I was among the youngest. She always had a warm, indulgent smile for me, perhaps because of my youthful exuberance, and as she said later, she always felt I was the daughter she never had.

After the war, we saw a good deal of Uppie when she was working in New York as Associate Professor of Nursing at Cornell, and Director of Nursing at Payne Whitney Clinic of New York Hospital. We lived a sixty-five-mile train ride north of Manhattan, so she spent many weekends with us, and Mel enjoyed her visits as much as I did, for she was a brilliant, compassionate woman with a marvelous sense of humor and infallible memory. When she retired and moved back to Keene, New Hampshire, to live in the hundred-year-old family home, we drove the three-hour trip to visit with her several times a year, and she always looked forward to those times. Uppie and I rehashed the war in between shopping expeditions. She had given up driving and was dependent on neighbors or taxi services for purchasing the necessities of life. We realized that her sight and hearing had deteriorated tremendously, the result of buzz bomb injuries suffered before and during the Battle of the Bulge, for which she had been awarded the Purple Heart, with two Oak Leaf Clusters representing additional combat wounds.

It was during one of these visits that Uppie made the request for obituary information. Trying to inject some levity into a serious discussion, I inquired, "Why? Are you planning to die soon?"

"Well, Phil," she replied, using my nickname from our army days, "my vision and hearing have gotten so bad that the VA physicians have advised that I will be completely blind within two years. My coordination and balance is so poor that I have fallen down stairs twice in the past two months, and my "English hack," the cough we all developed in England, seriously damaged my lungs. You are the only 'family' I have, except for my nephew in Arizona, whom I rarely see, and I want you to write up the story of 'our war' that was such an important part of my life. Your photo album with running commentary on each photo tells the complete story of the Sixteenth General Hospital, which I want, incorporated into my vital statistics information that I will provide my lawyer. I'm going to have a full military funeral, with all the bells and whistles, and if you and Mel aren't traveling somewhere, I hope you'll come."

Uppie moved to the VA Hospital in Manchester, New Hampshire, shortly after this discussion, where, true to their predictions, she was totally blind and had 90 percent loss of hearing in less than two years. She died from lung complications shortly after, escaping from her sightless and soundless existence. We didn't attend the funeral, as we were traveling at the time and only learned of her death from Uppie's lawyer on our return home. Along with his letter informing me of her death, he'd enclosed several copies of her obituary notice from a few different newspapers. Two of them detailed the history of our three years together as army nurses and the circumstances leading up to her Purple Heart awards. Several pictures of Uppie, which I had enclosed with her military history, were also reproduced in the newspaper articles. She did have the requested military funeral, with flag-draped coffin, a firing squad, and honor guard, and with "Taps" sounded. At the conclusion, the flag was presented to her nephew. As I read the details of the funeral, I thought, *Oh, how Uppie would have enjoyed all this.* Well, maybe she did. Mission Accomplished!

In July 1994, one year later, I received a phone call from a woman asking to speak to Mrs. Engelman. "Speaking," I replied.

"Muriel Engelman?" she inquired, continuing her questioning.

"Yes."

The caller seemed rather breathless. "Muriel Phillips Engelman of the Sixteenth General Hospital?"

She'll probably want my army serial number next, I thought. "That's right," I confirmed, "this is she."

She sighed, and the sound seemed to be one of relief. "It has taken me almost a full year to locate you, and I am so happy to have finally found you." Then she went on to introduce herself as Barbara Martin, calling from Santa Monica, the widow of the late Major Steve Martin of the Sixteenth General Hospital. Did I remember him?

Of course, I remembered him, as I did all fifty of the physicians and dentists in our outfit. I immediately visualized Steve, Chief of Orthopedics. He'd been of medium height and build, with light brown hair, and was very shy. Whenever he did appear at the Officers' Club, he usually had a book in his hand or sat and talked with other male officers. I never saw him dance to the jukebox music with any of the nurses.

I assured Barbara that I remembered Steve well, and his reputation as an orthopedic surgeon was outstanding. Now it was my turn to ask questions. "Why were you looking for me, of all the people in our outfit?"

Barbara replied that it was a long story and that she didn't want to take up too much of my time, but in brief, Steve had died three years previously, and with the fiftieth anniversary of World War II coming up next year, she had signed up for a tour of Normandy, which would be her private memorial to him.

"However," she said, "in all the years we were married, he would not talk about the war to me or our three sons, not even when they were in their teens and old enough to want to know about their father's war experiences. I knew from his letters when he was in England, France, and Belgium, but that's the extent of it. I learned from other officers' wives I met at your hospital reunions after the war that you lived through some terrible times, especially in Belgium, but when I asked him, he would only reply, 'I don't want to talk about it.' What I would like to do is find out every place your hospital was stationed, not just the country but the locale, and the dates you were there. When I have each destination fixed, I want to make my own pilgrimage with our youngest son, so we can see and feel and have insight into his experiences the years he was away from home."

I was deeply touched by her plan to reach out to her husband's past and my reply was: "It's a marvelous undertaking, Barbara, and I have all the information as to maps, dates, events, and places, and even some pictures of Steve in group photos. I'll be happy to send it to you."

Barbara was so profuse in her thanks for my offer, I knew from the emotion in her voice that she was close to tears.

But I wanted the answer to my question. "I still don't know how you happened to single me out for information, and how did you find me?"

"It seems you wrote an article for an obituary for one of the nurses in your outfit about a year ago that appeared in a New Hampshire newspaper, which credited you for the information," she said. "This obituary and article was sent by a friend of the deceased to a friend in Maine, who sent it to one of the officers' wives in Boston. She then sent it on to another wife in New York, whom I had met at your reunion and with whom I had been in contact since Steve died. When I told her I was so anxious to find the places Steve had been but had no idea where to start, she sent me the full page obituary and article. There was no address listed for you, so I called the New Hampshire newspaper and spoke to the writer of the article, who had your address and phone number in his files, and that's how I finally reached you."

Again, photos were reproduced and all information was sent out in time for Barbara to plan her itinerary to mesh with the Normandy ceremonies. About six week after the Normandy tour, I received grateful phone calls and letters from Barbara, detailing her journey to that missing part of her husband's life. Mission Accomplished! ❧

CHAPTER FIFTY-SIX

FLASHBACKS

HAVING REACHED THIS VENERABLE AGE of eighty-five, when most of life's experiences are behind me, it is more enjoyable ruminating on the past than on what the future could possibly hold for me. (Alzheimer's? Illness? Nursing home?) Flashbacks of individuals or memorable incidents pop up on my mental imagery board for rehashing, inviting a visit to times gone by.

We can't get away from the subject of politics these days, and I am so often reminded of our tour guide in Bangkok, who spoke English well, although as seems typical of many Asians, he had a problem pronouncing L's and R's. As our bus rolled through the Thai countryside, he apologized for not always recognizing the occupants of this particular tour bus because "All you Amelicans rook arike." A few minutes later, while discussing "Amelican" politics, a subject that he knew well, he was able to discourse in great detail all aspects of the coming "plesidential erection."

Politically speaking, I didn't garner too many high marks from a French secretary some time in 1990, when Mel and I were in Paris on a business trip. We had a tentative appointment with the president of a company that sold dental products, and I called from our hotel the morning of the appointment to confirm the time and address for our meeting with his secretary. The president's name was an unusually long one, with many vowels and consonants, but I was careful to write it out phonetically to help me pronounce it at our appointed time. We arrived at the business office on schedule, and I realized, with dismay, that I'd left my carefully written notes on the bedside table at the hotel.

Before being ushered in to see the president, I asked his secretary, "Comment s'appele le président?" ("What's the president's name?")

She looked at me with horror, disdain, and a look that clearly meant *you stupid American*, and then she replied in an icy voice, "Mais certainement, c'est Francois Mitterand." ("Of course, it's Francois Mitterand.") Two minds running in opposite directions, as if I didn't know the name of the president of France!

Mel and I first visited Paris in 1965, and while window shopping near our hotel, we passed a grocery store that featured in its store window several bottles of a fruit drink in flavors of orange, lime, and lemon. The name of the drink was spelled "Pschitt."

"Now, how do you think they pronounce it?" I asked Mel. We were so intrigued by the name, we purchased a bottle to take home for our bar, and for years enjoyed inviting our guests to try a drink of orange Pschitt.

In the spring of 1969, we took our two high-school-age children to Europe to experience foreign cultures and to visit historical points of interest they had studied in school. I had three years of Italian language classes under my belt and felt capable of being the family tour guide for the time we would spend in Italy. Before leaving home, I had been warned by friends just returning from Italy to watch out for the romantic Italian men who loved to pinch the rear ends of young women. I replied that I was forty-eight years old, and the bloom was definitely off the rose—even the garbage men didn't toot at me any more as they drove by.

Arriving in Florence after a couple of busy weeks sightseeing in Spain, Portugal, and Venice, it was planned that Mel would take the kids to the Pitti Palace to view the great works of art there. I wanted to shop for gifts in the many fine stores just up the street from our hotel, which was located on the banks of the Arno River, near the famous Ponte Vecchio. I savored my time alone, browsing and purchasing leather gloves and small, hand-carved gilded wooden trays. I was transfixed by the beauty of a window display in one store; it was of sculpted marble, alabaster, malachite, and stone objects, and as I stood at the window, admiring and calculating prices in dollars, a pleasant, melodious male voice behind me said in fluid Italian, "They are very beautiful, are they not?"

I turned to face the handsome, well-dressed gentleman, who seemed to be about my age. I answered him in my well-learned Italian, "Yes, they are beautiful, and I can't make up my mind which to buy." We kept up a steady conversation for several minutes about the items in the window, and then he remarked that he detected from my speech that I was not a native Italian (I saved that tidbit to repeat to my Italian teacher).

The gentleman became very interested when I said I was from New York, and then he asked where I was staying in Florence and could he have the pleasure of escorting me to my hotel. I figured my shopping spree was finished, and as I turned to go, he linked his arm through mine, and we set off in the direction of the hotel. Now I started to worry. This man hadn't pinched me yet, but he was getting rather chummy. He kept up a steady chatter about the sights he would show me in Florence and then asked if I would like to go dancing that evening.

I shook my head and replied that awaiting me at the hotel was "mio marito e mi bambini" ("my husband and children").

As if struck by a burning ember, my handsome Italian quickly disengaged his arm from mine, muttering, "Ah, marito e bambini, arrividerla, senora!" ("Ah, husband and children, good-bye, madame!")

I was relieved to see him go but thrilled at the idea that a man had tried to pick me up, at my age, no less. It was such a boost to my ego and far better than getting pinched in the rear. To this day, I remember my excitement as I burst into the hotel room to tell Mel and the kids that I'd been picked up by a handsome Italian. I never did find out what they saw at the Pitti Palace that afternoon.

One memorable incident I frequently recall occurred in a small backwater village on the banks of the Yangtze River in the mid 1980s. After debarking from our cruise ship and climbing up the steep, eighty to ninety wooden steps that ended in a dusty, flat plateau, we found ourselves in a civilization a century back in time. A dirt road comprised the main street of this hamlet, with merchants displaying their wares in open air on either side of the road. The butcher had his steer, sheep, or hog hanging from a metal rack, still dripping blood on the dirt below and swarming with thousands of flies and bees. Adjacent to the butcher was the shoemaker, who worked his treadle-operated sewing machine, repairing the sandals commonly worn by the village inhabitants.

The hardware merchant came next, with simple tools and knives displayed on a table, and he was busy sharpening the knives on a stone. When the knives were sharpened to his satisfaction, he placed them on the table. We rounded a curve in the road and came upon the village dentist at work, with his patient seated in a wooden straight-back chair at a wooden table. A filthy, blood-stained, ragged remnant of a towel that bore evidence of weeks of usage lay on the table in the midst of some rudimentary dental instruments. We watched quietly as the dentist proceeded drilling an upper tooth in the patient's mouth, oblivious to his audience. Suddenly, the drill loosened and fell to the dirt next to the patient's bare feet. Unperturbed, the dentist picked up the drill, and with the bloody towel, wiped off the loose dirt clinging to it, inserted it back into the hand piece, and resumed his treadle-operated drilling of the patient's tooth. He was in luck that surgical gloves weren't required then.

At the end of our Yangtze River cruise, we ended up in the large city of Chongqing, and en route to our hotel five miles out of town, we stopped at an electronics store to replenish our film supply. The store was filled with cartons of computers from floor to ceiling, the latest in modern-age miracles, and we were interested to note that the sales clerk totaled up the sales using his abacus. Once our purchase was completed, we headed for our hotel, which was made famous for us because Henry Kissinger had stayed there the previous week. The hotel was new and modern in style, though apparently constructed in a hurry to accommodate the sudden influx of tourists in China. Ceramic wall tiles were missing in the bathroom, and ceiling acoustic tiles had loosened and hung precariously over the bathtub. Mel sought out the housekeeping attendant, who was sitting in the laundry room at the end of the hall, and motioned for him to bring the vacuum cleaner to our room, where the carpeting was littered with dried tea leaves and dust balls. The attendant turned on the vacuum cleaner and pushed it back and forth, but left more debris than was there previously. No one had ever taught him that vacuum cleaner bags must be replaced when filled. He must have been the same room attendant who cleaned the room of a friend next door, who found a used condom under her bed.

The following morning, after finishing breakfast in the large hotel dining room, Mel remembered that he had left his sunglasses on the table and returned to the dining room to get them. That's when he saw the waiter pouring the dregs of everyone's coffee cups into a coffee pitcher. The waiter repeated this procedure at each table, probably to reuse it at the next sitting. You can be sure we were first in line at the dining room the following morning to assure freshly brewed coffee. Hopefully, Henry Kissinger took these same precautions.

During the war, when our hospital contingent moved to Liège, Belgium, while waiting to be assigned for hospital duty, a few other nurses and I decided to experience a Turkish bath that was located near our temporary quarters. After the sauna, where we had all worked up a good sweat, the manager asked the group, "Voulez-vous douchez?" ("Do you want to shower?")

That word "douchez" sounded obscene to us, and the poor guy never knew why we all chorused an emphatic *Non!* and stalked out in disgust.

Ah, a trip down Memory Lane is so good for the soul! ❧

CHAPTER FIFTY-SEVEN

LITTLE DARLINGS

AS SHE WOULD SWAT THE MOSQUITOES zooming in on her, my mother would declare, without fail, "The mosquitoes love me because I have sweet blood." Well, I don't know what flavors were floating around in my blood components, but at a certain period in my life, in my fifties, perhaps, I was attracting all varieties of wasps, with results more disastrous than mere mosquito bites.

Spring, summer, and fall, whether working in my gardens, swimming in the pool, enjoying a picnic lunch, or just minding my own business, I was attacked by these pesky critters. As long as I was out of doors in these seasons, I was targeted, often to the exclusion of the ten other people I might be with. On so many occasions, it never failed to amaze Mel and me that the flying enemy would single me out to buzz around ominously, forcing me to run for cover, with the wasp in hot pursuit. If he flew faster than I could run, then I was stung on any exposed bit of flesh. At first, I just exhibited pain and swelling at the site of invasion, which would subside in a day or two, but in time, these stings became more dangerous, requiring medical assistance in the form of cortisone shots.

Once, it became an "easy" way for me to get a new diamond-encrusted wedding band and new setting with extra diamonds for my engagement ring, though there must be easier routes for acquiring new jewelry. I was stung on the tip of my left ring finger at 4 p.m., as I stood in the shade, talking with Mel and his mom, at a time when all self-respecting wasps should be retiring to their hives or nests for the night. By 6 p.m., I was in Mel's office, where he used his dental instruments to cut off both rings from my purple swollen finger. Even with the rings off, the swelling continued to travel up my arm, which had ballooned out to immense proportions. By midnight, with the swelling shoulder high, we were in the emergency room for a cortisone shot, which halted its progress. Within two days, my arm was back to its normal size.

The next stinging episode was more scary. I was on my knees mid-morning, weeding the evergreen hedge, and I must have disturbed an underground wasp nest, for several angry wasps flew out, apparently the vanguard for the one that stung me under my left eye. Within seconds, my lips became numb, and my tongue started swelling. With visions of myself choking to death, I rushed indoors for the adrenaline kit, which I had kept on hand for years, in case of a reaction to my allergy vaccine which I administered to myself monthly. With shaking hands, I withdrew the adrenaline into the syringe, injected it into my thigh, and then called Mel's office, instructing his office manager to get him home immediately.

I then sat quietly in a comfortable chair on the back porch, telephone at hand, waiting for the adrenaline to work—to stop the tongue from further swelling before it obstructed my breathing. Mel arrived home to see me sitting peacefully in the chair, not knowing what to expect, but when I informed him of the sting, he was duly concerned and stayed with me until we were sure the tongue swelling was subsiding, although my lips and face were swelling by degrees. He had injected a patient with Lidocaine just before my call to his office and had rushed out, leaving the patient in the dental chair. After a half-hour or so, he felt it was safe to leave me to return to the office and continue with the patient's dental treatment.

There was no more gardening for me that day; I sat in the shallow end of the pool the entire afternoon, dunking my increasingly swollen face into the water, which unfortunately, did not alleviate the situation. My lips, cheeks, and forehead were so engorged, I couldn't open my eyes and felt that I must resemble a blind Ubangi. Making my way into the house by 4 p.m., I called Mel's office again, and soon we were on our way to the emergency room for a cortisone shot, which put a halt to the facial swelling.

After this episode, I really became paranoid at the sight or sound of a bee or wasp, and I didn't venture outdoors without protective clothing, a brimmed hat, and a can of spray insect killer. My greatest summer pleasures, gardening, swimming, and pool entertaining, were ruined, and at night I dreamed of having miles of highways covered with wasps as tanks rolled over their bodies. I just wanted all of them dead. We began investigating preventive measures against bee-sting reactions but at that time, the only treatments available were vaccines made up of a liquid solution and the ground bodies and venom sacs of the bees. These vaccines, which had to be administered weekly at first and gradually monthly for the entire year, were painful and not 100 percent effective.

Delving still further into medical records, we came upon information describing the newest bee-venom treatment; only one physician was on record for employing this treatment, but she guaranteed 100 percent immunity. Fortunately, this Dr. Loveless was only an hour's drive away, in Westport, Connecticut, which was feasible for us. We lost no time in making an appointment.

When we spoke on the phone, Dr. Loveless was all business, barking out instructions for a special diet full of protein for breakfast before my appointment—at least three strips of bacon, and two to three eggs. I was to bring someone else with me for the drive home, as I would have a sore arm. Last, she barked, "For God's sake, take down carefully the directions for finding my office, and don't get lost like all the other nitwits who come here for the first time." She sounded charming.

Following her instructions carefully, we still managed to get lost, for her home and office were located in a forested area with poorly marked winding roads, and there were no other homes in the area. We had left home early enough to give us extra time and were lucky to just happen to stumble upon her home/office. It was set off from the winding road where we spotted an arrow sign with *Dr. Loveless* printed on it in faded, almost indiscernible black paint. We drove into the yard on a sparsely graveled driveway and pulled up in front of a two-story white clapboard building in need of a new paint job and repairs to the sagging shutters hanging on one hinge. The front lawn was overgrown with weeds, and there were old flower beds that might have been colorful and pretty at some point in time, but which now sprouted tall weeds that strangled whatever flowers still survived. *This is a doctor's office?* I thought.

As we were about to head for the front door, an upstairs window was thrown open and a tousled white head appeared halfway out of the window, screaming, "What are you doing parking at the front door of my home? I told you to go to *my office* and park there, and that's on the other side of this building! The door is unlocked, so go in and sit in the waiting room until I get there!" A truly sweet lady.

We got in the car and drove to the rear of the building, and sure enough, a weathered sign reading "Office" was nailed over a doorway. *Maybe the office interior will look more like a physician's office than the exterior,* I thought. *You know, sort of sterile looking.* After we mounted the three steps and opened the door, I realized it was just a pipe dream. The waiting room was completely in harmony with the dilapidated and neglected outer grounds and building, with no resemblance to any physician's office we had ever frequented. It was about eight by ten feet in size, furnished with two faded chintz upholstered loveseats, one straight-backed wooden chair, a wrought-iron end table with a small reading lamp, and a large rectangular wooden coffee table. Health journals, dating back five years up to the present, were strewn on the coffee table, and the areas not covered with magazines were thick with dust, as were all flat areas in the room.

Our attention was caught by a wall rack that held dozens of different well-known medical journals, detailing Dr. Loveless' work with bees, and including her curriculum vitae, which was quite impressive. Up until this point, I'd been on the verge of fleeing back to our home, pristine by comparison, but as we read on, we were more encouraged. One of the early female graduates from Cornell Medical School, Dr. Loveless had pioneered in this field for years and had proven the efficacy of her method, though it had not been officially sanctioned by the American Medical Association.

The outside door opened and in walked Dr. Loveless, wearing a worn Hawaiian-print low-necked, loose-fitting muumuu and rubber thongs on her bare feet. *Do doctors dress like this?* She appeared to be in her mid-seventies, with an unruly mop of curly white hair that framed a florid face, bearing traces of a certain refinement and intelligence. Her blue eyes behind the wire-framed eyeglasses were piercing, as though she was peering right through us and reading our thoughts.

She offered no word of apology for keeping us waiting over a half hour. In a querulous voice, she commanded, "Come in, come in to my laboratory and let's not waste time." She motioned for Mel to follow also.

I'd hoped her laboratory would perhaps resemble a "doctor's laboratory," but again, I was doomed to disappointment.

It was a large room, about twenty by twenty feet in size, with wall cabinets hung from the ceiling, under which ran work countertops laden with flasks, white enamel instrument trays, cans of tuna fish, empty mayonnaise jars, and unrelated objects. A large, white, early vintage refrigerator rested on the worn and not-so-clean linoleum flooring next to a chipped, stained porcelain sink. Two stools were placed in front of the countertop, adjacent to the refrigerator, and a white plastic garden chair was on the opposite side of the room. These comprised the furniture in this lab.

Dr. Loveless directed me to sit on one of the stools and waved Mel to the chair with her hand, advising him, "There is to be no talking while I am working, and if you have any questions, save them for later. Make sure you pay attention to what I am doing, because in a few years you may be doing this procedure for your wife. I'm not getting any younger, and only the few physicians to whom I have taught this method of treatment will be available to carry on."

Well, she almost sounded human at this point.

Dr. Loveless then proceeded to describe my forthcoming treatment, which would consist of her using two forceps to place a live wasp, her Little Darling, on my upper arm. I was to click the stopwatch she had put in my opposite hand as soon as the wasp inserted his stinger under the skin. The theory behind it, according to her, was that one full minute of bee venom injected into my body would provide immunity for one year, as compared to the existing vaccines that were injected weekly and then monthly. They were not the pure, more potent venom I would be getting directly from the wasp. Before starting, as she bent over to apply the blood pressure cuff to my arm, I could see right down her low-necked muumuu to where her pendulous breasts were dangling on her abdomen. She didn't have a stitch of clothing on under this muumuu! *Female doctors don't wear underwear?*

Both Mel and I watched as Dr. Loveless opened the door of her almost empty refrigerator and removed a mayonnaise jar housing about five or six lethargic Little Darlings she had caught with her net earlier that morning about four miles away. When first caught and transferred to the jar, they flew around angrily in their glass prison. Being refrigerated for an hour or more quieted them down enough so she could work with them. With one forceps she removed a lethargic wasp by its wing, then covered the jar and replaced it in the refrigerator. She then applied a second forceps to the other wing and placed the wasp on my arm, crooning lovingly to this insect that was about to sting me as she held it in position.

Feeling both revulsion and fear, I watched as the Little Darling awakened from his lethargy and squirmed around on my arm, trying to shake loose from the forceps holding him in place, moving his stinger around but not yet inserting it under the skin.

"Be ready to click the stopwatch the second he injects," cautioned Dr. Loveless, and suddenly, he inserted the stinger under the skin and began pumping venom, as she screamed, "Click it! Click it!" I clicked, and we started timing the number of seconds, but about eight seconds later, the stinger was withdrawn. We had to wait for several minutes before the wasp, still squirming, finally inserted his stinger, and again, I clicked to time the seconds of the pulsating stinger. We actually got up to thirteen seconds of venom when again, he pulled out his stinger and refused to cooperate for the next ten minutes. Dr. Loveless then deposited him in an empty jar with air holes and retrieved another wasp from the refrigerator—and we went through the same procedure again. This one was more cooperative, maybe lulled by her crooning, and he inserted his stinger within a few seconds. We timed the pulsating stinger injecting his venom for another seventeen seconds before he withdrew, for a total of thirty-eight seconds so far. Twenty-two more to go. I was so intent on clicking the stopwatch and counting the seconds that I failed to notice the pain of the sting each time the stinger penetrated the skin. Little Darling number two horsed around for a while on my arm before finally finishing his job, for my actual total of sixty-five seconds of venom injected. I was now officially immunized against bee stings for the next year.

As Dr. Loveless gently deposited number two in the jar containing number one, she informed us that she would drive the four miles to where she had collected the wasps earlier and release them back in their home territory, none the worse for having donated their venom to me. I asked why she couldn't save herself the drive and release them in her own yard, where there were weeds and flowers. Dr. Loveless was horrified. "Oh no, my Little

Darlings go right back to their home territory, where I found them." She seemed to have more empathy for them than for me.

My blood pressure, taken again, was still within normal limits, and I was free to go, with her admonition to call her the following morning. "Call at 10 a.m. sharp, and I don't mean 10:30." I was to expect a certain amount of pain, which a couple of aspirin would control, and was to measure the amount of swelling with a ruler and report this to her. I was also to consume a high-protein diet for the next couple of days. We were glad to pay the hundred-dollar fee and leave. As we got into the car, Mel remarked, "Her name is very fitting. Who could love her?"

As predicted, the site of injection did swell and become red and painful, which a couple of aspirin relieved, and when I reported to Dr. Loveless the next morning at 10 a.m. sharp, she advised me to call her if I was stung at all over the year. I was to see her again the following summer. We had repeat visits to Dr. Loveless for several years, until she finally turned my treatment over to Mel, as she was retiring. Mel had received repeated instructions on how to proceed during previous visits. Under her watchful eye, he performed the procedure, and she only had to scream at him once, "Watch out! You're tearing the wing off my Little Darling, and he won't be able to fly again if you do!"

With final advice on attracting wasps with tuna fish, tomato, or melon and transferring them from the net into their bottle, our association with Dr. Loveless was finished.

Her method definitely worked for me, and even though I was stung a couple of times over the next twenty years, I had no allergic reaction whatsoever. I was able to resume my idyllic summer pastimes of gardening without protective clothing, swimming, and picnicking at the pool. Gone was my paranoia every time I heard the buzz of a bee, and no longer did I run for cover when they hove in sight. Gone also were my dreams of killing off every wasp in the world, for I was now in a "live and let live" frame of mind, thanks to Dr. Loveless and her Little Darlings.

Dr. Loveless' death was noted in the news media about three years later, though I never did learn whether her method had been recognized professionally. As Dr. Loveless admitted to us previously, however, there were very few physicians who were willing to take the time to collect live bees, let alone risk the stings one suffered when working with them. 🙂

CHAPTER FIFTY-EIGHT

PRESENTS

I AM MARRIED TO a man who enjoys shopping for presents, as long as he can order from mail-order catalogues or the Internet. Going from store to store isn't his bag, and in the early days, before the advent of computers, it was either catalogues or the *New York Times* ads. Mel always knows what he wants to purchase for me or the kids, whereas I never have ideas when it's my turn to buy a gift. I just wander aimlessly from store to store, checking prices, ending up empty-handed.

Mel has two theories when it comes to gift giving: if one is good, five are better; and if you like it, buy it! I learned this years ago, when we were first married, and Mel presented me with two pairs of pajamas at Christmas. They were just what I needed, and I quickly expressed my pleasure on the receipt of this gift. Two weeks later, for my birthday, I was the recipient of three more pairs of pajamas.

Mel never looks at price tags, while I, the cheapskate who shops around for the best price, only get practical gifts. I was brought up not to buy anything unless I really needed it; therefore, it was unsettling for me the years Mel attempted to purchase clothes for me from Saks, Bergdorf or Lord & Taylor catalogues. They usually went back to the stores as fast as they arrived. Not only was I horrified at the prices, but these clothes also were fashioned for tiny, long-waisted, flat-bellied women. I did not fit into either of these two categories with my thirty-two-inch waistline and big belly. Can you imagine me, wearing a four-inch-wide soft leather belt encrusted with semi-precious stones? Oh, yes, it was gorgeous, but I looked like a meal bag with a rope tied around the middle, bulging out above and below the rope.

I consented to keep the two-piece bathing suit that exposed six inches of my bare midriff, just to make him happy. You can be sure I remained covered with a beach robe until the very minute I entered the water, and the robe was hastily donned again as soon as I emerged. In those days, I called it a bikini, but it surely didn't compare to the couple of strips of cloth they call a bikini today.

One Christmas I received a beautifully wrapped package from one of his fancy stores and was nonplussed to find what was called a "cocktail lounging suit." I could have used a pair of dungarees for gardening but got this outfit instead, which consisted of plum-colored, clingy satin pants that really clung to me like the skin on a baloney. A gold accordion-pleated cummerbund accompanied the chartreuse, plunging-neckline blouse, which plunged right down to my belly button. It was a fascinating color combination that headed right back to the store in the first post-holiday mail.

For my birthday, a well known Fifth Avenue store was featuring some kind of "harem pants"—at least I think that's what they were called. I loved the wild colors of hot pink and purple, but I wouldn't be caught dead wearing those filmy, diaphanous things. All that was needed were castanets and tambourine, and I could be a belly dancer. It was about this time that Mel threw up his hands in despair, declaring, "I will never buy another stitch of clothes for you again!" I really felt guilty for raining on his parade so many times when his intentions were the very best, but my conservative tastes in clothes didn't quite mesh with his.

"You can give me gift certificates instead," I suggested, hoping to soothe his feelings.

But now that he didn't give me clothes as gifts, Mel turned to electric cooking appliances, like an ice-cream maker, a bread maker, carving knives, a meat-slicing machine, and a Cuisinart. The ice-cream machine languished in the basement for years, never used because it required heavy cream, which was fattening. The bread maker went back—I don't bake. I did use the electric carving knife and enjoyed the slicing machine, but I outsmarted myself when I sent back the Cuisinart. After all, I had a perfectly good cast-iron meat grinder that clamped under the kitchen counter, like the one my mother and grandmother had used. Five years later, I relented and requested a Cuisinart, which I couldn't possibly live without today, and newer models have replaced obsolete versions. Mel had the grace not to say, "I told you so."

Ever since Mel discovered a nationally known kitchen appliance store, he has enjoyed ordering their items for me, the latest being an electric rice cooker that took one full hour before the rice was soft enough to eat. I could have cooked it on the stove in fifteen minutes. I donated it to Goodwill for a tax write-off. Another recently returned gift from this store was a contraption which sliced, peeled, shredded, diced, grated, chopped—it did everything but tie your shoe laces. One needed a PhD in engineering to figure out how to remove and replace the different blades, and Mel did agree with me that it was too complicated to use without cutting body parts.

I don't mean to denigrate all the beautiful and useful gifts that I did receive from Mel over the years, which outnumbered the impractical ones by far. He really struck oil with works of art, jewelry, books, record albums of my favorite operas, and theater tickets for Broadway shows, and I didn't hesitate to express my enjoyment of them. Every once in a while, though, he'd stray from the beaten path and bestow something unusual upon me. For instance, one Mother's Day gift was a shiny, black, ominous-looking Colt .45 automatic pistol. Accompanying this expression of his love for me was a confirmation of reservation for a week's course of instruction for the two of us at Gunsite in Paulden, Arizona, four short weeks after Mother's Day. Our home had been burglarized a few times that year so it was understandable from whence this gift came. Just what I wanted!

The only prerequisites for class attendees were possession of the gun, a license for it, and three letters of character reference. I am sure my fellow classmates wished the Gunsite management had been a little more discriminatory in accepting students. There we stood in line, about fifteen men and two women, all of whom, except Mel and me, were in some form of police or security work. Pistols were loaded and safeties off. Each time the instructor yelled, "Muriel, for God's sake, keep your pistol pointed to the ground!" I was aware of those flanking me on either side, perceptibly moving as far away from me as they could. Mel was way down the line, so I couldn't glean any moral support from him.

It was a rough week, learning to shoot with live ammunition from different positions: standing, on our knees, or flat on our bellies, which I found to be the most difficult of all for hitting a target. I had a stiff neck for weeks afterward, from trying to fire in the prone position. This was one gift I could have done without. I must admit, though, I did have a sense of pride in belonging to this elite group as we walked through town at night, wearing the pistol belts that held our loaded pistols. You can be sure the safeties were on. The local townspeople were accustomed to seeing Gunsite students walking their streets and didn't flinch when they approached me, as did my classmates.

Once back home, Mel insisted on frequent practice sessions in our back acreage that sent all wildlife scrambling. Over time, these sessions became infrequent, gradually dwindling down to none. All I can remember from my week at Gunsite now is my stiff neck and, should I should ever handle the gun again, to keep the safety on with the gun pointed down.

Mel's imagination has tamed down in our senior years, and my gifts are quite civilized, like books written by his favorite authors; a gourmet meal in a five-star restaurant (I could enjoy four or five Chinese or Thai dinners for the price of this one meal); or my most recent birthday gift, a set of very sharp Japanese Shin knives. I've only cut my finger once since January. ❧

Muriel with her Colt .45, at gunnery school.

CHAPTER FIFTY-NINE

WORLD OF DREAMS

WHEN IT COMES TO DREAMS, Mel is an absolute dud. He says he doesn't dream, and if he does, he doesn't remember them anyhow. In our fifty-four years of marriage, he was only able to relate a dream to me three or four times, and then they were unremarkable—the usual "seeing someone you hadn't seen in years" variety.

On the other hand, my dreams run the gamut of experiences; besides meeting up with family and friends (dead or alive), there is travel, romance, frightening encounters, happy events—you name it, I dream it. If I recall and recount the dream immediately on awakening, I can remember it in detail; otherwise, it is gone forever. Upon awakening each morning, Mel usually asks, "Where did you go last night?" or "Who did you see last night?"

So many of my dreams actually have plots that when a distended bladder disturbs my sleep, I try to mark the place in my dream so I can continue with it on my return from the bathroom. It is very frustrating when the dream is lost.

When I am upset or worried, it is manifested in my dreams—I can be falling through space or confronted by crawling snakes, which I abhor. Once in a rare while, I'm running alone through a vast empty field, looking over my shoulder, trying to avoid a falling buzz bomb. It is such a welcome relief to awaken from one these nightmares that leave my heart racing. At that point, Mel asks, "What's bothering you?" Last week, when I dreamed an ugly, furry rat was running through our clothes closet, Mel wanted to know why I changed my allegiance from snakes to rats, a new addition to my worry list. Concern over mold in the closet must have prompted this unpleasant visitor.

For fifty years, we lived a few miles from the ancestral home of Franklin and Eleanor Roosevelt in Hyde Park, New York, and we frequently visited the homestead and museum there. Eleanor was still alive then and very much in evidence in the area as guest speaker for various causes. I admired her tremendously and sympathized strongly with this woman who, for so many years, had to live in her domineering mother-in-law's home and share the proximity to Franklin's bedroom with her. I'd be frigid, too.

My admiration carried over to having recurring dreams of my driving Eleanor through the back roads of Hyde Park in an open-topped four-door sedan, 1920 vintage, similar to a car owned by Franklin and on view in the museum. I was always the driver, while Eleanor sat in the passenger seat, and we had long conversations about current sociological and political topics. I am not the most relaxed driver and have absolutely no sense of direction, so I don't know why I occupied this exalted position of chauffeuring this eminent person.

During this phase of my life, my dreams also took me to London, where I often had afternoon teas with Queen Elizabeth at Buckingham Palace. I'm really not the afternoon-tea-drinking type, and though I liked and admired Queen Elizabeth as a young, dedicated ruler, she didn't inspire the fervor within me that Eleanor did. Perhaps I was aspiring subconsciously to elevate my social status in life by hobnobbing with two such celebrities, though I never considered myself that kind of person.

About this time, our daughter introduced me to her mentor, who was head of the psychology department at Georgia State University, where she was pursuing her PhD degree. Being a dream analyst, he enjoyed having me relate my dreams. For many years I would send him a report of an unusual nighttime adventure for his amazement or amusement. Over time, the reports gradually ceased until recently, when two most vivid and disturbing dreams occurred within the same week, which I reported to Suzy's mentor for analysis.

I awoke one morning to tell Mel that I was married to Max Resnick, whoever he is, as I don't know any one by the name of Max or Resnick. I described him in detail to Mel: medium height and weight, light brown hair, very pleasant-looking with a quiet demeanor. We were enjoying a very harmonious marriage. In the dream, I introduced him to Mel, who wasn't strenuously objecting to my changing partners, and I didn't have any guilt feelings, either, for leaving Mel and for being a bigamist. What I didn't understand about this dream was why I left Mel. If I had been angry at him that week, it would have made more sense, but we had no major or even minor disagreements prior to this dream. I asked Mel, "What did you do to make me mad enough to marry Max?" He couldn't dig up a good reason, either.

Then, to complicate matters, about five nights later, I was killing Mel off in my dream. It seems that Mel and I were at a circus, surrounded by hundreds of people, all rushing to get tickets. Mel instructed me, "Stay right here, and don't move. I'll stand in line and get tickets and then come back for you." I stood rooted to the spot, shifting from one foot to the other, waiting for his return. Finally, I set off in disgust to look for him, pushing my way through the crowd, in the direction he had taken. I approached the tent where tickets were being sold, and standing in front of one of the steel beams that supported the tent was Mel, his face white and drawn with pain, perspiration dripping from his forehead and chin.

"What happened to you?" I screamed, panic-stricken at seeing him in obviously severe pain. (Apparently, marriage to Max hadn't dulled my feelings for Mel.)

"I was standing next to this steel pole," Mel panted with difficulty, "and my hearing aid became magnetized to the pole, and now I'm being electrocuted."

Fortunately, the dream ceased at that point, and I was the one who awoke perspiring and panting, happy to hear Mel snoring gently in the adjacent bed. This dream was illogical, because I really should have killed Mel off before marrying Max and becoming a bigamist. It would have made more sense, but I guess that's why it's a dream. The analysis I received later didn't make much sense, either, or maybe I was too dense to understand it.

Even though I haven't encountered Max again in any of my dreams, he did make a strong impact on this household. Now, when Mel leaves home for an appointment or to run errands, he always reminds me, "Make sure you get rid of Max before I get home." ❧

CHAPTER SIXTY

FRAGILE CONNECTIONS

"SHOULD I? Shouldn't I? Should I? Shouldn't I?" This decision plagued me for weeks until I finally let my practical nature win out, and I told the persistent auctioneer to take the whole kit and caboodle and get it out of my sight before I changed my mind. This momentous decision concerned the one frivolous, financial expenditure I had made since becoming an RN and started earning real money. Oh, sure, I spent money for necessities, but to spend forty dollars on eight water and eight juice glasses when my mother already had water and juice glasses at home—this was sinful.

It all came about the winter of 1944, when our army hospital was stationed in Liège, Belgium, the main center of the Val Saint Lambert Christallers, world famous for the purity and exceptional brilliance of their hand-cut craftsmanship. Each piece carried its signature, certifying quality, origin and authenticity, not that this meant much to me. At that time in my life, a glass was a glass.

Some entrepreneur at Val Saint Lambert gave birth to the brilliant idea of exhibiting the glassware at U.S. Army installations in and around Liège. This would provide badly needed revenue for them after years of German occupation and also solved our problem of Christmas gifts to send home.

The large drawing room of the sixteenth-century chateau that housed the nurses was the site of the exhibit, with special lighting provided by the company for the occasion. As one walked through the double-door entry, it was akin to entering fairyland. Granted, we were all starved for beauty at that time, considering our olive-drab existence and long time use of aluminum mess kits, but the effect of the lighting on the dazzling display of transparent glassware was mind boggling. Rainbows seemed to dance around the tables from prism reflections, and each pattern of crystal was more beautiful than the previous one viewed. I moved, as if in a trance, wondering how I could ever make a decision of which to purchase when I wanted them all. Yeah, I was the one who had no intention of buying, and the only reason I was here was because everyone else in the outfit had already bought something, and I didn't want to be different.

Passing one particular table marked "Vignes," my attention was caught by an exquisitely hand-etched pattern of grape vines and bunches of grapes around the rim of a glass, with an interesting octagon-shaped base. I fell in love on the spot and ended up making my purchase, eight water and eight juice glasses, confident that this was a really different gift, one that my mother would appreciate. The transaction was completed, with directions for mailing, and it was received in perfect condition a few weeks later. As I surmised, my mother greatly appreciated it. She wrote to me, saying that she would enjoy the gift until such time when I married and had my own home, and then the glasses would be returned to me.

That time arrived a few years later, and those eight water glasses and eight juice glasses were my pride and joy, not only for their beauty but for the memories evoked of a special time in my life. The grape-and-vine pattern harmonized so well with the blue grape pattern of our Wedgwood dishes, which added to my enjoyment of setting the table for dinner guests. In time, I had to enlarge the set, because when I entertained, my sentiments were that if I had to cook for six or eight, I might as well cook for ten or twelve and get a few more obligations out of the way. So, for the next thirty-five years, I tracked down stores carrying my Vignes pattern, starting first in Belgium where we visited in 1965. We carried home enough glasses to complete place settings for twelve, at a price per glass that far exceeded the forty dollars paid originally for the original sixteen glasses.

Eventually, I was able to purchase them at an exclusive Fifth Avenue jewelry store in New York that carried the Val Saint Lambert line, and I was now addicted to the thin-stemmed water, wine, and champagne glasses, more graceful than the original octagon-shaped base. Only three to four glasses were ordered at a time, though, as the price increased by leaps and bounds each year, and when I stopped adding to my collection in the early 1980s, they were selling at well over one hundred dollars each.

But the rising prices did not diminish my joy each time I viewed the table set for a dinner party, the sparkling water and wine goblets flanking the blue grape dishes and gleaming sterling flatware on a pristine damask or linen and lace tablecloth from Italy or Spain. A fresh flower centerpiece set off by the silver candelabra completed the picture, and I reveled in the sight before my eyes. The pleasure of the beautiful table setting compensated for the nuisance of having to cook, not one of my most pleasurable pastimes.

The only fly in the ointment was the fragility of this crystal, for in time, slight nicks and chips would appear on the rims, which necessitated Mel taking the well-wrapped glass to his dental office lab and polishing the sharp-edged defect until it was smooth. Then, on two occasions, in the dishwashing process, the thin stem of the goblets fractured, leaving two separate entities in the dish drainer. Mel was able to rectify this situation with epoxy glue so that the glass was again usable, though I tried to segregate them in the china cabinet, for use only when necessary.

I became almost paranoid when it came to the care of these glasses, and each time we entertained, Joanne, the young neighborhood girl who came to do the dishes, was given strict orders: Glasses are to remain on the dining room table until all other dishes and silver are washed and put away. Only then may each glass be carried into the kitchen, washed separately in hot soapy water, rinsed, and placed in the dish drainer. When sufficiently drained and dried with a clean linen towel, then each glass may be carefully placed on its shelf.

This system seemed to work fine for protecting future fractures, and all went well until the evening when one guest to my right raised her wine glass and then, a strange, confused expression registered on her face. The reason was immediately obvious—the bowl of the goblet remained in her hand while the base and partial stem were left on the dining room table. Oh-h-h, apparently Mel's glue job wasn't holding too well, and now all eyes immediately focused on the puzzled guest. I jumped up to relieve her of this half a glass, that still contained a good measure of wine. I dumped out the wine in the kitchen sink and then retrieved another glass from the dining room china cabinet, hoping the replacement wasn't one of the defective ones. Well, we were among friends, and it was good for a laugh, but I worried each time that guest lifted her glass to drink. Those defective goblets looked so healthy and normal that I just couldn't think of retiring them. We'd just get a stronger glass cement the next time it happens.

Six months and a couple of dinner parties later, I received a phone call from Joanne's mother, who had the strangest question: "Muriel, have you been missing a dish towel?"

"Are you kidding? I don't count my dish towels. Why do you ask?"

"Well, I hate to have to tell you this, but when Joanne did dishes at your home a couple of weeks ago, one of the water goblets broke as she was drying it, and she was so terrified that she wrapped the two pieces in one of your dishtowels and brought it home. I was afraid you'd miss your towel as well as the glass, so I promised Joanne I would call you."

Oh, my God! A defective glass must have been in use that night and chose to become unglued while Joanne was doing the dishes! Poor Joanne! I felt so guilty for having traumatized her in this fashion, and I immediately assured her mother that the glasses had been glued, and it was not Joanne's fault. Between the constant polishing of the nicks and the unglued stems, the sparkle of my beautiful glasses was beginning to dim.

A year later, as we planned our permanent move to Florida, where all closet and cabinet space would be considerably downsized, this latest episode made it possible for me to part with my collection.

Hopefully, someone is enjoying the beauty of my Val crystal, while I entertain, completely headache-free, using an inexpensive set of glasses, probably from Wal-Mart or the like. 🙞

CHAPTER SIXTY-ONE

LITTLE RED BOX

IT HAS LITTLE MONETARY OR ARTISTIC VALUE and could probably be purchased in any Hallmark store for three or four dollars, but I treasure it for the memories and sentiment it evokes. This little red satin-covered box is about four inches long and two inches in width and depth and is topped by a clear Lucite lid. Lying on a bed of white satin under this lid and fashioned from a gold-colored metal is a delicately formed full-blown rose with a few leaves gracefully sprouting at different levels from either side of the stem.

This box, having traveled with me from our former New York home, has resided on one end of my chest of drawers for the six years we have been Florida residents, and if we should ever live elsewhere, it will be the first item to accompany me. When I awaken each morning, the bright red color automatically draws my eyes to it.

Sometimes, when I am a little remiss with my housekeeping and a thin film of dust covers the bureau and the Lucite cover, I chuckle inwardly as I think of my mother. Her house was clean by normal standards, but she wasn't a slave to it, and as she aged, she didn't have the time for it. Each morning, as she rushed off to her dress-shop business, the door to her bedroom was closed so no one could view the unmade bed or the dust on her bedside table that outlined the shape of her nighttime water glass. She would righteously declare, "This house will be here when I am dead and gone."

Yes, she is dead but not gone—some of her ashes repose under that gold rose on the white satin bed in the little red box, and as I gently wipe the dust off the cover, I am thinking, "Chip off the old block." ❧

CHAPTER SIXTY-TWO

A SHARED SECRET

THEY SAY THE WIFE is always the last to know when her spouse is playing around, but she was wise to him all along. She might have known for at least twenty years, when he went off for a week for the annual legal convention or for the state meetings every few months or for a "business meeting with a client" in a nearby town, when he would be gone overnight.

Certainly, no one in town was aware that this was anything but an idyllic marriage; they both played their parts perfectly. Active in professional, charitable, and social circles, they were two handsome people, always impeccably dressed in the height of fashion, though she was a little more avant-garde in her tastes than he. But he was one man who loved to shop with his wife, and she enjoyed having him select her clothes. They entertained often and were excellent hosts in their lovely home, a fitting reminder of his lucrative legal practice. He poured drinks and steered the conversation into interesting channels with an aplomb that she did not share, but her culinary skills and genuine warmth placed her on an equal basis with him, as a hostess enjoying her guests.

With all these odds in their favor, the news of their impending divorce hit their friends and family with the force of an exploding atom bomb. Especially upset and shocked was the one couple closest to them—they had shared carpools, baby-sitting, vacations, family sorrows, and joys over the years. Though they were of different religious denominations, they participated in each other's holidays and were considered *family*. They knew now that despite the intimacy between the two families, they had overlooked or missed the signals of problems fermenting in the home of the lawyer and his wife.

She might have put up with his affairs for another twenty years, but the saturation point was reached after his surgery to remove a brain tumor. In the previous five years, she had "been there" for him, with the doctor visits and hospital vigils during his bouts with colon cancer, gall bladder removal, and a fractured femur suffered on a ski slope. He had the capacity and will to bounce back quickly after each hospitalization, and the brain surgery recovery was no different. In fact, he recovered so quickly that two weeks post-operative, he had set up "a business meeting with a client" in the nearby town. This business call ended differently from previous ones, however, as his wife had done her homework and hired a detective, armed with a camera, which provided her with the evidence.

The loss of face and respect that he suffered from his family and close friends, plus the lack of home comforts that he could only appreciate after living in a motel room for over two months, seemed to bring him to his senses. When the full realization of the pain and shame he had inflicted on his wife finally penetrated his conscious mind, he was like a man bereft of his senses. He wept, he groveled, he swore to reform. He wooed her with flowers and love letters and fervent promises of the wonderful future they could still share together. And she finally capitulated because she still loved him, though she openly stated she could never trust him again. He moved back into their home and slept in the guest room in an icy isolation, but that gradually thawed with the passage of time.

Those close to the couple, especially their married children, were happy to see them gather up the shattered pieces of their lives, which were cemented in place when he retired, and they moved to a beach resort city in Florida. Their unhappy past was left behind and they were able to live in complete anonymity, in a different milieu, known to their new acquaintances only as a happy, loving couple. In no time, they became active members of the community, volunteering their services in charitable organizations and their church, and once again their home provided the setting for the same successful dinner parties they'd hosted over the years.

By a quirk of fate, their closest friends and confidants, who had shared so much of their lives in the past, moved to this same city in Florida two years later. They had inherited an eight room house near the beach and, after an exceptionally severe northern winter, did not hesitate to make the move. The newcomers anticipated renewing the warm relationship they'd had with their old friends; they had been, after all, a "family" for so many years.

However, a renewal of the old relationship between the two couples was not to be. Yes, the newcomers were invited to the home of their old friends, but only when no other guests were present. The phone calls between the two families that had been daily in former days were now once every two or three weeks, as if they were duty calls. They would meet in town for dinner occasionally, just the four of them, but the conversation on these occasions was always guarded. The past was never referred to, so they talked of their activities and the doings of their kids and grandchildren. The secret knowledge they all possessed lay heavily on their hearts and in their memories, and in time, the phone calls and dinner meetings ceased completely. ❧

CHAPTER SIXTY-THREE

WHEN YOU GOTTA GO

DIAMONDS MAY BE A GIRL'S BEST FRIEND but when you gotta go, one's best friend is a 100-percent-functioning flush toilet. I feel I can speak authoritatively on that subject, not only because of my advanced age, but also because I have had varied experiences with different types of toilets over the years.

Aside from a vague three-year-old's recollection of an outhouse in my grandparents' backyard, I took our mundane flush toilet pretty much for granted until I was twenty-two and joined the army. Under the auspices of Uncle Sam for three years, I was exposed to many ingenious forms of toilets or substitutes thereof, and not being in the category of military secrets, I can safely reveal this information to you.

The simplest form of toileting, used when on fifteen-mile hikes, was simply to find a clump of bushes and squat, being sure to bury the paper, as it was biodegradable. When crossing the North Atlantic on a Liberty ship in the midwinter of 1943, the flush toilets in the nurses' head required the use of a bath towel to mop up the deluge of salt water deposited on one's lower anatomy from each enormous wave that smacked the bottom of the ship. Upon arrival in England, and locked in a train compartment for hours at a time with five other nurses, we quickly learned there were other uses for our steel helmets than to protect our heads when under bombing attacks. The helmet was one of our most valued possessions for the two years spent overseas and was employed in this manner on the numerous endless train and truck rides that we endured without access to a latrine.

Also in England, we encountered the civilian water closet, or WC, which was a large rectangular water-filled box suspended close to the ceiling, with a pull chain dangling from it. It did happen that when one nurse pulled the chain too vehemently, the box came crashing down, fracturing her arm. This was our first casualty among the nurses. Incidentally, English toilet paper was abysmal, stiff and harsh, like the English pound notes we received monthly for salary. I lost my first month's pay by leaving the notes in my robe pocket when I went to the latrine, and I mistook them for toilet paper.

In France we had the opportunity to really enlarge our toilet repertoire via slit trenches, while living in tents in the Normandy cow pasture. When the GIs dug the slit trench for the nurses at the far end of our cow pasture, they patterned the width of it after the size of the rear end of our chief nurse, and that was *wide*. It was difficult enough to straddle the slit trench in good weather, but after several weeks of torrential rains, the slippery mud bordering the trench created additional balancing difficulties. That's the time we had the second casualty among the nurses when one of them fell in and had to be shipped back to the States with a fractured femur. Can you imagine the indignity of telling your grandchildren how you sustained your injury during the war?

Paris was a liberal education for us when we encountered the pissoir on every other street block. This was a black metal framework cage, about five feet high, with a foot of open space at the bottom. One could usually smell the pissoir long before approaching it, and pairs of feet standing in position were visible at the bottom. Another type of open-air pissoir was seen as a large, indented, ceramic tile wall built into a hill, with no screening whatsoever. One would walk nonchalantly past this area where men stood, their backs to the world, doing what they had to do. If they had pissoirs for women, I never came across them. In hotels, the neophyte Americans mistook the commonplace bidet for toilets, but they soon learned the difference.

We also discovered for the first time the bathrooms that consisted of a tile-lined hole in the floor, with foot outlines in the tile to indicate placement of the feet while squatting. One eighteenth-century chateau on the outskirts of Paris, where the nurses were housed for two weeks, contained flush toilets that had the most beautiful hand-painted chrysanthemums on the inside of the bowl. Ah, these aristocratic French, who loved art for art's sake!

And then we moved on to Belgium, where two-, four-, and six-holers were used on our tent hospital site, as well as in the sixteenth-century chateau occupied by the nurses. These wooden boxes with holes cut on the top surface housed pails directly under the holes, which were emptied daily by the POWs. There were many latrine tents throughout the hospital grounds, and the number of holes depended upon the amount of traffic generated in that particular area. They were most efficient and a lot more comfortable than helmets or slit trenches.

Back in civilian life, the greatest luxuries were hot running water and flush toilets, which I never fully appreciated until my wartime experience. In later years, when traveling in Europe and Asia, although the hotels all had flush toilets, public buildings still had the hole in the floor, and how I envied the Asian women who squatted as easily as they walked. Restaurants in Italy frequently featured unisex bathrooms—a separate entrance for men and women but once inside, you could meet up with your spouse, who you had just left at the men's entrance. In Egypt, my craziest experience was to find a turbaned Muslim male standing inside the ladies room at the Aswan airport, one hand holding a roll of toilet paper, the other hand outstretched. It was one tiny sheet per coin, and if you wanted two sheets, you paid another coin. I contributed to the economy that day for I purchased five sheets.

Once we moved to Florida I was ready to resort to army methods—our guest-room toilet either plugged up or overflowed every time we had houseguests. Knowing that all our neighbors had the same complaints with their guest-room toilets only strengthened our resolve to get to the bottom of the situation. We kept the plumbers well fed for years and amassed a good-sized collection of plungers, hoping for the magic one that would eradicate the anguished expression on a house guest's face each time he or she had to report a mishap. The crowning blow came when two consecutive visits by our favorite cousins resulted in the usual mopping and plunging. They were embarrassed, we were embarrassed, and I was mad.

Fate stepped in the very next day when a friend called to report on her newest acquisition, a Japanese flush toilet that worked like a charm—flush, whoosh, that's it. Guaranteed to work! I was so impressed, I ordered two, one for the guest bathroom and one for the master bathroom, and that one would be a treat for us, as it was elevated by three inches. The elevation is a boon to rusty hip and knee joints, and when sitting on this throne-like affair, I feel invincible. One year later, the plungers in the garage are covered with a thin layer of dust, and the plumbers have gone elsewhere for their business. 🙚

CHAPTER SIXTY-FOUR

RENDEZVOUS

IT WAS TWO MINUTES after 8 p.m., and the theater patrons began checking their watches—the performances *always* started on time. A pair of senior latecomers made their way up the few steps in the small Sarasota theater. His seat was the very last one in the row behind us, next to the wall, and hers was the last seat in our row, directly in front of him. These rows are notoriously narrow, so of course, we all had to stand to let these people through. Just as we seated ourselves, most of the theater lights dimmed. *They made it by the skin of their teeth*, I thought.

All talking ceased in the partially lit theater as a staff member positioned herself in front of the stage and welcomed the audience to the theater. She had just said, "At this time, please shut off all cell phones," when a voice behind us yelled out, "Call 911!" The staff member paused momentarily, disconcerted at the interruption, and began repeating her cell phone speech again. Several voices urgently called out, "Call 911!" and then another voice shrieked, "A man is dying here!" She got the message this time and moved quickly out of the theater into the lobby, while dozens of people retrieved their cell phones from pockets and purses, all dialing 911.

We looked behind us, and there, in the last seat in the row, was the male latecomer, his head thrown back over the seat, his face an ominous grayish-white, and without a rise and fall of his chest to indicate respirations. A woman directly in front of us had apparently succeeded in reaching an operator at 911 and was answering questions: "Yes, it's a man, and he doesn't appear to be breathing. He's in his seat; it's the Florida Studio Theater on North Palm Avenue. Your drivers must know where it is. Just get here."

Next, a voice in the audience called out, "Is there a doctor in the house?" A few seconds later a man, presumably a physician, made his way into the narrow row, now emptied of the shocked occupants, who congregated in the rear of the theater or in the lobby. Someone was standing behind the patient, attempting mouth-to-mouth resuscitation, which from that angle was pretty hopeless from the start. The physician vigorously thumped the chest of the patient several times, with no bodily response. The wife, sitting in our row and directly in front of all the activity behind us, was now standing and watching the activity, as if in a daze. Mel and I moved to the lobby and impatiently awaited the arrival of the ambulance, which arrived a few minutes later, though those few minutes seemed like an hour.

After quickly ascertaining the condition of the patient, the medical technicians extricated his lifeless body from his seat, and with great difficulty, maneuvered down the narrow aisle and managed to get him on the litter and into the lobby. They were followed by his wife, still too dazed to exhibit any sign of emotion.

The audience regained their seats while the emergency technicians worked over their patient in the lobby behind closed doors. A theater staff member informed the still-stunned audience that the performance would be delayed for a half-hour or until the ambulance departed. The low buzz of muted voices filled the theater. *Can we have the capacity to enjoy this comedy when we have just witnessed the death of a man?* I wondered. Then my thoughts wandered still further. *Who will drive her home from the hospital? Certainly, she will be in no condition to retrieve her car from the parking lot and drive herself home. Does she have kids or family in the area she can call for moral support? How can she walk into an empty house, alone now? Was the rush to get to their seats before the opening curtain responsible for this apparent heart attack?*

My one question was answered when the performance eventually commenced, and yes, we were able to put the gruesome events out of our minds and enjoy the comedy, but I'll never know the answers to my other concerns. And the man never knew, when he left home that night, that he had a rendezvous with death. ❧

CHAPTER SIXTY-FIVE

GUILT

THERE IT IS AGAIN! Each time I forage through my folders of army memorabilia, I rediscover this two-by-three-inch brown envelope containing a much-folded scrap of paper. I am well aware of the content of this missive, written in still legible ink, almost sixty-five years ago. Now, as then, I am swept by deep-rooted guilt and remorse. Why do I bother to keep this paper that provokes such troubling emotions?

I carefully unfold the paper and read the familiar fourteen lines of this love sonnet, poignant, haunting, and beautiful, and I am appalled at my behavior at the time, as I recall the happenings before and after the receipt of this poem.

It was April of '43, and I was the newest and perhaps youngest of the ten nurses comprising the nursing staff at the Station Hospital at Fort Adams, Newport, Rhode Island, my first army assignment. The hospital was small, with perhaps fewer than one hundred beds, in a country-club-like setting, overlooking the sparkling waters of Narragansett Bay.

By day we attended the sick with the usual variety of non-combat injuries or ailments, and by night we partied in the Officers' Club, and for the first time in my life, I was overwhelmed with dancing and drinking partners. It was a little heady, having grown men actually argue over whom I would dance with next, and I reveled in all this male attention, quite a change from the three years' cloistered atmosphere of our nursing school. I even graduated from the rum-and-Coke variety of drink to the more sophisticated liquors, like scotch and rye. I did notice during several evenings of merriment at the club that there was one young lieutenant who didn't join in the camaraderie but sat deep in conversation with another male officer, as they slowly nursed their drinks. Dancing past their table,

I was aware of his disdainful glances in my direction, his mouth slightly curved, as though smelling something unpleasant.

The time came for my frivolous evenings to be put on hold when I was assigned to a month of night duty at the Station Hospital, from 11 p.m. to 7a.m. My duties were to make the rounds of all the wards that were staffed by one or two corpsmen and administer medications or perform whatever treatments were necessary throughout the night. After each round was completed, I retreated to the nursing office to write my reports or to read a book I had brought on duty with me. The nights were long but quiet for the most part, and I had plenty of time to catch up on my reading, which at that particular time in my life was poetry.

Deeply involved in *Sonnets from the Portuguese* and savoring each line, I was gradually aware of someone standing in the doorway to the nursing office. I swiveled round in my chair to confront the six foot two, ramrod-straight slim figure of the serious lieutenant at the Officer's Club who seemed to disdain me or my dancing. I sprang to my feet as he introduced himself as Lieutenant Jonah Weil, from Medical Administration, doing his rounds as Officer of the Day. I reciprocated the introduction and answered his very businesslike questions about my most recent rounds of the various floors, and then waited for him to take his leave. He didn't seem in a hurry to leave, though, and as his eyes swept around the office, he spied the book I had hastily closed and casually asked, "What are you reading, Lieutenant.?"

Blushing, at being caught reading this romantic poetry, I showed him the title of the book, and he raised his eyebrows. I was sure he was thinking, *This party girl has something else besides dancing, drinking, and men on her mind?* He was very familiar with Elizabeth Barrett Browning, having taught English before the war, and as we talked about her poems and other poets, his reserve and sour look disappeared. He became more personal with his questions: How long had I been in the service? Where was I from? Where did I get my nurses training? Had I been to Newport yet to see the sights?

This was the beginning of Jonah's courtship, which I enjoyed at first, especially when I was on night duty. I looked forward to his nightly visits when he made the rounds with me, and then we sat in my office and talked about our previous lives, families, and ambitions for after the war. Jonah was full of plans for historical places of interest to show me in the Newport and Providence areas, and indeed, we did cover a lot of interesting territory on our days off, when he arranged his schedule to coincide with my free days. A ten-minute bus ride took us to Newport, where we explored the magnificent Victorian mansions or the historic Touro Synagogue, the oldest in this country. We always ended the afternoons walking the famous Cliff Walk at sunset, where we could still view the mansions from a different perspective and appreciate the sun setting on the ocean.

The relationship was progressing nicely until I mentioned to Jonah that I'd like to attend some of the dances at the Officers' Club, as I missed the new friends I had made there. At my insistence, he acquiesced, but the few times we went, we did not socialize with the other male and female officers but sat at a table by ourselves, sipping our drinks and dancing sedately to the slow numbers. No shag, jitterbug, or swing for us. No one else asked me to dance, and I was beginning to resent Jonah's possessiveness, always wanting to be alone with me when I wanted to be with the revelers. In my immaturity, I thought I could have it all, Jonah and all the others. When Jonah referred to the "drunken louts on the dance floor," I was both hurt and incensed, for these were the very officers who fought to dance with me a few short weeks ago and made me feel welcome in a sea of strangers.

The weeks went by and Jonah became more serious about me and even talked about marriage in the future, which scared the life out of me. I appreciated his very fine qualities and the fact that he cared for me, but I did not reciprocate his feelings. I wanted to be free to date other men, but I didn't have the guts to tell him so. Despite his possessiveness, he was a sweet, caring person and excellent marriage material—but not for me. I wasn't ready.

Fortunately, I had earlier requested overseas duty, as I didn't want to spend my army career nursing measles and appendicitis cases, and when an opportunity arose to be transferred to a hospital unit preparing for overseas duty at Fort Devens, Massachusetts, I grabbed it as my life line. I hoped with the distance between us, I could break off this relationship gradually and perhaps maintain it on a "just friends" basis. Oh, was I ever naïve to think he could turn love on and off at will! Jonah did visit me a few times at Devens, though I contrived to be on duty most of the days when he was free to come. We corresponded and spoke occasionally on the phone, which was fine with me, and the less I saw of him, the better I liked him. Once overseas, whether in England, France, or Belgium, and with the Atlantic Ocean between us, I felt safe and a lot kindlier toward him than I had when at Fort Adams. His letters were friendly and undemanding, and I was sure time and distance had dampened his ardor. I couldn't have been more wrong, and sending him the photograph started a chain of painful events I would rather have never happened.

It started innocently enough at the time I went to the photographer in Liège for my "glamour girl" photograph, and I was so delighted with this enchanting new me, I ordered a half-dozen copies. I never looked so good, even as a civilian, and I couldn't wait to send my photographs out to family members, signing each "With love, Muriel." One was left after my own copy and family was accounted for, and I made the fatal error by sending it to Jonah with the same inscription on it. So intent was I on displaying the glamour girl, I never realized how seriously I was toying with human emotions.

Jonah's receipt of my photograph elevated our previous friendly and undemanding relationship to a new level, but only in his mind. When our next batch of mail from the States arrived, I was horrified to read his letter, stating he was coming overseas within the next couple of months and couldn't wait to see me. Suddenly, the Atlantic Ocean wasn't wide enough. But the coup de grace was the handwritten poem he enclosed with his letter, which needed no clarification. I knew immediately that the photograph had reignited the flames I had hoped to quench in the past year and a half, and my sense of guilt knew no bounds. I think I was more upset at the depths of his feelings expressed in the poem than I was at the thought of his imminent arrival, and I never did find out whether he was the author of this exquisitely tender love sonnet, which I certainly did not deserve. I will reproduce it for my reader.

Darling, This Much

Darling, this much I've learned to understand,
And it has taken me a long, strange year,
A year I reached but could not touch your hand
And listened for your voice but could not hear.
Often I walked along our road in spring,
Silently asking strength, that I might bear
To watch the leaves and flowers unraveling
And feel the rain we loved and you not there
I thought I walked alone and wept that you
Walked somewhere far as lonely and alone.
I am much wiser now the year is through
And you are still away. I should have known
As I do now, there is no road or weather,
However dark, we do not walk together.

I didn't have time to stew over my problems with Jonah, for fate stepped in with the Battle of the Bulge beginning on December 16, 1944. For the next several weeks, we worked around the clock, caring for battle casualties and for patients and hospital personnel wounded from buzz bomb hits. And then, there was the Christmas Eve bombing and strafing of the hospital tents, when the Germans were only ten miles away. Our work so engulfed us so that Jonah's imminent arrival was the last thing on my mind. Finally, the Germans were pushed back into Germany, and we all started to breathe freely again.

I was breakfasting with other nurses and physicians after night duty, when the mess sergeant approached me and announced, "You have a visitor, Lieutenant."

My heart sank as I looked up to see Jonah standing in the tent entrance. I walked over to him slowly, forced a happy smile on my face, and offered my cheek for a chaste kiss. Someone brought him a plate of food, and I sat there with him, as he related how he had arrived in France about twenty-four hours ago and driven all night long. Despite Jonah's fatigue, he was brimming over with happiness at seeing me, while I was ready to crawl under the floor and die. I had hoped that perhaps when I saw him after all this time, I might feel a spark of something for him, but nothing was there.

My spark had been quietly ignited by a fighter pilot, who had completed his missions and returned to the States that week. I knew I'd never see him again, as we both realized ours was just a wartime attraction. I was still mourning his departure and certainly not in the mood for Jonah's declarations of love that night as we sat in the nurses' lounge of our chateau in front of the fireplace. Jonah had his arm around my shoulder, and when I didn't respond to his attempted kisses, he demanded, "What in the world is going on here? Don't you feel the way I do? And if you don't, why did you send me that photograph signed 'with love'?"

I confessed that I had signed all the photographs that way for family members, and his was among them. I also inferred that there had been someone else on my mind the past few months, who had just returned home.

Jonah's face turned white with anger. He jumped to his feet, declaring "You are the cruelest person I know! I never want to lay eyes on you again!" He strode out of the room while I slunk into the corner of the couch, not blaming him at all for his outburst and feeling as low as a human could possibly feel. Is it any wonder I have such feelings of guilt each time I unearth his love sonnet? Perhaps I am punishing myself by keeping it, and yet it is so beautiful, I am loathe to discard it.

Our paths were to cross again. Six months later, when our hospital had moved back to Chalons-sur-Marne, France, a sleepy little town in the dustbowl area on the Marne River, I saw him. I was meandering through the town on my day off and was about to cross the street, when a long convoy of jeeps and trucks came suddenly into view, preventing me from crossing. I waited on the curb for the convoy to pass, and I recognized the markings and insignias on the vehicles as those of Jonah's company. As the first jeep drew abreast of me, not eight feet away, there was Jonah sitting in his usual ramrod position next to the driver, staring straight ahead. Had he seen me? I wanted to run away but stood there, mesmerized, glued to the spot. The convoy passed, and I continued on my way, shaken by the almost-confrontation and reliving his last words, "I never want to see you again!"

Well, he did see me again, some thirty-five years later. I was lounging around the pool with Joe, a friend who had recently retired from his government job in New York. He handed me the newsletter from his former office so that I could read the announcement of Joe's retirement award, which was presented by the head of the government office, Jonah Weil. How many Jonah Weils could there be? It wasn't a common name. As I described Jonah's physical characteristics to Joe, he agreed this person had to be the very same Jonah I'd known in my army days. Joe was acquainted with Jonah on a personal basis and informed me that Jonah and his wife had a summer home in the mountains, not too far from us.

This was such a coincidence that I had to write a brief note to Jonah, in which I asked if he was the same Jonah Weil who knew a Muriel Phillips at Fort Adams so many years ago. If so, my husband and I would like to have him and his wife stop off to visit us when en route to their summer home. Was this ever chutzpah? Was I expecting absolution? I just had to know whether he still despised me.

Surprisingly, I received an immediate and cordial reply, acknowledging his remembrance of me and mentioning that he and his wife would be happy to stop off for a visit, which they did a week later. His wife, Julie, was a pretty, warm, soft-spoken woman, who radiated tranquility and appreciated that she was well cherished by her husband. I was relieved that Jonah didn't seem to harbor any ill feelings toward me, though we avoided any personal issues of the past and just discussed mutual friends we had known in the military. We visited with each other a few times over the next three years, until we received the sad news from Jonah that Julie had lost her battle with cancer. He was obviously devastated by his loss, and we never heard from or saw him again.

Yes, I still suffer pangs of guilt each time I unearth Jonah's poem, but happily, once the poem is back in its little brown envelope and out of sight, so, too, are my feelings of guilt. ❧

CHAPTER SIXTY-SIX

MIXED SIGNALS

MOVING TO FLORIDA IN 1999 meant leaving the house in the woods that we loved and where we'd lived for fifty years. We had weathered enough of New York's winters of ice and snow, however, and were now ready to leave for tropical climes in our senior years.

Once in Florida, we kept in close contact with friends by frequent e-mails, phone calls, and personal visits on our biannual family trips to New York and Connecticut. As for neighbors who lived a quarter-mile or half-mile down the road, we exchanged Christmas cards, which usually included an extra insert page of handwritten news. Over the years, though, we didn't party or dine out with most of the neighbors, although we were still friends, sharing the same neighborhood problems, happy for them when good things happened within their families, and consoling them in times of sorrow.

Six years into permanent Florida living, I was stunned one evening by an unexpected phone call and a male voice that asked, "Are you Mrs. Engelman?

"Yes, I'm Mrs. Engelman."

"Well, how are you, Mrs. E.? Do you remember me?" It was sort of a stupid question, as he hadn't talked long enough for me to identify him, even though I am usually quick to recognize voices of long-forgotten people.

"I don't recognize your voice, so who are you?"

"I'm your old neighbor, Vic, who lived down the road from you, across the highway."

"Oh, my gosh, of course I remember you, Vic Clarke! It's so nice to hear your voice after all these years. And how are you and how is your family?" He was one neighbor who hadn't sent Christmas cards, and I had almost forgotten about him until this phone call, which evoked instant memories of him.

Vic was the kind of guy that no neighborhood should be without; there wasn't anything he couldn't do—except to remain in the job he had at Texaco for twenty years. Once he was diagnosed with myasthenia gravis, he was retired on medical disability, but even with this diagnosis, nothing held him down. Except for his drooping eyelids, he seemed the picture of health as he plowed, shoveled, and mowed for us. He also was a general consultant about pool problems, damp basements, and insects invading the vegetable garden. He was a true powerhouse of information and could discourse on any subject, including politics, world news, and the weather. He also didn't mind sharing any juicy neighborhood tidbits, especially when it came to the newcomer who had built a big, expensive home down the road from Vic's house. Vic's home was a lovely eight-room ranch house on four acres, with a circular driveway set into the well-manicured front lawn. The foundation plantings of evergreens were always perfectly pruned, and in springtime, especially, the flowering trees that dotted the property were a gorgeous sight to behold. A twenty-by-forty-foot swimming pool could be seen on a rear lawn, and off to the side was Vic's workshop, which housed numerous tractors, mowers, snowblowers, motorcycles—all sorts of mechanized equipment to be repaired.

Vic wasn't more than five foot eight and had a stocky build, but with his clean-cut features, he had an air of authority about him. Mel and I always chuckled at Vic's penchant for starting off every few sentences with "Like I sez …" Despite his outward appearance of being physically fit, Vic made frequent trips to Johns Hopkins for medications and treatment of his disease, which seemed to keep it under control, though his eyelids always remained at half-mast. Occasionally, Vic would admit to having had a bad few days, when arm and leg muscle weakness kept him off the job, but for the most part, he was there when needed.

For the many years we availed ourselves of his services, we always discussed our kids and their activities and exchanged flowers and vegetables from our gardens, so we were more like old friends, not just a serviceman and employer. Familiar as we were, Vic always addressed me as Mrs. E.

and Mel as Doc, and even now, Vic inquired, "How is Doc, and is he still following the gold market?" This was an interest mutually shared.

We talked for an hour, or I should say that Vic did, for he did most of the talking, filling me in on all the neighborhood gossip; the enormous amount of building construction that had taken place in the area since we left and resultant traffic generated on the roads because of this; local politics that had the residents in an uproar; neighbors who had died and others who had sold their homes, and that the upkeep of our former property, Nutmeg Hill, was not up to snuff, which saddened both Mel and me. Throughout this hour-long spiel, Vic continually inserted his old familiar "like I sez" before most sentences, and time seemed to stand still.

I really enjoyed hearing all the news about people and places from our former life, but I kept wondering throughout Vic's ramblings, why he'd really called. I wondered if perhaps he was coming to Florida and wanted to stop off for a visit. Finally, I posed the question. "Vic, do you ever get to Florida with your family? If so, we'd love to have you stop off and visit us."

"Nah," replied Vic. "We used to have a time-share at Fort Myers where we'd go to every winter, but it's too far to drive now, so we rent a place for a couple of weeks on the beach at Hilton Head in the late fall."

OK, he wasn't looking for an invitation to Florida, but I felt it was so strange that he called out of the blue, six years after we moved away, just to talk about our old neighborhood. Either way, I did enjoy the phone visit.

One week later, I discovered the reason behind Vic's call. Again, my phone rang, but this time a high-pitched, emotional-sounding voice said, "Mur?" I recognized it as that of my dear friend Val, a former neighbor, who'd lived a half-mile down the road from us (in the opposite direction than Vic) with her husband, Bill. They'd sold their home two years after we moved away and relocated to Cape Cod, where they'd been busy restoring their historical landmark home. Val and I remained in frequent contact by phone and mail, though sometimes two or three months might elapse between calls.

I detected a sense of urgency in Val's voice, so I quickly replied, "Val, it's so good to hear from you. How's everything?"

"Oh, Mur," she replied with relief, "you don't know how good it is to hear your voice." Then, slightly hesitant, she asked, "How is Mel?"

"Mel's fine, happily sitting at the computer, as usual. How's Bill?"

"Oh, Bill's fine, but I'm just happy knowing that you and Mel are OK."

"Val, what in the world are you getting at? Is there any reason, aside from our age, that we shouldn't be fine?"

Val explained that she'd been traveling in Europe with their daughter, Pam, for the past two weeks and had just gotten home a half-hour ago. "Bill said I *had* to call you immediately," she said, "as he had received a very disturbing call from Alice!" Alice was one of our former neighbors, a friend to both Val and me, and it seems that Jimmy, our local farmer who lived close to Vic, had told Alice something alarming. "He said that one of the Engelmans had died!" she went on. "This scared the life out of me, and I just had to call. Thank God, you're both OK!"

"I wonder which one of us is supposedly dead?" I inquired, amused by the idea, but also aware that it could have been true, for we aren't exactly in the spring-chicken category anymore.

Now I had the answer for Vic's prolonged phone call. He had heard the rumor from his neighbor Jimmy and called to verify it, but he'd had the sensitivity not to disclose the reason for his call, once he learned we were both very much alive.

Wow! Someone's signals surely got mixed up, and I'm more than happy to say we're still here. A little older and with less zip in our movements, but we're here. ❧

CHAPTER SIXTY-SEVEN

COINCIDENCE

IT WAS MAY AGAIN, and time for us to start packing for our annual move to Leisure World, a community of eighteen thousand seniors in Southern California, a few miles from Laguna Beach. We did not enjoy the heat and humidity of the Florida summers, and at our daughter, Suzy's, urging seven years ago to "Try it," we did, and we liked it, finding the weather to be perfect for us. The mornings and evenings are cool, it's pleasantly hot during the day, and there's always a gentle breeze. We've been returning every summer.

Several months before we left Florida, I had responded to an ad in the Leisure World newspaper for a five-day Shakespeare Festival tour in Medford, Oregon, at the end of August. We had never been to Oregon, and as it was a good fifty years since we had last attended a Shakespeare Festival at Stratford-on-Avon in Canada, it was time for us to avail ourselves of a little culture and see something of this beautiful state we had heard so much about.

I submitted our application with accompanying down-payment check, and a couple of weeks later, I received an acceptance letter from Sylvia, the tour director. She advised me to call her after our arrival at Leisure World to finalize the details about the tour, which I did.

Once Sylvia and I took care of official business, Sylvia remarked, "It's so strange; you come from Florida to California, my home state, and next month, I'm going to Florida, your home state."

"Really?" I asked incredulously. "Why would anyone in her right mind leave this heavenly climate to visit Florida in the summer, home of heat, humidity, and hurricanes?"

"Oh, we wouldn't be going if it wasn't to celebrate the birthday of an aunt I have always adored. And kids, grandchildren, and cousins, are coming from all over to celebrate her one hundredth birthday the first weekend in August."

"That is so funny! My husband Mel's uncle in Florida is celebrating his one hundredth birthday the same weekend, and family will also be coming from all over to celebrate. We won't be there, though, as we felt it was too much of a trip to make for a few days in the heat of the summer, especially because the humidity there bothers my asthma."

"Where in Florida does your uncle live?" Sylvia inquired. "In a retirement community somewhere in Hollywood."

"Hollywood? That's where my *aunt* lives. In a retirement community called Classic Residence Hyatt. What's the name of your uncle's place?"

I couldn't remember his address, but Sylvia persisted. "Do you know *where* in Hollywood your uncle's home is? Have you ever been there?"

"Oh, yes," I replied. "We were there just a year ago. We took a right exit off of I-95 and drove a few blocks to a very lovely retirement community, built in a residential neighborhood. The buildings all looked quite new, and there were several of them spread out over a large area."

Now Sylvia was really excited. "That sounds like the directions to my aunt's Classic Residence. Wouldn't it be a riot if your uncle was living in the same place? We'd have to introduce them to each other. What's your uncle's name, so I can ask my aunt, just in case it happens to be the same place?"

"Milton Engelman, and if this is the same place, he must know her. When we visited him there three months after he moved in, he seemed to know everyone's names. The guy is amazing, in good health mentally and physically, and always impeccably dressed, whether in sports or evening wear. He's still a handsome man."

On our visit, Mel and I had marveled at Uncle Milt's interests. He was on the computer daily, checking out his stock portfolio. He participated in the daily tai chi classes, which he loved. He played cards with the other residents and enjoyed the comforts of his own well-furnished apartment, replete with the same familiar pieces of furniture from the apartment he'd shared for years with his wife, Mattie, whom he still lovingly referred to as "my Mattie," a good eight years after her death.

"If you talk to your Uncle Milt, ask him if he knows a Helen Sherman, who will be in a wheelchair. When I speak to her this weekend, I'll ask her if she knows him."

"OK, and in the meantime, I'll get his address from Mel's cousin, and check it against yours."

Well, of course it was the same retirement community, and when I called Sylvia a few days later, she had already spoken to her aunt, who knew Uncle Milt well. "A very fine man," she said.

That weekend, when Mel and I called Uncle Milt, he confirmed it. "Oh yes," he said, "I know Helen Sherman very well, a lovely lady."

Of all the thousands of retirement communities in this country, it was indeed coincidental that two people who had never met, except by phone, were able to pinpoint the exact location and acquaintance of two individuals, an uncle of one and aunt of the other, both celebrating their one hundredth birthday on the same weekend. 🙡

CHAPTER SIXTY-EIGHT

LOST AND FOUND

I OPENED THE FRONT DOOR and bent down automatically to pick up something that should have been there but wasn't. I straightened up, turned back into the house, slammed the door, and stormed into the den. "Mel!" I roared, "they did it again! This is the second time in a month they didn't deliver the Sunday paper."

Mel looked up from his computer keyboard, visibly annoyed at the news, and said, "Call them then, and find out what happened, and if they're planning to deliver later in the day."

"Fat chance I have of talking to a live voice," I muttered, "but I'll give it a try." As expected, I got the usual menu of "Press one for this, and two for that, and finally, three for delivery." As directed, I pressed three and received the following canned message: "If you are experiencing delays or no paper at all, we are sorry to inform you that due to problems in our printing department, no further papers will be delivered today. Most neighborhood stores will be carrying the *Orange County Register*."

"Which means one of us will have to go to Staters," I told Mel.

"Sure, I don't mind going," Mel said agreeably. Staters, the local supermarket, was about four miles away. "And if we need anything else, let me know."

Mel's really good about running unexpected errands, while I do a lot more complaining. "Well, as long as you're going, and it will save me a trip later this week, you could also get some green bananas, and they're having a sale on Tropicana orange juice this week, so get a couple of half-gallons. And if you see any interesting flavors of ice cream, pick out something you like." *That should sweeten the trip*, I thought, *letting him pick out the flavor that he likes—coffee—and while he's gone, I'll work on breakfast.*

If you're not retired, then you have no conception of what sheer luxury it is to sit at the breakfast table with a mug of coffee and the daily papers and spend an hour at least perusing the pages. Sunday is the best day of the week, as we can spend a good two hours lingering at breakfast, with all the different supplements to read and my favorite funnies in color. That's why any interruption in our routine, especially Sundays, is almost catastrophic.

Forty minutes later, Mel came in, carrying the bags of groceries, plus our precious newspaper, which he parceled out on the table for us to read as we ate. While I was putting the food stuffs into the refrigerator, Mel quietly remarked, "You know, I think I lost my wallet. It's not in my pocket, and I must have dropped it at Staters, or perhaps I left it on the checkout counter. I'll have to go back and see if they have it."

"Oh, God!" Having been through stolen identities and lost wallets a few times, I could immediately visualize canceling all our various charge and credit cards, applying for a new driver's license, and worrying over all the other cards in a wallet that verify we are who we say we are. In a panic mode, I could feel my blood pressure jumping fifty points while my complexion probably turned lily white. Mel is much calmer than I in emergency situations.

"Before you go," I exclaimed, "wait a minute, and let me call the store and see if anyone found your wallet. And give me the purchase slip so I can try to identify the checkout aisle you used. Who knows? Maybe there are still some honest people in this world."

I dialed the store phone number printed on the slip, fervently hoping I wasn't going to get a busy signal, and was relieved when the call was immediately answered by a crisp feminine voice. "Staters. This is the cashier's department. How can I help you?"

I identified myself and told the cashier the reason for my call: that my husband had been there a half-hour ago and apparently had lost his wallet in the store or at the checkout counter while paying for the groceries.

The cashier's voice softened considerably as she sensed my panic. "I'm sure we can help you," she assured me. "Just relax while I ask you a few questions. First of all, do you have the purchase slip handy?" From the purchase slip, she was able to determine the time that Mel checked out and which checkout line he was in. Next, she asked me to describe the clothes

Mel was wearing and his general appearance. All these questions seemed so superfluous, but I did as she asked, even though I just wanted to know if someone had found the wallet and returned it, rather than his being solicited for a centerfold picture in *Playboy*.

A few seconds elapsed after I fed the cashier that information, and then she announced, "Mrs. Engelman, your husband did not lose his wallet in this store."

I was unconvinced. "What makes you so sure it's not on the floor somewhere or on the counter?"

"Mrs. Engelman," she replied, "the camera on the checkout you indicated shows me a picture of your husband at that time, and after he made the purchases it shows him putting his wallet in his back pocket. If he went straight home after he left the store, then it is probably on the seat of your car. Please have him check the car, and I'm sure that's where his wallet will be."

Bingo! And that's exactly where it was. Sunday breakfast was behind schedule, but we doubly enjoyed reading the *Orange County Register* that day, with Mel's wallet back where it belonged. 🙶

CHAPTER SIXTY-NINE

QUEEN FOR A MONTH

I DON'T ENVY THE QUEEN OF ENGLAND. Until she abdicates, she has to be queen, with its inherent duties, living in a goldfish bowl, year in and year out. I was Queen for a Day, which extended to Queen for a Month, and I loved every day of it. But I didn't have to ride a horse in the rain for Trooping the Colours on my birthday, with the whole world watching on TV. I just had loving family and friends to share in my eighty-fifth birthday celebration, which was the biggest surprise of my life. Weeks later, I am still basking in the glow of it.

So, how did I get to be Queen for a Month? It's sort of a long story, but you really have to understand all the background to fully appreciate how I got my title.

Every December, Mel and I always head for California to spend Christmas with Suzy and her husband, Dennis, and our two grandsons, Morgan and Aaron. This past December was no exception. The difference was that this year, we arrived two weeks earlier so we could embark with friends on a Hawaiian Island cruise out of San Diego, which is only a forty minute's drive from Suzy's home. While we were at sea, our older grandson, Morgan, would be celebrating his fifteenth birthday, and we were going to miss the party, so we promised to take the family out for a birthday dinner on our return to California. This was scheduled for the night before we were to head back to Florida.

The morning of the planned birthday dinner, I asked Suzy, with some trepidation, in what restaurant we would be dining. I use the word "trepidation" because we would be paying for this meal, and Morgan, who has an extremely healthy appetite, has been known to order from every course on the menu. He also has champagne tastes, running to the likes of lobster and shrimp. When Mel and I take the kids out for a meal, we always put a price limit on their menu selection, but this time, we were going to be big spenders, without any price ceiling.

"Ask Morgan," Suzy replied. "It's his birthday."

Morgan's choice of restaurant, called Brio, was perfect, because they served great Italian food, which we had enjoyed in the past, and the prices were fairly moderate for gourmet food and quality dining, so I was able to relax and forget finances for the rest of the day. I'm the cheap one in the family and never outgrew my upbringing, when my mother always urged me to order the cheapest dish on the menu when I was dating. The first time I ever went out for dinner with Mel, he warned, "When you're out with me, you don't look at the right side of the menu," which was very impressive, but I still do.

The day passed as a normal one in that household, Suzy and Dennis were in and out, running errands, returning Christmas gifts. Then Dennis had to go to the office in Newport Beach to sign some papers. He took Aaron with him and promised to meet the rest of us at the restaurant at 6 p.m. In honor of Morgan's birthday, Dennis and Suzy dressed more formally than usual. Dennis wore a jacket, and Suzy looked stunning in a form-fitting black dress and high heels. Mel and I were passably present-able, wearing the clothes we planned to wear for the return plane trip the next day, but my old-lady-looking SAS bone-colored oxfords didn't impart any glamour to my black wool slacks and white blouse. Morgan and Aaron combed their hair and wore shirts that had color as well as collars, so they were really dressed up for the occasion.

Suzy herded us into the restaurant at 6 p.m., after parking the car in a lot off to the side of the restaurant, where, she said, she wouldn't have to worry about someone putting a dent in her fairly new car. It made a lot of sense. We walked through the length of the restaurant into the private dining room, which would give us privacy for our small family dinner, and then … pandemonium broke out—a roomful of people burst into the familiar "Happy Birthday" ditty. Momentarily, I thought the song was for Morgan's birthday, but as I looked at the people sitting at three large, round tables, I made out the familiar faces of our close California cousins and our neighbors and friends from our summer rental at Leisure World.

Someone, I think it must have been Suzy, planked a hot-pink plastic tiara on my head, which upon later close examination was crown-like in style, very similar to that worn by Queen Elizabeth. It was studded with faux pink diamonds and rubies, set on a base of feathery hot-pink fluff. A voice from the crowd called out "You're Queen for the Day" and indeed, I felt like one as I surveyed the smiling faces of the occupants of each table.

The incredible fact was that Mel and I had lunched or dined with some of these people before our Hawaiian cruise and had spoken on the phone to the rest of them, and our parting words had been "We'll see you next summer." Not one of the approximately twenty-five people in this room had spilled the beans. This included the couple we had traveled with just a few short days ago, as well as Mel's cousin, whom I had called that very afternoon to report on our Hawaiian trip, while her husband and son were motioning for her to get off the phone so they could leave for the long trip to the restaurant. I really couldn't believe my eyes, to see each and everyone of them here, and I could only gasp with each new face, "Oh, my God!" The surprise was compounded by the fact that my actual birthday was two weeks later, so a birthday party was the farthest thing from my mind at this point.

After all the individual greetings had been made at each table, and I had simmered down enough to seat myself, the full impact of all the behind-the-scenes preparation began to emerge. Even days later, I was still getting bits and pieces of the true happenings before the party. It seems that Dennis hadn't really gone to his office to sign papers, and Suzy wasn't exchanging Christmas gifts—they'd been running back and forth to the restaurant, decorating the private dining room in a manner commensurate for a big birthday bash. They were also greeting the guests who had arrived well before 6 p.m., and Dennis and Aaron were being hosts until Mel and I arrived with Suzy and Morgan. Now I understood why Suzy parked the car so far from the entrance to the restaurant—nothing to do with not getting a dent in her car; she didn't want us to recognize any of the cars already parked there. Ah, intrigue abounded!

As facts unfolded slowly in my state of amazement, my attention was called to an enormous red-and-yellow, professionally lettered, six-foot-wide sign reading "Surprise! Happy 85th Birthday, Mom Muriel—Hooray!!!!"

Then I was directed to the walls, upon which hung dozens of photographs of my life, before marriage and after, with husband and kids, enlarged to mammoth proportions. Many of these had been gleaned from old photo albums and from the ten thousand colored slides that Mel is slowly putting on CDs for the kids. They included Mel and me at various occasions in our marriage, Suzy and her family, and our absent son and daughter-in-law, Curtis and Anita, living three thousand miles away and unable to come for this occasion. There was even one of me holding my "granddog" Lizzie, with whom I share a special affinity.

I was in an absolute daze, not knowing later what I ate or to whom I spoke, though I did remember downing a raspberry-flavored vodka martini in no time. It seems as though everyone was taking photos, and from the ones that Cousin Sharon sent, my facial coloring was sky high from a combination of the excitement and the vodka. From those photos, I learned the room was decorated with balloons and snowmen and teddy bears that I have no recollection of even seeing that night. I do remember the birthday cake well, though, because it was so gorgeous, and I *am* a chocoholic. It was a large, square chocolate cake, centered with red roses and lots of flickering candles that took two big breaths to extinguish. As for the eating, it was heavenly—and sinful.

I briefly remember thinking about my mother's reaction to a surprise ninetieth birthday party we gave her. She was in such a state of shock, she kept repeating, "Don't ever do this to me again!" That wasn't my reaction, though, because I was loving every minute of this party, though parts of it are still a complete blank. Some of the guests told me about the beautiful party invitations Aaron had concocted on his computer, which they had received weeks before, but I still haven't understood how Suzy was able to get names and addresses for so many of our friends.

Gifts were piled on a table under the wall of photos, and on this same table was a 2½ foot birthday card with a Lizzie look-alike dog (a Bichon) on the cover. Inside, both sides of the card were filled with pictures of all the common breeds of dogs and birthday messages from all the guests. Of course, I was still in such a stage of excitement that I wasn't able to fully realize or appreciate the card until Suzy mailed it out to me a few days later, and I was able to coherently read all the inscriptions. Can you believe spending almost seven dollars to mail out a birthday card, albeit a giant one? Like her father, she always goes whole hog; if one is good, ten are better.

We were still in a party mood early the next morning as we prepared to leave for the airport, especially since Morgan plopped the tiara/crown on my head and gave me orders. "Nana, you have to wear your crown home." Never did I realize the reaction this little plastic hot-pink tiara with false diamonds, rubies, and hot-pink fluff would create! In the airport and on the plane, I was the recipient of warm, indulgent smiles, with questions such as "Celebrating your birthday?" or "Celebrating New Year's Eve early?" I was constantly addressed as "Queen" or "Princess" or "Your Majesty." Prior to my attaining royal status, this very senior citizen was just one of thousands, but now I really stood out in a crowd, and I was enjoying it.

New Year's Eve in Florida came up shortly, and of course, I wore my emblem of royalty on that night, achieving the same results—more attention. During the following two weeks we were treated to birthday lunches and dinners in restaurants, so I wore my crown/tiara, and I learned some restaurants even serve free ice-cream sundaes for birthday people. In one restaurant, the waitress curtsied to me as we were leaving, after addressing me throughout the meal as "Your Highness." I have one more birthday luncheon coming up later this week, to which I shall wear my eye-catching headpiece, and then perhaps I might retire it for a while. I will have milked it for all it was worth for a month and don't really want to overdo it.

In the meantime, the humongous birthday card, wall photographs, and Happy Birthday sign are still on display in our living and dining rooms, and I may just keep them there for a while, so I can still enjoy the thrill of a lifetime—tangible evidence of the love and caring that elevated me to the rank of Queen for a Month. ❧

The Queen wearing her tiara.

CHAPTER SEVENTY

PARKING LOT LESSONS

I AM A VERY FORTUNATE WOMAN. How many eighty-five-year-old females do you know who have a rendezvous five days a week at 6:40 a.m., with not one but two men? Not only that, but Mel, my spouse of fifty-seven years, drives me to this rendezvous. It doesn't seem to rattle Mel much, though, perhaps due to the fact that we meet in a public parking lot at Clubhouse No. 5, and what mischief can one do out in the open at this ungodly hour? Besides, one of the men, Joe, is a ninety-three-year-old widower, and Sid, the younger of the two at eighty-nine, has a wife my age.

The setting for this intrigue takes place at Laguna Woods Village (formerly called Leisure World) in Southern California, a retirement community for seniors, age fifty-five and older. To my way of thinking, a fifty-five-year-old is a kid, certainly not a senior. We have spent seven summers in a rented condo here, mostly because of the marvelous climate, but also for the opportunity to see more of Suzy and Dennis and our two grandsons, who live eleven miles away. Just a ten-minute drive from Laguna Beach on the Pacific Ocean, cooling breezes keep Laguna Woods homes pleasant and comfortable, so that doors and windows can remain open, and air conditioners are seldom used. (This past summer was an exception, as it was the hottest summer on record, even surpassing Florida temperatures a few times.)

In California, I can maintain my daily form of exercise, which consists of a two-mile walk early each morning, which Florida humidity prevents, even at 7 a.m. So for at least five mornings a week, I am out there in the parking lot, doing my thing. Why a parking lot when sidewalks abound for walking? It's because this part of the state is so mountainous, one would have to be a mountain goat (or have the lungs of a two-year-old) to hike the seven blocks from our condo to the huge, almost level parking lot at Clubhouse No. 5. Mel drives to his fitness center at the same time each morning, so he drops me off here, where I begin my seven revolutions of the lot, which equals two miles of walking. This is where I have been rendezvousing over the years with Joe and Sid. When my two-mile stint is finished, I can head home on foot, as it's mostly all downhill—no stress to the lungs.

Joe is usually midway in his walking laps by the time I arrive. As I alight from the car, I can see him, ramrod straight, about five foot seven, immaculately dressed in his razor-sharp creased beige pants, windbreaker jacket, and visor cap. He walks with firm steps, arms swinging slightly with the momentum of his stride. We'll wave to each other as I start my walk in the opposite direction. I do this purposely, as I walk faster than he does and don't want to risk catching up with him, when I'd have to slow down to match his pace. More important, Joe's conversation drives me nuts.

I learned through trial and error that when walking with Joe, one becomes a captive audience, hearing every detail of Joe's devoted care of his wife, as she was bedridden for two years before she died nine years ago. It's very commendable for a spouse to be so caring, but after the first six years of listening as we walked, I got smart and changed my walking pattern. How often can one listen to his organ recital of massaging and bathing her, giving her manicures and pedicures, preparing special recipes and cooking for her—enough was enough already. And his recitation of those darned recipes and procedures for freezing cuts of meat, fish, and casseroles—those were the worst offenders of all. Cooking is not my favorite pastime so having to listen to someone's recipes is akin to slow-drip torture for me.

Now you know why I learned to walk in the opposite direction. When our paths do cross at some point, we stop for a minute or two to discuss my recent arrival, the weather, or our mutual friend Sid, who was either late or early today. I learned, too, that my friend Joe is a little bigoted when it comes to certain ethnic groups that abound in this part of Southern California. Once he starts in on them not performing their landscaping jobs efficiently, I interrupt with, "I gotta go; I'm behind schedule," and I take off like a big bird, leaving Joe carping away in mid-sentence.

I try to execute four laps of the parking lot before joining Sid, sitting on the bench near the clubhouse entrance, and after my visit with him, I'll be ready for the last three laps of my exercise regime. Sid usually arrives at the parking lot well before I do because he is an early riser, and while his wife is still sleeping, he gets his exercise for the day. Sid is much taller than Joe and would probably be close to six feet in height if he wasn't stoop-shouldered. With his shoulders forward bent, he creates the sensation of a man walking directly into a gale wind. He's still a good-looking man, with a thin, white, Clark Gable-type moustache and full head of white hair, visible only when he removes his visor cap momentarily.

As I plank myself down next to him on the bench, his standard greetings consist of "Mel is still driving too fast, and he'll get a ticket one of these days" or "You're late [or early] today" or "What happened to you yesterday? You didn't show up" or "Today is going to be a hot one." And thus, our visit begins. Sid doesn't discuss recipes or his dead wife, because she is very much alive, and there are frequent references to his wife, Selma, who suffers from arthritis. Because of this, they have had to curtail their usual lifestyle of traveling to Chicago, Arizona, or distant parts of California to visit various family members. And relatives, he has them by the hundreds! Furthermore, he has acquainted me with most of them, but he forgets he has already talked about them, so I hear the same stories over and over about each one. Sometimes, I wonder if it would be easier to learn how to prepare fish for broiling than to hear about Sid's kids, siblings, and nieces and nephews.

Sid was blessed with nine brothers and sisters, most of whom have predeceased him, but they left behind numerous sons and daughters, all of whom stay in close contact with Sid and occasionally visit him in Laguna Woods. An impending visit brings forth an often-repeated recitation of the history of that particular individual, his or her location on the family tree, occupation, spouse, number of children, business acumen, and financial standing.

I have learned over the years that all of Sid's relatives are extremely gifted; they all have the most important jobs; they are the most brilliant; they all live in the most beautiful and the biggest of homes; their cars are the latest and most expensive models; and they are all very wealthy. The only failure in his family was Sid's older brother, a building contractor who became a multimillionaire at the height of a building boom. However, he didn't heed Sid's advice, lost four of his five homes, and died practically penniless a few years later, while Sid survives in relative financial comfort. After all, Sid had a very high-level job in the clothing industry in New York for many years, and you didn't have to be in the *shmatte* (colloquialism for clothing or rags) business not to recognize that here was a man who knew everything about the business world.

Despite Sid's preoccupation with his productive and brilliant family, I've always found him to be very likable, with a good sense of humor. When I can divert his attention to other subjects, he'll offer the latest news on his neighbors or his Wednesday night poker games with "the boys" (all of whom are at least ninety years old). A couple of times a week Sid and Selma meet friends for dinner at a local restaurant, and the following day I'll get the critique about that particular restaurant. Once in a while, Sid asks about my family, and I'm only too happy to do a little bragging about my kids and grandchildren, and he seems interested enough—until one of my anecdotes reminds him of one of his grandnieces or grandnephews, and he is off on a tangent about them.

Eventually, I look at my watch and grouse, "Sid, you kept me here too long, and I still have three more laps to go. You've already done all your laps." Of course, Sid is a slow walker, and every year he does fewer laps around the parking lot. When we first met, he was doing the same seven revolutions that I do, and now, he only does three. Sometimes he cheats and only does two, depending on how well or poorly he slept the previous night.

Sid will glance at his watch and drag his body off the bench, as he mutters, "I should have left earlier. Selma will be awake, and I always make breakfast and serve it to her in bed. I'll see you tomorrow." And he heads off in the direction of his condo building. As I pick up steam on my fifth lap, I'm annoyed at myself for overstaying my rest time on the bench, listening to Sid's stories. Now, I still have to finish my laps when I should have had them done and over with by now.

I have learned how to curtail Joe's recipes without alienating him—by walking in the opposite direction but when I am getting a needed rest on the bench between laps #4 and 5, I have yet to learn how to cope with Sid's illustrious relatives. 🐌

CHAPTER SEVENTY-ONE

KIDNAPPED

IT WAS THAT TIME OF THE YEAR AGAIN, Mel's birthday, when he would not only reach my age but also my wisdom level. Six months earlier, on my eighty-fifth, I taunted him with the time-worn adage, "With age comes wisdom," so now he was about to become as smart as I, but for six months of the year only. We were in California for this milestone, as we had been for my eighty-fifth (Queen for a Day party).

"Do you think Dad would like a party something like yours, Mom?" Suzy asked.

I seriously pondered the question for a day or two before I responded. "I don't think Dad would enjoy a surprise party with a bunch of people around as much as he would like just being somewhere with his own little family. If we could find a place not too far away, it would be fun to 'kidnap' Dad and go there, perhaps a couple of weeks before the actual day, so it would really be a surprise."

That sounded workable to Suzy, and a few days later she called with the perfect destination in mind—Mexico. One of her psychology colleagues owned a three-bedroom vacation condo, located directly on the Pacific Ocean in Rosarita, a resort town about a three-quarter-hour drive from the Mexico/San Diego border. With luck, from Suzy's home in Dana Point, it could be a about a three-hour drive to Rosarita. It sounded ideal for our needs; the price was right, and Suzy proceeded to finalize the rental agreement for five days.

As we'd discussed, planning it for two weeks before his actual birthday would contribute to the surprise aspect, but what was the next step? Every summer Mel and I "baby-sit" our grandsons (ages twelve and fifteen at this point) so Suzy and Dennis can get away by themselves for a few days, so this presented a perfect excuse for keeping these days free on our calendar. Mel loves being with his grandsons and swallowed that idea beautifully. A couple of days later, I casually informed Mel that this year, Suzy and Dennis were going to the del Coronado Hotel in San Diego for a change of scene, rather than their usual favorite hotel in Laguna Beach.

"Good, let them go wherever they want," he replied.

Next in this pattern of intrigue was Suzy's idea that Mel and I should plan to take the kids to the San Diego Zoo, which they loved visiting but hadn't been there for a couple of years. And as long as we were going to the zoo, we could drop off her and Dennis at their hotel, and they would rent a car when they were ready to return home. It had been twelve years or more since Mel and I had been to the zoo, and we knew that many changes and improvements had taken place. Experiencing these changes with our grandsons was appealing to Mel, and he was happy to acquiesce.

The "Kidnapping Day" arrived, and we appeared at Suzy's home at the appointed hour, twelve noon, when Dennis was expected home from the office. Expectations didn't quite measure up to realization, though, for it was one o'clock, then two o'clock, and still no Dennis. Mel exasperatedly told Suzy, "At this rate, by the time we get there, it will be time to come home, just at the height of rush hour." We knew from past driving experience in San Diego that bucking traffic at rush hour could be a nightmare.

"Don't worry, Dad," Suzy countered, "they have marvelous sleeping accommodations at the Wild Animal Park for nighttime exhibits. We did that with the kids before, and it was fun, so that's what you'll plan on. Maybe Dennis and I will plan to sleep there, too, and go on to our hotel in the morning."

Then Aaron chimed in, anxious to placate his grandfather, "Oh, yeah, Bumps, the zoo at night is even more fun than during the day." (Bumps was the name given to Mel—for "Gramps"—when Morgan was born, and Bumps it is to this day.)

Dennis' car rolled into the garage at 2:30 p.m., but it was another half-hour before we piled into the car for San Diego. The kids were settled in the back of the van with their electronic gadgets, Mel and I were in the middle seats, and Dennis was at the wheel, exchanging news of the day with Suzy, the navigator. Maps were on her lap, water bottles distributed, and we were finally off. There was an underlying feeling of excitement and intrigue in the car, palpable to all of us—except Mel.

We were just in time to hit the weekend traffic, so what should have been a drive of less than an hour turned out to be closer to two and a half hours. Exit signs for the San Diego Zoo began appearing, which Mel took note of and mentioned to me, "We'll be turning off on one of the exits very soon." He knew Suzy was navigating and directing Dennis, so he didn't want to impinge on her territory. Signs also began appearing for the San Diego/Mexico border crossing, but Dennis was busy talking to Suzy and didn't appear to be noticing. Mel, slightly concerned but attempting to be casual, offered, "Dennis, I guess we'll be taking the next exit, won't we?"

Dennis's reply was vague, "Yes, but don't worry. Suzy will tell me when it's time to turn off." And the car flew on.

Mel gave me a look of frustration as we passed a sign indicating it was the last turnoff to the zoo. "I think you missed the last turnoff," he offered quietly.

"Oh, no, I think there's one more," Dennis's replied. And the next thing we knew, we were at the border crossing, with no turning back. We were in Mexico.

At that point, Dennis turned to Suzy, and seemed to explode. "Suzy, what happened? You're watching the maps and were supposed to tell me when I was to turn off! Now we're going to have to find a left exit somewhere and find our way back so we can get to the zoo. Some navigator!"

Very apologetically, Suzy admitted she goofed because they had been talking, and she had failed to pay attention. The kids in back were trying to stifle their laughter as they heard Dennis chastising Suzy. Mel was annoyed at both of them but assured Dennis that there should be a left turnoff soon that would get us back to the zoo exit. He strained forward in his seat as he scanned the road ahead and then advised, "I think there's a left turnoff just ahead that will do the trick. See? There's a sign for the border."

"Where?" Dennis innocently asked, as we sailed past the sign.

"You missed it, but there's bound to be another, as we're still so close to the border."

We rounded a curve and for a few minutes were so engrossed at the shocking panorama of Mexican slum living on our left that we momentarily forgot about the exit. Poverty in its worst guise was before us, with hundreds of cardboard, corrugated-metal, or packing-box shacks that actually housed whole families. These hovels were erected so close to their neighbors on both sides, they actually seemed to be attached. The area was peopled mostly with children in ragged clothing, racing around at play, oblivious to their poverty. Women of all ages were watching the children, hanging clothes on an outdoor line, or chatting with their neighbors. A few grizzled old men were dozing in the sun immediately in front of their packing boxes or lean-to's.

Once out of sight of that disturbing intrusion into Mexican poverty, we again turned to the problems of the road. Mel tried again. "Dennis, there seems to be an intersection up ahead, and you can probably make a left turn there."

"OK," replied Dennis. "We'll try for that one." Then he deliberately engaged Suzy in conversation, as Mel called from the back, "Turn here! This is it!"

"Already? Oh, gosh, I was so busy talking to Suzy, I missed it."

By this time, Mel was thoroughly exasperated and leaned back against the seat, sputtering to me, "That's it. I'm finished. Let him find the way back himself, and I'll just enjoy the scenery!"

We drove on in silence for another ten miles or so, while Mel stared out the window with an "I don't care what you do" attitude.

Suzy finally broke the silence. "There's a building up ahead, and we'll stop there and see if I can get directions for getting back to the border." Dennis turned into the driveway of what was a rental condominium building and parked the car next to the caretaker's office. Suzy got out and advised us all to alight and stretch our legs, while she went in search of the condo manager for directions. We poured out of the van, checking our immediate surroundings, as we awaited Suzy's return. This five-story building seemed to be of new construction, and there was a handful of cars with Mexican license plates parked in the allocated slots.

Ten minutes later, Suzy emerged from the building with a deep smile upon her face. "OK, everybody, I made a deal with the manager, who is really hungry to sell or rent a couple of these condos. He said he would gladly escort us back to the border if we would at least come up to look at one or two of his condos, and I told him we would." This sounded like a waste of time to Mel, but we locked the car and followed her over to the building.

We reached our third-floor condo via an elevator that felt so rickety, I was sure it would never get us to our destination. When I voiced my doubts about it, my precious grandsons immediately began stamping their feet and jumping so that the elevator swayed and groaned ominously. For a new building, this elevator sounded, acted, and felt ancient. Not only that, but one of the condo occupants apparently thought it was a garbage disposal, for a bag of garbage sat in one corner of it. *We're in Mexico*, I thought. I was beginning to feel some apprehension about the condition of the condo we would be inhabiting for a few days, but I was happily surprised when the condo manager opened the door to an immaculate, beautifully furnished, three-bedroom apartment.

We had no time to really check out the apartment, for Suzy was opening the sliding glass doors to the enormous patio, calling out, "Just get out here and see this gorgeous view." Indeed, it was breathtaking. The calm, sparkling-blue Pacific stretched endlessly to the horizon under a cloudless blue sky, against which were silhouetted a few boats. The patio was tastefully furnished with comfortable lounge chairs and even a large, glass-topped dining table set. "See, we can play dominoes here at night," Suzy smilingly announced, as we gravitated toward the table. At that point, taking a cue from Suzy, we all burst into the "Happy Birthday" ditty for Mel, while he stood there, mouth agape, looking utterly confused, not yet understanding the conspiracy.

"But what about the zoo?" he asked. We then explained that the zoo was just a ploy to spirit him away for his birthday, and we had no intention of going there. "And you don't know what thoughts I had about Dennis' failing to make those left turns all this time!" he laughed.

Mel and I were the honored occupants of the large master bedroom that opened on to the patio, and we appreciated the fact that we would have the magnificent panorama of ocean and sky to awaken to each morning. We quickly explored the other rooms to find a small but compact kitchen unfolding into the modern well-furnished living room. A large fireplace took up a good portion of one wall, above which Suzy had already hung

"Happy Birthday" decorations for her dad, with cards and gifts stacked under it. Upon checking out the kitchen, we did find a few discrepancies—one cabinet door could not be opened because it hit the refrigerator; another cabinet door could not be opened because it hit the microwave. Then the kids discovered that the TV wasn't hooked up—that was the biggest calamity at the moment. Yes, we were in Mexico. The manager vehemently protested that he had called the serviceman, who apparently never did come to hook it up. To appease Morgan and Aaron, who had been promised a working TV, he allowed them the use of the television set in the next-door condo, which was empty at the time. Peace reigned.

We stood at the patio railing, sipping our birthday cocktails, surveying the lovely grounds and gardens below, which seemed well tended, until our eyes focused on the pool, in which a few children were frolicking. We could hear them conversing in Spanish as they played. The aqua water sparkled in the setting sun, and it looked enticing, until Suzy spotted an electric light fixture with its wire trailing, floating lazily in the middle of the pool. "No one is going in that pool," she declared, "unless you want to get electrocuted." No one did.

Next on the agenda was shopping for food in the *Mercado*, a few miles down the road, and Suzy did well in her Spanish/English dialect, picking out the foods she wanted to supplement the ones she had brought from home in the massive cooler. Once the groceries were unloaded into the refrigerator, we readied for dinner in a recommended restaurant a couple of miles away. The restaurant was a recently constructed stone building bordering the ocean, with only a couple of tables occupied. We were not only tired but starved by the time we were seated, and we were confident the service would be rapid with so few tables occupied. Hah! We should have eaten our newly purchased groceries at home—it took two hours before we were served our entrées. Remember, we were in Mexico!

The following two days passed in shopping orgies and sightseeing en route to more shopping. The miles between our condo and Rosarita abounded with shopping bazaars, teeming with colorful ceramics, lawn and house ornaments, bird and animal figures, paintings, jewelry—everything to draw the eye and empty the purse. Once arriving in Rosarita, we parked the car for the day and walked the few blocks to the main shopping area, a duplication of what we had seen along the highway, only on a much larger scale. The bazaars, teeming with people bent on shopping, covered an area that equaled several city acres in size. Every object one could possibly desire was sold, after much haggling, of course. The price was always lowered as one started to walk away, when the dealer realized his customer could go to an adjacent booth that carried the same merchandise and make his purchase there. He usually capitulated with, "Because you are my friend, I will give it to you at your price." And the deal was made. We were in Mexico—and yet we could also be in China or Turkey for this scenario.

It was fun to wander the bazaar and purchase a ceramic bird mobile for a friend's balcony and a sterling silver bracelet for myself that I doubt is really sterling, despite the markings that indicate it is. If we hadn't seen so many pirated watches, cameras, clothing articles, and pocketbooks, I might not have been so suspicious. Suzy bought a number of large ceramic jars and animals for their home and patio, which are great mementos of our trip each time we visit their home.

After two days of shopping the bazaars in Rosarita and a neighboring town, where the merchandise was identical, we were satiated with shopping and ready for a change of pace. With one full day of our mini-vacation left, we planned to visit the large resort hotel in Rosarita for some gourmet dining and checking out the hotel for a possible future vacation destination.

The following morning we awakened to the unhappy realization that there was no water whatsoever in our condo—not for cooking, washing, or flushing. Someone had shut it off, and the condo manager to whom we might have complained wasn't on the premises. No one was in the business office that day. Suzy put in a call to her colleague, the condo owner, who promised to try to contact the manager. With our bottled water and fruit juices, and using the toaster and microwave, we did have breakfast, but felt like the great unwashed. Yes, we were in Mexico.

The amenities of the Hotel Rosarita were much appreciated by all of us who took advantage of the running water in the bathrooms there, and we were able to brush our teeth, albeit, much later than normal. Several hours were spent in this modern hotel, and after our morning ablutions were performed, we were taken on a sightseeing tour of the facilities to investigate the different bedrooms and suites for future reference. Meals were sampled in the dining room and hors d'oeuvres in the cocktail lounge, where we could watch the swimmers cavorting in the pool and on the beach. After an early dinner, we headed back to our waterless condo, stopping en route for some last-minute shopping. There was still no sign of the absent manager. Occupants of other condos reported no water problems, so why were we the chosen ones?

On our departure day, leaving the condo in the same pristine condition in which we found it on our arrival was impossible without water. Unwashed dishes would be left in the sink and toilets left not flushed. Then someone came up with the bright idea of using the facilities of the next-door condo that the manager had allowed the boys to use for TV watching. Just as we were about to start our parade there with soap and towels, a serviceman appeared at our front door, claiming to be the one who had inadvertently shut off our water supply, thinking we had returned to California a day earlier. If we had only known the turnoff handle was immediately outside our front door! One flip of his wrist and voilà, we had water!

The trip back took much longer than anticipated, as we were diverted by Mexican police to another border crossing, where we sat in line for three hours until the guard finally poked his head through the car window. "Anything to declare?" he asked. Satisfied when we answered no, he waved us on our way. We played enough word games in those three hours of waiting to last a long, long time. "I'm thinking of an animal or a country or a flower that begins with A or B or C" still rings in my ears.

We knew our kidnapping trip to Mexico was finished when we stopped at a Chinese restaurant in a shopping mall, several miles over the border. The birthday boy was back in civilization and happy, even if he never did get to the zoo. ❧

Birthday boy kidnapped to Mexico blows out the candles, except for two resistant candles.

CHAPTER SEVENTY-TWO

DECISIONS, DECISIONS

THIS YEAR IS DIFFERENT, and I don't know why. Does being eighty-seven and not eighty-six change one's outlook on life? So far, we're still doing everything we want to do, albeit a little slower, but we get there. We make plans for next year and the year after, as though we're going to live forever. We have very good reason to be optimistic about our longevity. A couple of years ago, our internist told me that I would live to be one hundred and twenty, thanks to my extremely high *good* cholesterol count. Mel's count isn't as good as mine so he is only promised one hundred and ten years, but I'm not complaining.

We were given food for thought when our kids mentioned, we should consider living near one of them, now that we were getting up in years. We agreed in principle, but did nothing about it. This is a big decision to make and we're not ready to make it right now. After all, we practically had a guarantee that we were good for another twenty-five years, so what's the rush?

And then the unexpected happened. The week before our annual trek to California for the summer, Mel was diagnosed as "a walking time bomb," in need of abdominal surgery as soon as possible. Suzy took over immediately; through her intervention, moral support, and perseverance in finding the right surgeon for the job, the "walking time bomb" was defused.

We don't know whether Mel's surgery influenced the attitudes of our grandsons, now fourteen and seventeen, but we can feel that there is a change in their behavior. In past years, when we'd appear at their home after a hiatus of several months, they were sprawled out in the family room, deeply engrossed in a TV program or games. We'd get a wave and a "Hi,

Nana" and "Hi, Bumps," and if we were lucky, they might rise and give us a quick kiss before slumping back down to their floor cushion or rocker. They were not impressed by the uproarious welcome we get from the dogs, Casper, the yellow Lab and Lizzie, the white Bichon ball of fluff.

So what was different about this year when we arrived? Had they suddenly become aware of our advanced years and approaching mortality? Their former quick kisses were enhanced with long hugs, comments, and questions:

"How was the trip?"

"Nana, I can't wait to show you my new skateboarding trick."

"When are you going to move out here for good?"

Formerly, we could have flown in from the moon and made no impression whatsoever.

Then, our younger grandson wrote in his thank-you note for holiday gifts, "It is such an awesome treat to have you guys down here for the holidays," and we knew it had come from the heart. Even better was the reply we received from his brother, acknowledging a check we had sent to help defray incidental expenses when he flew to Oregon for his girlfriend's school dance. After expressing fervent thanks for the check, he wrote the following: "When Mom has to put you and Bumps into an old people's home, I'll make sure she gets you a real good one."

I guess if the grandsons are thinking "old people's home" for us, maybe it's time we make a decision and take the advice of our kids to be near one of them. Naturally, it will be the balmier climate of Southern California, rather than the snow and ice of New York State winters. But, we *do* have to stop procrastinating and face the physical discomforts of moving, uprooting ourselves and leaving behind the close friendships we have made.

Our ten years of Florida living seem to have flown by faster than the fifty years we lived in New York, where we had established roots and raised a family. It proves the theory, "The older you get, the faster time goes." And what happened to all those years before marriage: my years in the army, in nursing school, girlhood in Connecticut? All, another lifetime ago, when I visualized myself as remaining eternally young.

The mirror tells me otherwise these days, and while we are still walking and breathing on our own, we had better make the decision to GO. We'll be adjusting to a new life and so little time remains. That clock hasn't stopped. ❧

BIBLIOGRAPHY

Excellent sources for detailed information concerning the period June 7, 1944, to May 7, 1945, may be found in the following:

C.R.I.B.A. Centre de Recherches et d'Informations sur la Bataille des Ardennes *(Center of Research and Information on the Battle of the Bulge)*, http://www. criba.be.

Ambrose, Stephen E. *Citizen Soldiers: the U.S. Army From the Normandy Beaches to the Bulge to the Surrender of Germany, June 7, 1944-May 7, 1945* (New York: Simon & Schuster, 1997).

Caddick-Adams, Peter. *Snow and Steel: the Battle of the Bulge*, 1944-45, (New York: Oxford University Press, 2015).

Monahan, Evelyn M. and Neidel-Greenlee, Rosemary. *And If I Perish; Frontline U.S. Army Nurses in World War II*, (New York: Alfred A. Knopf, 2003), pp. 405-426.

Schrijvers, Peter. *Those Who Hold Bastogne: The True Story of the Soldiers and Civilians Who Fought in the Biggest Battle of the Bulge*, (New Haven and London: Yale University Press, 2014).

Weintraub, Stanley. *11 Days in December, Christmas at the Bulge, 1944* (New York: NAL. Caliber, 2007).

Made in United States
North Haven, CT
10 August 2022

22509616R00202